"Reaching the world  r
greatest passion. No one— n
Adoniram Judson, America y
represents the official birth ?r
enshrines the Judsons in the missionary hall of fame, but that is just the beginning of the story. This book is history, biography, theology, and missiology all wrapped into one. In some aspects ground-breaking, it is well researched, well written by a crack team of Baptist scholars, and well edited by Baptist historian Jason Duesing. Every missionary should own it; every pastor should read it; every Christ should be inspired by it to win the world to Christ. The Judsons' flaming torch continues to burn."

David L. Allen
Dean, School of Theology
Southwestern Baptist Theology Seminary
Fort Worth, Texas

"Jason Duesing's *Adoniram Judson* is a book of historical, theological, missiological, and pastoral consequence. The all-star ensemble of authors for this edited volume provides essays that appreciate Judson's monumental life and work, but do so in an appropriately critical manner, avoiding the hagiography often present in missionary biographies. In this book, the reader is provided with an excellent and concise biographical treatment of Judson in historical context, followed by a theological and missiological evaluation of his life and ministry, and finally concluding with a homiletical interpretation of Judson. I highly recommend this book."

Bruce Riley Ashford
Dean, College at Southeastern
Southeastern Baptist Theological Seminary
Wake Forest, North Carolina

"Adoniram Judson and his wives continue to be key figures in Baptist studies and international Christian missions. This volume illustrates the widespread renewed scholarly interest in the Judsons, offering new insights and raising important questions."

The Rev. William H. Brackney
Millard R. Cherry Distinguished Professor of Christian Thought and Ethics
Director, Acadia Centre for Baptist and Anabaptist Studies (ACBAS)
Vice Chair, Board of Governors, Canadian Bible Society
Acadia Divinity College
Faculty of Theology, Acadia University

"In the current debate about the formulating of a list of Baptist 'saints,' Adoniram Judson would surely have a secure place, not only for his own work but for the part he played in initiating the great missionary movement in nineteenth-century America, a movement that is happily still continuing and that helps us to fulfill both the biblical mandate to remember [Deuteronomy 8] and yet also to forget [Isaiah 43], or to stop being imprisoned in history focusing only on past achievements, developing instead the eyes of faith to perceive what God's ongoing initiating grace is doing in the world in our own day. Remembering and forgetting are important, because both relate to the witness that God Himself leaves on the pages of history. This volume helps us with both tasks—to understand the pioneering significance of Judson's labors, duly contexted, theologically and historically, but also to be faithful to that compelling example by our own engagement in Christian mission today."

John H. Y. Briggs
Director Emeritus, Baptist History and Heritage Centre
Regent's Park College, University of Oxford

"Jason Duesing and his colleagues have produced a fine work with a beneficial balance of scholarship, human interest, and practical call to action. As a pastor, I find this volume a wonderful resource for preaching and for leading the church to a renewed commitment to the Great Commission. Judson still speaks. Those who take the time to dig into these reflections on the life and work of Judson will find themselves driven to the field. Please, come and dig."

D. Hance Dilbeck
Senior Pastor, Quail Springs Baptist Church, Oklahoma City, Oklahoma
Chairman, Board of Trustees, Southwestern Baptist Theological Seminary

"I congratulate Jason Duesing on bringing together a fine team of writers to provide a fresh interpretation of the life and ministry of Adoniram Judson for Baptist theology, history, and missiology. This useful volume not only offers a clear appraisal of the historical and biographical material but also explores the issues of Judson's day in light of their importance and significance for twenty-first-century Baptist life. This well-designed bicentennial celebration of the pioneer American missionary is a welcomed addition to the field of Baptist studies."

David S. Dockery
President, Union University, Jackson, Tennessee

"Adoniram Judson was much like the apostle Paul in his devotion and service to Jesus Christ. He was a theologian, missionary, church planter, and sufferer for the cause of the gospel. I commend Jason Duesing and those who collaborated on this fine bicentennial project describing the life, theology, and influence of Judson. I was encouraged and deeply challenged by the noted Burmese missionary. I encourage all believers in Jesus to read it with this caveat: prepare yourself for a great blessing and also the challenge to go on mission with Christ to a distant shore."

Danny Forshee
Pastor, Great Hills Baptist Church, Austin, Texas

"Come and read and 'dig up a buried stone' and remember a hero of Christian missionary history. Jason Duesing has done an incredible job of editing and writing a book about the life impact of Adoniram Judson that will challenge and encourage a new generation of mission-minded, hot-hearted, young missionaries to go to the unreached unengaged Burma's of our generation and hold forth the timeless message of our Savior."

Gordon Fort
Vice President, Office of Global Strategy, International Mission Board, SBC

"Adoniram and Ann Judson, along with their friend Luther Rice, are the great pioneers of missionary awakening among Baptists in America. This well-wrought volume brings together timely perspectives on Judson and his legacy. Two centuries later, Judson's vision still burns brightly in a dark world. May the Judson bicentennial contribute to a new missionary awakening for our time."

Timothy George
Founding Dean, Beeson Divinity School, Samford University
Birmingham, Alabama
General Editor, Reformation Commentary on Scripture

"On Sunday afternoons after the members of Kenwood Baptist Church have gone home, a church made up of Chen people, refugees from Burma, uses the building to worship in their own language. When we first met them and received their request to worship in our building, these refugees from the country now called Myanmar told us that they know the gospel because of the work of Adoniram Judson. Jason Duesing has given us the right book, with the right contributors, on the right man, at the right time. May the Lord so use it that centuries from now people will be referring back to missionaries who were compelled to go just as Judson was, that the glory of the Lord might cover the dry lands as the waters cover the sea."

James M. Hamilton Jr.
Associate Professor of Biblical Theology, Southern Seminary
Preaching Pastor, Kenwood Baptist Church, Louisville, Kentucky

"While most Southern Baptists would readily acknowledge our denomination's commitment to the missionary enterprise, perhaps few could articulate why this is so. Of course, the biblical mandate is clear. But God has also blessed us with many voices crying in the wilderness for the church to passionately embrace its calling to and the great adventure of world evangelization. Through a careful examination of the historical, theological, and practical implications of the life and ministry of missionary Adoniram Judson, the contributors of this volume have masterfully expounded not only the 'what' of missions, but also the 'why' of missions. With each chapter my own personal commitment to world missions was both challenged and reaffirmed. With God's help may Adoniram Judson's story be my story."

Mark Howell
Pastor, First Baptist Church, Daytona Beach, Florida

"Every generation, God sends a world-class leader among His people to stir their passion for taking the gospel to the ends of the earth. But it's a truly remarkable man whose impact is felt, not for a generation, but for two centuries! The contributors to this volume have provided a comprehensive study of Adoniram Judson—not just as another historical collection but to once again allow his life to motivate us to missionary-living. Judson's sacrifice and service are a timeless example, and a modern motivator, for every believer to give his or her life for what matters most—the gospel to the nations."

Jeff Iorg
President, Golden Gate Baptist Theological Seminary
Mill Valley, California

"As a pastor for more than fifty years, I am always blessed when I go back to read about the heroes of the Christian faith. This volume on the life of Adoniram Judson brings into perspective the historical situation and theological events used by God to call and shape Judson into the image of Christ. It refreshed my spirit and inspired me to remember the faithfulness of God and His determined love for every person on planet earth. I am so grateful for Dr. Duesing's excellent compilation of materials that paint such a powerful portrait of our first Baptist missionary and his family. What a timely message to the church as we reach out to the unsaved both near and far. This book is a tonic for the soul of growing followers of Christ.

Jimmy Jackson
Pastor, Whitesburg Baptist Church, Huntsville, Alabama

"Jason Duesing has brought together a gifted set of scholars to discuss the life and influence of the magnificent Adoniram Judson, the father of the American missionary movement. Christians of all faith traditions will be both informed and inspired by the various chapters that shed new and inspiring light on this great Christian saint and his remarkable impact on missions in the generations that have come after him."

Richard D. Land
President, Ethics and Religious Liberty Commission, SBC
Nashville, Tennessee

"This work is more than the story of a missionary. It is a confrontation with mediocre Christianity, a clashing of the twenty-first-century American church with the sacrificial living of its forebears. It is the story of a real man with real problems, real struggles, and a real Great Commission drivenness. I agonized at times as I read this account in the warmth of my home, with multiple study Bibles on my desk and sermon podcasts on my computer . . . but I could not put it down. Read it. Be challenged. Hear the cry of nations that to this day remain in darkness."

Chuck Lawless
Vice President for Global Theological Advance,
International Mission Board, SBC
Distinguished Professor of Evangelism and Church Growth
Southern Baptist Theological Seminary

"Here you'll find hot-hearted historians, missiologists, and preachers telling the story of one of the most significant Baptists of all time. It's an exciting story that many have not heard. Judson's life, convictions, and ministry touch on the full span of Baptist doctrine and practice. This thorough treatment of those events and issues will teach every reader something valuable. At the very least, the modern reader will be struck by the contrast between the hearty commitment of our forebears and our often pale efforts at world evangelism. As Paige Patterson promises in the volume's introduction, this book is truly 'a chronicle that will inspire faith and courage in all who venture into its pages.'"

Gary Ledbetter
Director of Communications, Southern Baptists of Texas Convention

"Jason Duesing and a fine list of contributors have done Baptists a great service. This volume has both the scholarly aptitude and the captivating retelling that Judson's life warrants. After reading this volume, Baptists will know the life, mind, and heart of one our greatest missionary heroes. In the words of the editor, 'come and dig' into Judson and you will find out about his mission and the Savior who motivated him."

Jason K. Lee
Professor of Historical Theology, Southwestern Baptist Theological Seminary
Fort Worth, Texas

"Two hundred years after the father of American missions first embarked on a missionary life that would reset the course for how the Western church does missions, this fresh and very honest look back on Adoniram Judson's life and ministry has the potential to bring tremendous renewal to the missionary spirit of our churches. At times as absorbing as a fiction thriller, the book utilizes a matrix of historical, biblical, and methodological components that leaves the reader feeling compelled to discover and fulfill their own role in Christ's global missionary enterprise. The presentation of the content hides the academic aspect of the book, making this a very good equipping resource for the Christian reader and the local church. I look forward with anticipation to the effect this book will have on our church."

Nathan Lino
Pastor, Northeast Houston Baptist Church, Houston, Texas

"As American Christianity refocuses on what it means to recover a radical gospel, this book drives us to an old vision of what could be. Adoniram Judson abandoned everything for what seemed to be certain failure. As this group of stellar historians reflect on his life and legacy, this book will drive you to gratitude and to the gritty determination to see Christ praised among all the peoples of this planet."

Russell D. Moore
Provost and Dean, Southern Baptist Theological Seminary
Louisville, Kentucky

"I wholeheartedly recommend *Adoniram Judson: A Bicentennial Appreciation of the Pioneer American Missionary.* Editor Jason Duesing and his awesome team of contributors have blessed the church with this significant work, celebrating the life and achievements of Adoniram Judson. It encouraged my heart and cast significant vision in my mind to hear of Judson's remarkable commitment. As a pastor, I pray that God will use this work to raise up a new generation of Judsons who will take Christ's gospel to the darkest corners of the world where He has never been named. I totally endorse this work. Anyone who gets their hands on this book will be blessed!"

Jeremy Morton
Pastor, Cross Point Baptist Church, Perry, Georgia

"I encourage everyone to read this new book on Adoniram Judson. You will find in these pages a tremendous story from various perspectives of one of the great pioneers of our mission endeavor. You will read of courage, of sacrifice, but most of all, of a commitment to the Great Commission of our Lord Jesus Christ. You will read how the life of Judson has touched so many significant leaders in the past as well as in our own present experience. My hat goes off to Duesing for pulling together this compilation, which adequately and accurately honors the legacy of this great mission pioneer. I have said many times that we have a marvelous heritage and must never forget those who have gone before. Adoniram Judson is truly one of the greats!"

Frank S. Page
President and Chief Executive Officer, SBC Executive Committee
Nashville, Tennessee

"It is right that in 2012 a volume should be produced that recognises and reflects on the departure of Adoniram and Ann Judson for Burma in 1812 and the missionary service that ensued. This book admirably introduces Adoniram Judson, a pioneer American missionary and one of the most significant figures in the history of global Baptist mission, to a new generation of readers. Jason Duesing has gathered together historians, theologians, and missiologists who through their fine essays contribute not only to a full-orbed picture of Judson and his context but also to a volume that contains the continuing challenge of commitment to world mission."

Ian M. Randall
Senior Research Fellow, Spurgeon's College, London, England

"Jason Duesing used an exceptional collection of writers to craft a kaleidoscope showing the many facets of Adoniram Judson's life and ministry. It is intellectually stimulating and spiritually compelling. Another generation of believers is reintroduced to the call of missions through a bigger-than-life man of God, Adoniram Judson. Through Jason's work we can experience the stirring of the call of God upon our own lives to live closer to Jesus while sacrificing more for His great name!"

Jim Richards
Executive Director, Southern Baptists of Texas Convention

"The life of Adoniram Judson is simply overwhelming. For this reason, the scope of his life is best studied with the aid of several scholars. This allows one to understand the challenges of his family life, the tenacity of his missionary fire, and the longevity of his missionary strategy. Dr Jason Duesing and this stable of writers bring all that to the reader with succinct clarity and rich scholarship. Read and be provoked."

Steven W. Smith
Dean, The College at Southwestern
Southwestern Baptist Theological Seminary
Fort Worth, Texas

"This bicentennial appreciation of Judson's historic journey to India—and eventually to Burma, today's Myanmar—is a treasure for the church, church historians, and missionaries. Judson's famous journey launched America's involvement in the foreign missions movement. Just as important, it led to the rise of Christianity in Burma, a land where Christian faith is difficult and sometimes even dangerous. Judson's bold witness and careful work on the Burmese Bible remain an inspiration today. I pray that the stories in this volume will inspire you to pray and work for the spread of the Word of God throughout the world in years to come."

Douglas A. Sweeney
Trinity Evangelical Divinity School
Deerfield, Illinois

Adoniram Judson

A BICENTENNIAL APPRECIATION OF
THE PIONEER AMERICAN MISSIONARY

Mom and Dad,

To two incredible people who made me who I am — I hope you enjoy the story of Adoniram and especially Ann, Sarah, and Emily. They have inspired me so much!

Love you madly!

Candi

B&H Studies in Baptist Life and Thought Editors

Series Editor

Michael A. G. Haykin
Professor of Church History and Biblical Spirituality
and Director, Andrew Fuller Center for Baptist Studies
The Southern Baptist Theological Seminary
mhaykin@sbts.edu

Associate Editors

Gregory Alan Thornbury
Dean of the School of Theology and Missions
and Professor of Philosophy
Vice President for Spiritual Life
Union University
gthornbu@uu.edu

Malcolm B. Yarnell III
Associate Professor of Systematic Theology
and Director, Center for
Theological Research and
Editor, *Southwestern Journal of Theology*
Southwestern Baptist Theological Seminary
ctr@swbts.edu

Consulting Editors

Peter Beck
Assistant Professor of Religion
Charleston Southern University
pbeck@csuniv.edu

Daryl Cornett
Senior Pastor
First Baptist Church, Hazard, Kentucky
hazardfbcpastor@windstream.net

Roger Duke
Assistant Professor of Religion
and Communications
Baptist College of Health Services
Rogerdduke@aol.com

Nathan Finn
Assistant Professor of Church History
Southeastern Baptist Theological Seminary
nfinn@sebts.edu

Timothy George
Dean, Beeson Divinity School
Samford University
tfgeorge@samford.edu

Lloyd A. Harsch
Associate Professor of Church History
New Orleans Baptist Theological Seminary
LHarsch@nobts.edu

Michael McMullen
Professor of Church History
Midwestern Baptist Theological Seminary
MMcMullen@mbts.edu

James A. Patterson
University Professor and Associate Dean
School of Theology and Missions
Union University
jpatters@uu.edu

Jeff Straub
Professor of Historical and Systematic Theology
Central Baptist Theological Seminary
jstraub@centralseminary.edu

Earl Waggoner
Associate Professor of Theology
and Church History
Golden Gate Baptist Theological Seminary
EarlWaggoner@ggbts.edu

Thomas White
Vice President for Student Services
and Communications
Southwestern Baptist Theological Seminary
TWhite@swbts.edu

Gregory A. Wills
Professor of Church History
and Director, Center for the Study of the SBC
The Southern Baptist Theological Seminary
gwills@sbts.edu

Adoniram Judson

A BICENTENNIAL APPRECIATION OF
THE PIONEER AMERICAN MISSIONARY

BY

JASON G. DUESING

STUDIES IN BAPTIST LIFE AND THOUGHT
MICHAEL A. G. HAYKIN, SERIES EDITOR

NASHVILLE, TENNESSEE

Adoniram Judson: A Bicentennial Appreciation
of the Pioneer American Missionary
Copyright © 2012 by Jason Duesing

All rights reserved.

ISBN: 978-1-4336-7765-6

Published by B&H Publishing Group
Nashville, Tennessee

Dewey Decimal Classification: 266.92
Subject Heading: JUDSON, ADONIRAM \ FOREIGN MISSIONS \ MISSIONARIES

Scripture quotations marked ESV are taken from the *The Holy Bible, English Standard Version*. Copyright © 2001 by Crossway Bibles, a division of Good News Publishers.

Scripture quotations marked NKJV are taken from the New King James Version. Copyright © 1982 by Thomas Nelson, Inc. Used by permission. All rights reserved.

Printed in the United States of America

1 2 3 4 5 6 7 8 9 10 • 17 16 15 14 13 12
VP

Dedication

---

*To Adoniram Judson (1788–1850),
of whom the world was not worthy (Hebrews 11:38),*

*And to the modern-day Judsons,
the unknown heroes
who make known God's saving power among all nations
(Psalm 67:2).*

Contents

Contributors	xvii
Foreword — Tom Elliff	xix
Preface: A Bicentennial Appreciation in 2012–13 — Jason G. Duesing	xxi
Introduction: From Judson's Prison to the Ends of the Earth — Paige Patterson	1

Historical Foundation

Chapter 1
Just before Judson: The Significance of William Carey's Life, Thought, and Ministry — Michael A. G. Haykin … 9

Chapter 2
New England's New Divinity and the Age of Judson's Preparation — Robert Caldwell … 31

Biographical Presentation

Chapter 3
Ambition Overthrown: The Conversion, Consecration, and Commission of Adoniram Judson, 1788–1812 — Jason G. Duesing … 55

Chapter 4
"Until All Burma Worships the Eternal God": Adoniram Judson, the Missionary, 1812–50 — Nathan A. Finn … 77

Chapter 5
So That the World May Know: The Legacy of Adoniram Judson's Wives — Candi Finch … 101

Missiological and Theological Evaluation

Chapter 6
The Enduring Legacy of Adoniram Judson's Missiological Precepts and Practices — Keith E. Eitel … 129

Chapter 7
From Congregationalist to Baptist: Judson and Baptism — Gregory A. Wills … 149

Homiletical Interpretation

Chapter 8
Marked for Death, Messengers of Life: Adoniram and Ann Judson
— Daniel L. Akin   167

Conclusion
Please Come and Dig — Jason G. Duesing   179

Name Index   183

Contributors

Daniel L. Akin, Ph.D., University of Texas at Arlington, serves as President of Southeastern Baptist Theological Seminary. He is the author of several essays, articles, commentaries, and books including *Ten Who Changed the World* (B&H, 2008).

Robert Caldwell, Ph.D., Trinity Evangelical Divinity School, serves as Assistant Professor of Church History at Southwestern Baptist Theological Seminary. He is the author of several essays and *Communion in the Spirit: The Holy Spirit as the Bond of Union in the Theology of Jonathan Edwards* (Paternoster, 2007) and coauthor of *The Trinitarian Theology of Jonathan Edwards* (Ashgate, 2012).

Jason G. Duesing, Ph.D., Southwestern Baptist Theological Seminary, serves as Vice President for Strategic Initiatives and Assistant Professor of Historical Theology at Southwestern Baptist Theological Seminary. He is the coeditor of and a contributor to *First Freedom: The Baptist Perspective on Religious Liberty* (B&H, 2007), *Restoring Integrity in Baptist Churches* (Kregel, 2008), and *Upon this Rock: The Baptist Understanding of the Church* (B&H, 2010).

Keith E. Eitel, D.Theol., University of South Africa, DMiss, Trinity Evangelical Divinity School, serves as Dean of the Roy Fish School of Evangelism and Missions and Professor of Missions at Southwestern Baptist Theological Seminary. He is the author of several essays, articles, and books including *Transforming Culture: Developing a Biblical Ethic in an African Context* (Evangel Publishing House, 1986), "Echoes from the Past: The Theological Significance of Carey's Enquiry for Contemporary Global Evangelism," in *An Enquiry into the Obligations of Christians to Use Means for the Conversion of the Heathens*, by William Carey, revised edition edited by John L. Pretlove (Criswell Publications, 1988), and *Paradigm Wars: The Southern Baptist International Mission Board Faces the Third Millennium* (Regnum/Paternoster, 2000).

Candi Finch, Ph.D. candidate, Southwestern Baptist Theological Seminary, serves as Assistant Professor of Theology in Women's Studies at Southwestern Baptist Theological Seminary.

Nathan A. Finn, Ph.D., Southeastern Baptist Theological Seminary, serves as Associate Professor of Historical Theology and Baptist Studies at Southeastern Baptist Theological Seminary. He is the author of several essays and articles and coeditor of and contributor to several books including *Domestic Slavery Considered as a Scriptural Institution* (Mercer, 2008), *Calvinism: A Southern Baptist Dialogue* (B&H, 2008), and *Southern Baptist Identity* (Crossway, 2009).

Michael A. G. Haykin, Th.D., Wycliffe College and University of Toronto, serves as Professor of Church History and Biblical Spirituality at Southern Baptist Theological Seminary. He is the author of several essays, articles, and books including *The Spirit of God: The Exegesis of 1 and 2 Corinthians in the Pneumatomachian Controversy of the Fourth Century* (Brill, 1994), *One Heart and One Soul: John Sutcliff of Olney, His Friends, and His Times* (Evangelical Press, 1994), *Kiffin, Knollys and Keach: Rediscovering Our English Baptist Heritage* (Reformation Today Trust, 1996), *"At the Pure Fountain of Thy Word": Andrew Fuller as an Apologist* (Paternoster, 2004); *Jonathan Edwards: The Holy Spirit in Revival* (Evangelical Press, 2005), *The God Who Draws Near: An Introduction to Biblical Spirituality* (Evangelical Press, 2007), and *Rediscovering the Church Fathers* (Crossway, 2010).

Paige Patterson, Ph.D., New Orleans Baptist Theological Seminary, serves as president of Southwestern Baptist Theological Seminary. He is the author of several essays, articles, commentaries, and books including the New American Commentary volume on *Revelation* (B&H, 2012).

Gregory A. Wills, Ph.D., Emory University, serves as Vice President for Research and Assessment; Associate Dean, Theology and Tradition, and Professor of Church History at Southern Baptist Theological Seminary. He is the author of several essays, articles and books including *Democratic Religion: Freedom, Authority, and Church Discipline in the Baptist South, 1785–1900* (Oxford, 2003) and *Southern Baptist Theological Seminary, 1859–2009* (Oxford, 2009).

Foreword

Few people would dare question Adoniram Judson's impact on the history of modern missions. By both example and precept, Judson stirs up our hearts, compelling us to look to the harvest fields and pay whatever price necessary, including our very lives, to work there in fulfillment of the Lord's Great Commission.

Shortly after being asked to write this brief foreword, I received a note from one of our International Mission Board trustees and my friend, Nathan Lino, with the following lines:

> The June 1913 issue of the *Foreign Mission Journal* recounted the presentation of the Board's [Adoniram] Judson Centennial fundraising movement at the Convention's annual meeting in St. Louis. One statement made and recorded from that Convention [is interesting], "The mighty significance of the Judson Spirit is not the fact that when a missionary is left alone with his Bible he becomes a Baptist, but the significant thing is that when a Baptist is left alone with his Bible he becomes a missionary."[1]

Captured in those few words above is the impact of Judson's life and ministry. Now, you hold in your hands a tribute to Judson, flowing from the hearts and pens of some of America's greatest theologians and missiologists, and edited by Jason G. Duesing, a man whose heart is aflame for the spread of the gospel across the world.

In the pages that follow, Adoniram Judson will, once again, walk through the hallways of your own heart, stop occasionally to focus his piercing gaze upon you and pointedly challenge you to a level of commitment few are ever willing to experience.

Coming to you on the bicentennial of Judson's remarkable ministry, this book is not meant to merely inform but to inspire. God is looking for a new generation of Judson-like men and women to complete the task Judson and his contemporaries felt compelled to take up two centuries ago. As you read these pages, you will be forced constantly to ask, "Lord, what is my role in the fulfillment of your commission?"

---

[1] *The Foreign Mission Journal* 63, no. 12 (June 1913): 355.

While missional paradigms are always in a state of flux, two things remain constant, the simple clarity, authority and purpose of our Lord's commission and the utter abandonment of life to Christ that commission's fulfillment requires. No finer examples of these two guiding necessities can be found than in the life of Adoniram Judson, a life captured in the moving accounts recorded in these pages. We are indebted both to Jason Duesing and to these who have meticulously and movingly recorded both the events and the spirit marking Judson's life.

My simple prayer for you, the reader, is that your own heart will be opened to God's plans for your participation in His great work for this hour. Your history has yet to be written. Will that history be filled with pages that record an unqualified obedience to the Lord's commission, "Go . . . teach all nations"? And will those pages reveal a spirit of absolute surrender, the kind of sacrifice necessary if the gospel is to reach sin-darkened hearts in the remotest corners of this world?

Following Judson's example, the greatest hours in the history of missions could be immediately upon us!

Yours for the vision!

Tom Elliff
President, International Mission Board
Southern Baptist Convention

Preface
A Bicentennial Appreciation in 2012–13

On February 19, 1812, Adoniram Judson, his wife Ann, and a few others set sail for the East from their native America. The launching of these missionaries by a newly formed missions society marked the beginning of Americans formally joining the modern missions movement. Later that year, Judson stated, "American Christians pledged themselves to the work of evangelizing the world. They had but little to rest on except the command and promise of God."[1] Therefore, the year 2012 marks the bicentennial anniversary of Judson's departure and the official start of the American missionary enterprise.[2] However, the Judson bicentennial can and should last through the year 2013, as Adoniram and Ann Judson did not reach their Burmese destination until July 13, 1813.[3] *Adoniram Judson: A Bicentennial Appreciation of the Pioneer American Missionary* joins a lengthy procession of volumes that have sought both to interpret Judson's life and mission and to retell his story for new generations.[4] Seeing the two-hundredth anniversary of Judson's departure as a fitting context for such a presentation, the authors of this volume have sought not only to remember what took place in the past, but also to forecast what we hope will take place in the future.

---

[1] Adoniram Judson, "Parting Address of Mr. Judson," in *Southern Baptist Missionary Journal* (July 1846): 31–33.

[2] As Nathan A. Finn notes in this volume, it is right to recognize George Leile, an African American who left the United States in 1782 to evangelize and preach in Jamaica, as one of the first, if not the first, "informal" or unofficially commissioned missionary from America.

[3] In 1913, American Baptists celebrated in Burma the Judson Centennial. See *The Judson Centennial, Celebrations in Burma* (Rangoon: American Baptist Mission Press, 1914). Marked by the distribution of "Centennial Medals," the anniversary was also recognized in the United States throughout 1914 to mark the founding of the American Baptist Foreign Mission Society. See Howard B. Grose and Fred P. Haggard, eds., *The Judson Centennial, 1814–1914* (Philadelphia, PA: American Baptist Publication Society, 1914), 280, and *Missions* 5, no. 2 (February 1914): 157–58, 163. Southern Baptists started a Judson Centennial Campaign in 1913 to raise funds to meet equipment needs on the mission field. See *Foreign Mission Journal* 63, no. 12 (June 1913): 345–55, 363–64. American Baptists marked the Judson Sesquicentennial in 1962 with an anniversary issue of *Missions* (March 1962).

[4] For an overview of the many Judson biographies published in the 1800s, see Joan Jacobs Brumberg, *Mission for Life* (New York: The Free Press, 1980), 1–19.

A word should be said regarding the nature and aim of evangelical biography. Too often, in the name of inspiration or education, well-intentioned authors create hagiography or, as Carl Trueman explains, "the uncritical and adulatory description of the life of a hero of the faith."[5] Joan Jacobs Brumberg argues that in the 1800s this often appeared in works concerning Adoniram Judson reasoning that, "Biography, particularly the biography of the trials of sincere individuals, regardless of denomination, had unlimited potential as a molder of character, a socializing agent."[6] Regardless of the motive, hagiography ultimately does not serve the reader. Instead, Trueman advises that

> a warts-and-all portrait is perhaps a better apologetic in the long run: to ignore or hide the problems is arguably to produce a deceptive account, especially when those problems play directly to the kind of overall balanced assessment of life, character and ministry for which a good biographer should be striving. A writer does not have to record every act of jay walking or breaking the speed limit, but should not shy away from evidence that is relevant.[7]

This is not to say that inspiration should have no place in the agenda of an author or that works of hagiography have no edifying value or contribution. Rather, as we hope is the case in this volume, authors should seek a balanced approach to writing evangelical biography.[8] Such an approach presents the facts critically while commending the faith and zeal in the life under examination. Yet it refuses to ignore the errors or inconsistencies of that life. The life of Adoniram Judson helped start an American evangelical embrace of the peoples of the world. Further, as W. O. Carver noted, the life of Judson has had an effect "not only in drawing men into service, but rather more, perhaps, in sustaining men in service."[9] Therefore, those who have contributed to this volume hope that their readers will not only gain a renewed desire to see the gospel reach those peoples

---

[5] Carl Trueman, "Writing on Athanasius: A General Note on Hagiography," *Reformation21 Blog*, June 2, 2011, available from http://www.reformation21.org/blog/2011/06/writing-on-athanasius-a-genera.php.
[6] Brumberg, *Mission for Life*, 11.
[7] Trueman, "Writing on Athanasius."
[8] For more on a balanced approach for what he terms "Christian biography," see A. Donald Macleod, "The Joys and Frustrations of a Christian Biographer," *The Gospel Coalition Blog*, September 2, 2011, available from http://thegospelcoalition.org/blogs/tgc/2011/09/02/the-joys-and-frustrations-of-a-christian-biographer.
[9] W. O. Carver, "The Significance of Adoniram Judson," *Baptist Review and Expositor* 10 (October 1913): 478.

still unaware of the name of Jesus Christ (Rom 15:20), but also find encouragement to persevere in the ongoing pursuit of the Great Commission.

To that end, Paige Patterson gives a first-person account of Judson's impact on his own life and ministry in the Southern Baptist and evangelical context for more than 50 years. Creatively recounting his journeys in Judson's footsteps, Patterson's introduction begins the volume with a needed focus on Judson's missionary calling.

Michael A. G. Haykin, a leading church historian in the United States, Canada, and the United Kingdom, begins the historical foundation section with a description of the father of the modern missions movement, William Carey. Haykin shows how Carey's labors, two decades in advance of Judson, charted a course for and ignited interest in the world mission endeavor of Judson and his contemporaries. Robert Caldwell, a Jonathan Edwards scholar, then explains the theological and historical setting of New England, in which Judson was reared, converted to Christianity, and called to missionary service.

Jason G. Duesing, Nathan A. Finn, and Candi Finch provide the biographical presentations of Judson's life. The volume's editor tells the story of Judson's early years to his preparation for the departure overseas. Finn, a prolific evangelical and Baptist historian, recounts Judson's life from his embarking to his death, including his acquired conviction regarding believer's baptism and later trials and sufferings. Finch, a lecturer of theology in women's studies, presents the story of Judson, a widower twice over, from the perspective of his three wives: Ann Hasseltine, Sarah Hall Boardman, and Emily Chubbuck.

Keith Eitel evaluates Judson's missiological principles. Eitel, seminary dean and missiologist, brings to the effort decades of missions experience both as a practitioner and an educator. Gregory A. Wills, a leading Southern Baptist historian, examines Judson's theology of baptism as it developed during the early years of his missionary service.

Daniel L. Akin lends a homiletical interpretation of Judson's life in a sermon on Rom 8:28–39.[10] A renowned preacher and teacher of preachers, Akin's chapter helpfully ties together the entire volume with a call to follow not only Judson, but also the God who sustained him. The editor concludes the volume with a brief recollection of his own experience tracing Judson's footprints.

---

[10] Judson's life has served as the subject of previous homiletical interpretations in both F. W. Boreham, "Adoniram Judson's Text," *A Temple of Topaz* (London: Epworth, 1928), 130–41, and John Piper, "'How Few There Are Who Die So Hard': The Cost of Bringing Christ to Burma," *Filling Up the Afflictions of Christ* (Wheaton: Crossway, 2009), 85–107.

In addition to the contributors to this volume named above, the editor would like to acknowledge the much needed assistance of Zachary Bowden, PhD student in church history at Southwestern Baptist Theological Seminary. In addition, at Southwestern Baptist Theological Seminary, Kelly King, Berry Driver, and Dorothy Patterson have all provided significant aid to various parts of the compilation of this volume, as did Cory, Carla, and Joshua. Bill Sumners and Taffey Hall at the Southern Baptist Historical Library and Archives, as well as Betsy Dunbar at the American Baptist Historical Society, were gracious and eager to help during visits to their archives. Special thanks is extended to Keith Eitel, dean of the Roy Fish School of Missions and Evangelism at Southwestern, who in 2010 provided a way for the editor to teach in an adjacent setting that allowed for a firsthand visit into Myanmar. In late 2009, the concept for this volume was first presented to Michael A. G. Haykin, and from that day forward he became the project's number one advocate and promoter. Without the vision and support of Christopher Cowan and Jim Baird at B&H, a volume celebrating the bicentennial of Adoniram Judson would not have materialized in 2012.

As a former dean of mine once said, we are always making and writing the history of the future. This is true even for those of us who prefer to examine and reflect on the past. With the future in mind, it is a great joy to play a part in presenting the life of Adoniram Judson for my children, Gracyn Elisabeth, Ford Martyn, and Lindsey Joy. To my enduring and cheerful wife, Kalee, I reserve the last and cherished thank you.

Jason G. Duesing
Scarborough Hall
Southwestern Baptist Theological Seminary
September 2011

Introduction

From Judson's Prison to the Ends of the Earth

Paige Patterson

The walls of Let-Ma-Yoon death prison had long ago vanished. The odd sight of four American visitors lying on their backs with bare feet lifted in the air for a photo op amid the ample cockleburs seemed both to perplex and amuse the Burmese onlookers. But from our prone position one could view the scene exactly as Adoniram Judson would have experienced it. A few massive trees offering the only solace from the oven-like heat of the Mandalay sun, the leaning pagoda and the walls of the ancient monastery were all visible.[1]

The journey from Mandalay to Inwa, the ancient capitol of Ava, was not long, but its difficulty that day atoned for the relative proximity. Snarled in traffic in Mandalay, we finally arrived at a tributary of the surging Irrawaddy River. But how to cross? A rickety ferry with no side rails or ropes appeared. With local workers, goats, dogs, one cow, and an assortment of commercial baggage, Richard Headrick and I got our wives as close to the middle of the unstable craft as possible and prayed for safe passage. On the other side the mode of transportation declined. A small horse-drawn wagon appeared. We paid the fee—quite exorbitant, but we were Americans. Potholes in the "road" looked to me much like slightly smaller versions of the Arizona meteor crater. I never thought the wagons would survive the shaking, but finally we arrived at the lonely, overgrown location of Judson's imprisonment.

Lying there, to relive what I had read about so often was not difficult. We could imagine Ann Hasseltine Judson pleading with the "spotted faces," criminals turned jailors, to relent in their harsh treatment of her husband Adoniram, who lay helpless, feet suspended high on a bamboo pole, head resting on his precious translation of the Bible,

---

[1] The name "Let-Ma-Yoon" translates as "Hand, Shrink Not," a reference to the relentless abuse inflicted on those incarcerated. Edward Judson, *The Life of Adoniram Judson* (New York: Anson D. F. Randolph, 1883), 218–81, describes his father's experiences in prison with vivid detail. Colin Matcalfe Enriquez, *A Burmese Enchantment* (Calcutta: Thacker, Spink, 1916), 239–41, 251–66, recounts the local geography as found in 1916, most of which remained unchanged since Judson's imprisonment and continues as relatively untouched even today. For further description of the location, see Rosalie Hall Hunt, *Bless God and Take Courage* (Valley Forge, PA: Judson, 2005), 106–29, 252.

which he had done directly from Hebrew and Greek into the Burmese language—a gift that continues to bless Burmese Christians to this day 175 years later.[2]

The impetus for this pilgrimage to Judson sites in February 2002 began in 1957, when my dad, Thomas Armour Patterson, a missionary-hearted pastor, placed a book in my hands and urged that I read it carefully. Courtney Anderson's biography of Judson titled *To the Golden Shore* wrapped its tentacles around my heart, mind, and soul when I was a red-haired young teen.[3] And until this day, I read it often, unable to shirk the adventure, the love, the risk, the suffering, the faith, and the courage that leap from every page, grasping the reader and choking his spirit into submission.

In a sense, I was an unlikely mission candidate. A puckish prankster almost from the womb, not much in the world seemed very serious to me. I roamed the woods of Southeast Texas without my parents' knowledge or permission by the time I was 10, caught the sunning cottonmouths with my bare hands, and hunted with a contraband .22 pump rifle, which no one knew I had. (I have conveniently forgotten how it came into my possession.) I loved the woods, football, baseball, basketball, and ping pong. I loved my parents and my childhood sweetheart, Dorothy Kelley, but marveled at how little they all seemed to know of my escapades.

Because I had a better than average awareness of my rather remarkable capacity for sin, my conversion to Christ at age nine was vivid to the point that now, nearly 60 years later, I remember every detail. With it came a commitment to the ministry in answer to God's call, which I grasped fully. Conversion healed immediately the more gross of my sinful impulses, but I fear that the prankishness and love for exploration and adventure were only exacerbated. The sometimes stodgy Adoniram had another side to him, I learned. He loved to laugh and could evidently spin a yarn or two himself. And, as I read the pages of *To the Golden Shore*, two different but not at all contradictory notions were stoked into a raging fire that has never been quenched.

First, the desire to see the world, to embark on a great adventure gripped my soul. And to attempt this journey bearing the gospel of Jesus the Christ as the sole solution to the agonies of life only made such an enterprise seem more essential. Now, after visiting more than 125 countries and having countless adventures, including several brushes with death and a couple of arrests, my aging body makes it more challenging but my thirst for more is not slaked in the least.

---

[2] For further presentation of these events, see the chapters in this volume by Candi Finch and Nathan A. Finn.
[3] Courtney Anderson, *To the Golden Shore: The Life of Adoniram Judson* (New York: Little, Brown, 1956).

More important, if the Judsons could sacrifice as they filled up that which remained of the sufferings of Christ (Col 1:24), then it dawned on me that lost people, people outside of Christ, must really matter. As Judson put it,

> The poor Burmans are entirely destitute of those consolations and joys which constitute our happiness; and why should we be unwilling to part with a few fleeting, inconsiderable comforts, for the sake of making them sharers with us in joys exalted as heaven, durable as eternity! We cannot expect to do much, in such a rough, uncultivated field; yet, if we may be instrumental in removing some of the rubbish, and preparing the way for others, it will be a sufficient reward. I have been accustomed to view this field of labor, with dread and terror; but I now feel perfectly willing to make it my home the rest of my life.[4]

Clearly for all the tragedy that engulfed them, the Judsons believed that the lost of Burma and the saving message of Christ were more important than all else in life. This forced me to reconsider the atoning sacrifice of Jesus and the lives of Jesus, Paul, Peter, and John.

As a 16-year-old-evangelist, I may well have been more of an eminent danger than a blessing, but I could identify with the prophet who said he had a fire in his bones and he could not keep silent (Jer 20:9). In the company of my parents, I traversed the whole circumference of the globe, preaching in 13 countries to the precious lost for whom Christ died.

Though I envy those called of God to permanent mission assignments, especially those in exotic and difficult places, the Lord never led me to those. Rather, for the last 36 years I have followed what I believe to be the leadership of the Spirit of God to train missionaries and mission-hearted pastors so that no one is left without an opportunity to know of the Savior who could save even a freckled-faced, red-headed, hot-blooded prankster—a preacher's kid in Beaumont, Texas. And the impact of Adoniram Judson played a major role in my life's work.

The reader will easily comprehend why I am enthusiastic about the volume you hold in your hands. The story of God's amazing work through the Judsons in Burma must be rehearsed afresh for every generation. First, it must be told as a chronicle that will inspire faith and courage in all who venture into its pages. Second, the Spirit of the living God will surely use the book to awaken a love for the lost and a thirst for taking the gospel

---

[4] Ibid., 166.

to the ends of the earth in the hearts of many. In fact, I might almost caution against the reading of this volume if you cherish comfort and do not wish to be deeply disturbed by the prospects of people on their way to hell.

Somewhere in my journey I discovered this poem, which, written from the perspective of Judson just prior to his final return to Burma, encapsulates the convictions that drove the great missionary. May it bless your soul also.

JUDSON LONGING FOR HIS BURMAN HOME[5]
H. S. Washburn

A stranger in my native land!
   O home beyond the sea,
How yearns with all its constant love,
   This weary heart for thee.

I left thee, when around my hearth
   Was gathering thickest gloom,
And gentle ones have since that hour
   Descended to the tomb.

A flower has withered on thy breast,[6]
   Thou wilt that treasure keep;
And sweet her rest, whose grave is made
   Away upon the deep.

I once trod lightly on the turf
   That I am treading now;
The flush of hope was on my cheek,
   And youth was on my brow—

But time hath wrought a wondrous change
   In all I loved—and *me!*
I prize thee, native land—but more,
   My home beyond the sea

---

[5] John Dowling, ed., *The Judson Offering* (New York: Lewis Colby, 1848), 293–94.
[6] This refers to an infant son of Mr. and Mrs. Judson, who died in Burma after their departure for America.

O Burma! shrouded in the pall
    Of error's dreadful night!
For wings—for wings once more to bear
    To thy dark shores the light:

To rear upon thy templed hills,
    And by thy sunny streams,
The standard of the Cross, where now
    The proud Pagoda gleams.

One prayer, My God! Thy will be done—
    One only boon I crave:
To finish well my work,—and rest
    Within a Burma grave!

Historical Foundation

Chapter 1

Just before Judson
The Significance of William Carey's Life, Thought, and Ministry[1]

Michael A. G. Haykin

The long eighteenth century (1688–1815) saw the English-speaking people, in the face of almost constant war with their French neighbors, establish themselves as the masters of a far-flung empire that encircled the globe. It was in the middle of this century that British troops under the command of Robert Clive (1725–74) defeated a French army in India at the battle of Plassey, which paved the way for the British conquest of Bengal and later all of India. Two years later on September 13, 1759, General James Wolfe (1727–59) defeated the French General Louis Joseph Montcalm (1712–59) at the battle of the Plains of Abraham, then outside the walls of the city of Quebec. Though Wolfe was killed in this engagement, the British victory meant the end of French rule in Canada. Ten or so years later, Captain James Cook (1728–79), a British naval officer, entered upon his world-changing discoveries in the South Pacific, discovering and mapping the coastlines of New Zealand and Australia. There was, of course, one notable loss during this century, namely, the jewel of this empire, the American colonies, who revolted in the final third of the century and established a nation independent of their fellow Anglophones's empire.

Running parallel to this empire building by the British, though distinct from it, came the kingdom building by English-speaking missionaries. Until the latter part of the eighteenth century, evangelical Christianity was primarily confined to northern Europe and the Atlantic seaboard of North America. But suddenly in the last decade of the century, it was especially English-speaking evangelicals who began to launch out from these two geographical regions and establish churches throughout Asia, Africa, and Australasia. This endeavor, which is often called the modern missionary movement,

---

[1] Parts of this chapter have appeared as monthly installments throughout 2011 in the magazine *The Gospel Witness* (published by Jarvis Street Baptist Church, Toronto). Used by permission.

made of Christianity a truly global faith and must be regarded as the most salient event in the history of Western churches since the Reformation. To be sure, the eighteenth-century missionary movement had earlier historical precedents,[2] but the energy with which and scale upon which Western Christian missionaries set out to evangelize the world was a tremendously important turning point in the history of Western Christianity.

Among these missionaries is, of course, Adoniram Judson (1788–1850), the main subject of this book. The shape of Judson's cross-cultural ministry, though, would have been completely different without another central figure in this missionary movement, namely, William Carey (1761–1834), who has often been described as "the Father of modern missions." Since there were other Europeans and Anglophones involved in cross-cultural mission before Carey, some have argued that this moniker is quite inaccurate. Ultimately, though, it is a moot point, for there is absolutely no gainsaying the fact that Carey played a major role in the genesis of the modern missionary movement and in shaping Judson's ministry. This chapter examines the formation of Carey as a mission-minded Christian, along with key aspects of his thought and ministry, both of which influenced Judson and make for an instructive comparison with those of Judson.

How to Interpret the Life of Carey

"Such a man as Carey is more to me than bishop or archbishop: he is an apostle." This was the estimate that the evangelical Anglican John Newton (1725–1807) once expressed about Carey while the latter was still alive. On another occasion, Newton wrote that he did not look for miracles in his own day on the order of those done in the apostolic era. Yet, he went on, "If God were to work one in our day, I should not wonder if it were in favour of Dr. Carey."[3] Interestingly enough, when, in 1826, two missionaries by the names of George Bennet and Daniel Tyerman happened to visit Carey in India (by that time he had been laboring there more than 30 years), they were struck by what they called his "apostolic appearance."[4]

---

[2] For a brief summary of some of the most significant Protestant missionary work before the rise of the modern missionary movement, see Timothy George, *Faithful Witness: The Life and Mission of William Carey* (1991 ed.; repr., Worcester, PA: Christian History Institute, 1998), 38–45.

[3] *The Autobiography of William Jay*, ed. George Redford and John Angell James (1854 ed.; repr. Edinburgh: The Banner of Truth Trust, 1974), 275; S. Pearce Carey, *William Carey* (London: Hodder and Stoughton, [1923]), 134.

[4] Tom Hiney, *On the Missionary Trail* (London: Chatto & Windus, 2000), 222.

But Carey's opinion of himself was quite different. He once told his nephew Eustace Carey (1791–1855) that he was essentially "a plodder."[5] In other words, his achievements were not the work of an inspired apostle, but the product of grit, gumption, and, he would have wanted to add, divine grace. Carey was quite conscious that he did not merit being decked out with a halo like some medieval saint, something that the later Baptist and evangelical tradition—following Newton's lead?—has done. In the final analysis, Carey was convinced that he had simply done his duty as a servant of Christ.[6] And for Carey that duty had begun about 55 years prior to his death, when he first fled to Christ for "strength and righteousness."

CAREY'S FAMILY BACKGROUND

William Carey was born of poor parents in 1761 in a tiny village called Paulerspury in the heart of Northamptonshire. Carey's parents were staunch Anglicans. His father, Edmund (d.1816), the schoolmaster of Paulerspury, was what was known as the parish clerk. According to William Cowper (1731–1800), the evangelical hymn-writer and close friend of John Newton, the parish clerk had to "pronounce the amen to prayers and announce the sermon," lead the chants and the responses during the church service, keep the church register of baptisms, marriages, and burials, and chase "dogs out of church and force . . . unwilling youngsters in."[7] Thus, young William was regularly taken to church. Of this early acquaintance with the Church of England, Carey later wrote:

> Having been accustomed from my infancy to read the Scriptures, I had a considerable acquaintance therewith, especially with the historical parts. I . . . have no doubt but the constant reading of the Psalms, Lessons, etc. in the parish church, which I was obliged to attend regularly, tended to furnish my mind with

---

[5] According to Eustace Carey, William, his uncle, once told him: "If, after my removal, any one should think it worth his while to write my life, I will give you a criterion by which you may judge of its correctness. If he give me credit for being a plodder, he will describe me justly. Any thing beyond this will be too much. I can plod. I can persevere in any definite pursuit. To this I owe everything" (*Memoir of William Carey* [London: Jackson and Walford, 1836], 623, henceforth cited as Carey, *Memoir of William Carey*).
[6] A. Christopher Smith, "The Legacy of William Carey," *International Bulletin of Missionary Research* 16, no. 1 (January 1992): 2.
[7] Mary Drewery, *William Carey: A Biography* (London: Hodder and Stoughton, 1978), 10.

a general Scripture knowledge. [But] of real experimental religion I scarcely heard anything till I was fourteen years of age.[8]

A Passion for Flowers

Also living in Paulerspury was William's uncle, Peter Carey. Peter had served with General James Wolfe in Canada during the French and Indian War (a.k.a. the Seven Years' War), and had seen action at the British capture of the citadel of Quebec in 1759, two years before William was born. Peter subsequently returned to England and worked in Paulerspury as a gardener. His tales of Canada almost certainly awakened in young William an unquenchable interest in far-off lands.

Peter also implanted in young William a love of gardens and flowers that remained with him all of his life. When, years later, Carey was established in India, he had five acres of garden under cultivation. Cultivating this garden served as a welcome means of relaxation amid the stresses and strains of ministry in India. It was of this garden that his son Jonathan later remarked, "Here he [i.e., his father] enjoyed his most pleasant moments of secret meditation and devotion."[9]

John Warr

Not surprisingly, so much did young Carey love gardening that he wanted to become a gardener like his uncle Peter. At this point in his life, however, Carey suffered from a skin disease that made it very painful for him to spend large amounts of time in the full sun (it is interesting to note that when Carey went to India, he spent a considerable amount of time in the sun, but with no recurrence of this skin disease). And so, in his mid-teens, his father apprenticed him to a shoemaker named Clarke Nichols who lived in Piddington, about seven miles away from his home.

This apprenticeship was to have very significant consequences for William, for one of his fellow apprentices was a Christian. His name was John Warr. He was a

---

[8] Carey, *Memoir of William Carey*, 7.
[9] Ibid., 398. For this area of Carey's life, see Keith Farrer, *William Carey: Missionary and Baptist* (Kew, Victoria, Australia: Carey Baptist Grammar School, 2005). The importance of Carey's Indian gardens and botanical work to the missionary's life can be seen when it is recognized that the gardens which Carey created at Serampore were so extensive it took 50 gardeners to look after them (Farrer, *William Carey*, 83).

Congregationalist and was used of God to bring Carey to Christ. It was known for a long time that Carey's salvation had come partly as the result of the witness of one of his fellow apprentices. Until the First World War, however, the name of this apprentice had been completely lost. During that war it was found in a letter of Carey's that had only then come to light. It is a powerful illustration of how the faithful witness of one believer can have immense significance.

At first, when Warr shared his faith with Carey, Carey resisted. It is vital to recall that he was the product of a staunch Anglican home and that he had learned to look down on, indeed despise, anyone who was not an Anglican, that is, not part of the state church. For many, to be English was to be Anglican. But John persisted in his attempts to win Carey for Christ. He lent him books and then invited him to attend on a regular basis the mid-week gathering of Congregationalists in Hackleton, a nearby village, for prayer and Bible study. Carey went and came under deep conviction. He tried to reform his life: to give up lying and swearing, and to take up prayer. But at this point he did not realize that a definite change in his lifestyle could only occur when he had been given, in the language of Scripture, a new heart.

Coupled with Warr's testimony was an important lesson that young Carey learned from a traumatic incident that took place at Christmas, 1777. It was the custom for apprentices at that time of the year to be given small amounts of money from the tradespeople with whom their masters had business. Carey had to go to Northampton to make some purchases for his master as well as for himself. At one particular shop, that of an ironmonger—that is, a hardware dealer—called Hall, he was personally given a counterfeit shilling as a joke. When Carey discovered the worthless coin he decided, not without some qualms of conscience, to pass it off to his employer. Appropriating a good shilling from the money that Nichols had given him, he included the counterfeit shilling among the change for his master. On the way back to Piddington, he even prayed that if God enabled his dishonesty to go undetected he would break with sin from that time forth!

But, Carey commented many years later, "A gracious God did not get me through."[10] Carey's dishonesty was discovered, he was covered with shame and disgrace, and he became afraid to go out in the village where he lived for fear of what others were thinking about him. By this means, Carey was led, he subsequently said, to "see much more of myself than I had ever done before, and to seek for mercy with greater earnestness."[11]

---

[10] Carey, *Memoir of William Carey*, 12.
[11] Ibid.

That mercy he found as over the next two years he came to "depend on a crucified Saviour for pardon and salvation."[12]

BAPTIST CONVICTIONS AND MEETING JOHN RYLAND

William Carey continued to go with John Warr to the prayer meetings in Hackleton, but it was not until February 10, 1779, that he actually attended a worship service. On that particular day a man named Thomas Chater (d. 1811), a resident of Olney, was preaching. Chater's text has not been recorded, but in his sermon he did quote that powerful exhortation in Hebrews 13:13 (KJV): "Let us go forth therefore unto him [i.e., Jesus] without the camp, bearing his reproach." On the basis of this verse Chater urged upon his hearers "the necessity of following Christ entirely." As Carey listened to Chater's exhortation, his interpretation of this text and of the preacher's words was one that he would later describe as "very crude." He distinctly felt that God was calling him to leave the Church of England, where, in his particular parish church, he was sitting under "a lifeless, carnal ministry," and to unite with a Dissenting congregation. Since the Church of England was established by the law of the land, he reasoned, its members were "protected from the scandal of the cross."[13] So Carey became what he had long despised—a Dissenter.

During the first few years after his conversion, Carey struggled "to crystallize his beliefs, to establish foundations on which to build his faith."[14] "Having so slight an acquaintance with ministers," he later wrote, "I was obliged to draw all from the Bible alone."[15] His study of the Scriptures soon led him to the realization that infant baptism, as practiced by Anglicans and Congregationalists, had no real scriptural authority behind it. So, in 1783, he approached a Baptist pastor named John Ryland Sr. (1723–92), pastor of College Lane Baptist Church in Northampton, for baptism. Ryland, in turn, asked his son, John Ryland Jr. (1753–1825), to baptize Carey.

Thus, in the early hours of October 5, 1785, the younger Ryland baptized Carey in the River Nene that then flowed through Northampton. Obviously at the time, neither of these two men realized what the future would hold; they would become firm friends and co-laborers in a great work of God.

---

[12] Ibid., 14.
[13] Ibid., 12.
[14] Drewery, *William Carey*, 23.
[15] Carey, *Memoir of William Carey*, 14, 16.

A Growing Passion for Missions

Around the time of his baptism Carey came across accounts of the voyages of discovery undertaken by James Cook in the Pacific, which involved, among other things, the discovery of Tahiti and the charting of the unknown shores of New Zealand and Australia. Iain H. Murray has rightly observed that "the end of Cook's geographical feat [was] the beginning of missionary enterprise."[16] Carey would later say regarding his perusal of these volumes: "Reading Cook's voyages was the first thing that engaged my mind to think of missions."[17] Through these accounts, Carey's boyhood desire to know about other lands was given substance and shape. More importantly, through the written account of Cook's voyages, Carey began to gaze upon wider spiritual horizons than the fields of Northamptonshire and to reflect on the desperate spiritual plight of those who lived in the countries that Cook had discovered. Many of them had no written language, certainly none of them had the Scriptures in their own tongues, and there were neither local churches nor resident ministers to share with them the good news of God's salvation. "Pity, therefore, humanity, and much more Christianity," he wrote only a few years after reading Cook's journals. The heathen nations called "loudly for every possible exertion to introduce the gospel amongst them."[18] Over the next eight years one of his main preoccupations was the collection of information, especially geographical and religious, about these and the many other nations of the world that had never heard a word of the gospel.

Carey's growing passion for the evangelization of nations outside of Europe did not cause him to forget the need at his own backdoor. Through his witness, for example, his two sisters, Mary and Ann, were won to Christ. As is often the case with the members of one's own family, William had not found it at all easy to speak to them concerning their need of Christ. But he persevered in praying for them, and when Mary Carey thought back on this period of her life, she could only exclaim, "O what a privilege to have praying relations, and what a mercy to have a God that waits to be gracious!"[19] The two sisters were baptized in 1783.

Carey's formal ordination occurred on August 1, 1787, in the village of Moulton. Taking part in his ordination that day were three Baptist pastors who would become

---

[16] Iain H. Murray, "Divine Providence and Captain Cook," *The Banner of Truth* 274 (July 1986): 7.
[17] Carey, *Memoir of William Carey*, 18.
[18] William Carey, *An Enquiry into the Obligations of Christians, to Use Means for the Conversion of the Heathens* (1792 ed.; repr., Didcot, Oxfordshire: The Baptist Missionary Society, 1991), 40–41.
[19] Carey, *Memoir of William Carey*, 32–33.

lifelong friends and who would be the pillars of the Baptist Missionary Society (BMS) that sent him to India: John Ryland, Jr.; Andrew Fuller (1753–1815), later Secretary of the BMS; and John Sutcliff (1752–1814), pastor of Olney Baptist Church, where Carey had his membership for a couple of years. It is quite misleading to suppose that it was Carey's singlehanded effort that brought about the founding of the BMS and enabled him to accomplish all that he did in India from 1793 till his death more than 40 years later. Carey was part of a close-knit circle of likeminded friends, without whom little of what he longed for would have been realized. A Scottish Baptist by the name of Christopher Anderson (1782–1852), who was well acquainted with a number of Carey's close friends, maintained during Carey's lifetime that it was the "strong personal attachment" of these friends to one another that lay behind the "usefulness" of the BMS: Carey, Joshua Marshman (1768–1837), and William Ward (1769–1823)—the Serampore Trio—abroad in India; Sutcliff, Fuller, and Ryland at home.[20]

CAREY REBUKED[21]

Carey's pastorate at Moulton admitted him to meeting periodically with other Baptist ministers who pastored churches in what was called the Northamptonshire Baptist Association. This association provided a forum for the exchange of ideas, a meeting place for fellowship as well as mutual spiritual encouragement. At a meeting of the pastors of this association on September 30, 1785, one of the senior pastors of the group, John Ryland Sr.—who, the reader will recall, Carey had approached regarding baptism—is said to have asked Carey and another young pastor, John Webster Morris (1763–1836), pastor of Clipston Baptist Church in Northamptonshire, to offer those gathered that day some topics for conversation. Carey suggested a question that had been running through his mind for some time: "Whether the command given to the apostles to teach all nations was not binding on all succeeding ministers, to the end of the world, seeing that the accompanying promise was of equal extent." Carey's question obviously grew out of meditation upon Matt 28:18–20. If, Carey reasoned, Christ's promise of His presence

---

[20] Christopher Anderson, *The Christian Spirit which Is Essential to the Triumph of the Kingdom of God* (London: Holdsworth, 1824), 22–27.
[21] For what follows in this section, see Michael A. G. Haykin, *One Heart and One Soul: John Sutcliff of Olney, His Friends, and His Times* (Darlington, Co. Durham: Evangelical Press, 1994), 193–96. See also the discussion of this event by Brian Stanley, *The History of the Baptist Missionary Society 1792–1992* (Edinburgh: T&T Clark, 1992), 6–7.

with His people is for all time (v. 20), what then of His command to "teach all nations" (v. 19a)? Was it not a requirement for the church till the end of history as we know it?

According to Morris, Ryland responded with some vehemence to Carey's suggestion and bluntly told the young pastor:

> You are a miserable enthusiast for asking such a question. Certainly nothing can be done before another Pentecost, when an effusion of miraculous gifts, including the gift of tongues, will give effect to the commission of Christ as at first. What, Sir! Can you preach in Arabic, in Persic, in Hindustani, in Bengali, that you think it your duty to send the gospel to the heathens?

John C. Marshman (1794–1877), the son of Carey's coworker in India, Joshua Marshman, had a similar report about the words of the elder Ryland. As Marshman reported the incident, Ryland apparently dismissed the proposed topic with a frown and told Carey: "Young man, sit down. When God pleases to convert the heathen, he will do it without your aid or mine!" On the other hand, John Ryland, Jr., the son of the elder Ryland and in time one of Carey's closest friends, strongly asserted that his father never uttered such sentiments. The burden of proof, however, does seem to indicate that Carey did indeed receive some sort of stinging rebuke from the elder Ryland.

Now, the standard interpretation of the elder Ryland's reasoning has been to trace it back to the influence of hyper-Calvinism.[22] Although this author doubts that this is an adequate theological explanation of Ryland's outburst,[23] there is little doubt that hyper-Calvinism was a major challenge with which Carey and his circle of Baptist friends had to contend. Hyper-Calvinists in this period maintained that because the unsaved could not respond to the call of Christ in the preaching of the gospel without the enablement of God, then it was not their responsibility to repent and believe; consequently, pastors had no duty to exhort the lost to come to Christ.

Carey's close friend, Andrew Fuller, had handily refuted this error in his tremendous exegetical study *The Gospel Worthy of All Acceptation* (1785; 1801 [2nd ed.]). In

---

[22] See, for example, F. Deaville Walker, *William Carey: Missionary Pioneer and Statesman* (1925 ed.; repr., Chicago: Moody Press, n.d.), 55, who attributes Ryland's remarks to "ultra-Calvinistic theories"; George, *Faithful Witness*, 54–55; Malcolm B. Yarnell III, *The Heart of a Baptist* (White Paper, no. 2; Fort Worth, TX: The Center for Theological Research, Southwestern Baptist Theological Seminary, 2005), 2–3.

[23] See Iain H. Murray, "William Carey: Climbing the Rainbow," *The Banner of Truth* 349 (October 1992): 20–21; Michael A. G. Haykin, "John Collett Ryland and His Supposed Hyper-Calvinism Revisited" (*Historia Ecclesiastica*, October 9, 2007; http://www.andrewfullercenter.org/index.php/2007/10/john-collett-ryland-his-supposed-hyper-calvinism-revisited).

this work, Fuller demonstrated from the Scriptures that it was the duty of sinners to believe the gospel even though the power to believe was entirely dependent on God's grace. He also showed that the gospel must be freely offered to sinners far and wide. Carey took Fuller's theology in this regard as his own starting-point. Further, in his written defense of cross-cultural missions, *An Enquiry into the Obligations of Christians, to Use Means for the Conversion of the Heathens* (1792), he noted that some of his contemporaries had argued that the command to make disciples from all the nations was no longer incumbent upon the church.[24]

Given this theological atmosphere it is not surprising that people could react to Carey in the manner described by the younger John Ryland as follows. This description comes from Ryland's diary entry for July 8, 1788:

> Asked Brother Carey to preach. Some of our people who are wise above what is written, would not hear him, called him an Arminian, and discovered a strange spirit. Lord pity us! I am almost worn out with grief at these foolish cavils against some of the best of my brethren, men of God, who are only hated because of their zeal.[25]

Carey was a Calvinist, but an evangelical one of the same ilk as John Bunyan (1628–88), the powerful preacher of the previous century; Jonathan Edwards, the great New England theologian of revival; and George Whitefield (1714–70), the leading evangelist of the eighteenth century. In his theology, Carey married a deep-seated conviction in God's sovereignty in salvation to an equally profound belief that in converting sinners God uses means.[26]

THE ENQUIRY

Carey wrote one truly seminal work, *An Enquiry into the Obligations of Christians, to Use Means for the Conversion of the Heathens*. With a minimum of emotional coloring and rhetoric, this tract argued that the mandate which Christ laid upon the church in

---

[24] Carey, *Enquiry*, 8.
[25] Cited in A. de M. Chesterman, "The Journals of David Brainerd and of William Carey," *The Baptist Quarterly* 19 (1961–62): 151–52.
[26] David Kingdon, "William Carey and the Origins of the Modern Missionary Movement," in *Fulfilling the Great Commission* (London: The Westminster Conference, 1992), 88.

Matt 28:18–20 to evangelize the nations of the world was binding for all time. It was thus incumbent upon local churches of Carey's day to determine what were the appropriate means for accomplishing the task. While it does not appear to have been a best seller at the time of its publication, this tract has been aptly described as "the classical presentation of the argument for the World Mission of the Church."[27]

When this tract was published in 1792, it contained five sections. In the first, Carey tackled head-on the theological objections raised by Hyper-Calvinists to the evangelization of other nations. Some argued that the mandate to evangelize the nations of the world as found in Matthew 28 was required only of the apostles and they had actually fulfilled it in their lifetime. In fact, this line of argument was not uncommon in various European Protestant circles, where it was supported by reference to proof texts like Mark 16:20; Rom 10:18; and Col 1:23. Even an author as astute as the Puritan John Owen (1616–83) asserted that no local church has the authority to "ordain men ministers for the conversion of infidels." Since the cessation of the apostolic office, Owen maintained, only God by an act of "divine providence" could send men overseas to establish churches in those lands where the gospel was not known.[28] A more pragmatic line of reasoning also declared that there was "enough to do to attend to the salvation of our own countrymen" without sailing to the ends of the earth.[29]

Carey's response to the first of these arguments was drawn directly from Matt 28:18–20. If the commission with regard to evangelism that Christ gave in this passage applied only to the apostles, should not this also be the case for the direction to baptize those who became His disciples? Since Carey's tract had as its principal audience fellow Baptists who obviously took very seriously the command to baptize, this would have been a telling point. Then, what of those individuals who have gone to other nations and planted local churches? If the Hyper-Calvinists were correct, they must have gone without God's authorization. Yet, as Carey would show in section II of the tract, God has been with these men and women and blessed their efforts. Finally, Christ's promise to be with His church till the end of time made little sense if the command to evangelize the world was to be completed by the end of the first century AD.

Turning to the argument that there was enough to do at home, Carey readily agreed that there were "thousands in our own land as far from God as possible." This state of affairs ought to spur the Baptists on to yet greater efforts to plant local churches

---

[27] J. B. Middlebrook, *William Carey* (London: The Carey Kingsgate Press, 1961), 19.
[28] John Owen, *The True Nature of a Gospel Church and Its Government* in *The Works of John Owen*, ed. William H. Goold (1850–53 ed.; repr., Edinburgh: The Banner of Truth Trust, 1968), 16:93.
[29] Carey, *Enquiry*, 35–36.

throughout Great Britain from which the gospel could be faithfully proclaimed and these thousands reached. Yet, it still remained a fact that most of the nations of the world of that day had no copies of the Scriptures in their own tongues and no means of hearing the faithful proclamation of the Word.[30] In this section of the tract, Carey showed that missionary work was not reserved for a bygone era but was the present duty of the church. As one of the keywords of the tract's title stated, Christians had an obligation to engage in missions.

HISTORY, GEOGRAPHY, AND REALITY: SECTIONS II TO IV OF THE ENQUIRY

Section II of the tract traced the history of missions down to Carey's own day, which demonstrated that God had blessed missionary endeavors beyond the apostolic era. Following it was a section primarily composed of a statistical table of all the countries of the then-known world, detailing their length and breadth in miles, the size of their respective populations, and the religious affiliation of the majority of their inhabitants. None of this was guesswork. It was the fruit of many hours spent scouring the latest geographical handbooks and the *Northampton Mercury*, the local newspaper, for facts and notices about the nations of the world.[31] From this spare table of facts and figures, Carey concluded that the vast majority of the world was sunk in "the most deplorable state of heathen darkness, without any means of knowing the true God, except what are afforded them by the works of nature," and "utterly destitute of the knowledge of the gospel of Christ."[32]

The fourth section of the tract demolished the practical obstacles that Carey's contemporaries were wont to raise in response to what he was proposing. Confronting the real problems posed by keeping life going in other nations of the world, their distance from Great Britain, their different languages, their supposed "barbarism" and purported treatment of Europeans, Carey cogently argued that none of these rendered the evangelization of these nations impracticable.

---

[30] Ibid., 40–41.
[31] Ernest A. Payne, "Introduction" to Carey, *Enquiry*, 20–21.
[32] Carey, *Enquiry*, 88.

Practical Issues

Section V, the final section of the tract, was concentrated on outlining what was entailed in the other keyword of the work's title, "means." First in importance among these means was "fervent and united prayer."

> However the influence of the Holy Spirit may be set at nought, and run down by many, it will be found upon trial, that all means which we can use, without it, will be ineffectual. If a temple is raised for God in the heathen world, it will not be by might, nor by power, nor by the authority of the magistrate, or the eloquence of the orator; but by my Spirit, saith the Lord of Hosts. We must therefore be in real earnest in supplicating his blessing upon our labours.[33]

As missiologist Andrew F. Walls has noted, this text cannot be fully appreciated apart from the background of prayer meetings for revival that had been going on since 1784 in the Baptist circles in which Carey was now moving. Carey was thoroughly convinced from the record of Scripture and the history of the church that "the most glorious works of grace that ever took place, have been in answer to prayer."[34] Prayer therefore had to be the first resource or means that the church used to fulfill Christ's mandate.

Prayer was vital, but, Carey argued, there were other means which Christians could employ. Turning to the world of eighteenth-century commerce for an analogy, Carey noted the way in which merchants would form trading companies, outfit ships with care and then, venturing all, "cross the widest and most tempestuous seas," face inhospitable climates, fears and other hardships to successfully secure material wealth. They do such things "because their souls enter into the spirit of the project, and their happiness in a manner depends on its success." The truest interest of Christians, on the other hand, lies in the extension of their Lord's kingdom. Carey thus made the following suggestion:

> Suppose a company of serious Christians, ministers and private persons, were to form themselves into a society, and make a number of rules respecting the regulation of the plan, and the persons who are to be employed as missionaries, the means of defraying the expense, etc., etc. This society must consist of persons

---

[33] Ibid., 103.
[34] Andrew F. Walls, "Missionary Societies and the Fortunate Subversion of the Church," *The Evangelical Quarterly* 60 (1988): 144; Carey, *Enquiry*, 104.

whose hearts are in the work, men of serious religion, and possessing a spirit of perseverance; there must be a determination not to admit any person who is not of this description, or to retain him longer than he answers to it.[35]

Out of the members of this society a small committee could be established which would oversee such things as the gathering of information and the collection of funds, the selection of missionaries and equipping them for missions overseas. "All of this sounds so trite today," Walls comments, "because we are used to the paraphernalia of committees and councils of reference and subscriptions and donations." To Baptist churches in the eighteenth century, however, all of this would have been quite new and, in some ways, quite extraordinary. Carey had no desire at all to subvert the primacy of the local church, but he had grasped the simple fact that the way that Baptist congregations were then organized made it next to impossible for them to engage effectively in missions overseas.[36] Here, Carey was drawing upon a tradition in English Protestant circles in which voluntary, religious associations were formed in order to achieve specific goals.

Early Trials and Blessings in India

What Carey formulated in his *Enquiry* was realized at Kettering later that year. On October 2, 1792, 14 men, including Carey, Fuller, Ryland, and Sutcliff met in the back parlor of the home of a Martha Wallis (d. 1812), the widow of a deacon of Kettering Baptist Church, and formed the Baptist Missionary Society (at the time called "The Particular Baptist Society for propagating the Gospel amongst the Heathen"). Carey, then aged 31 years, became the Society's first appointee, along with John Thomas (1757–1801), a doctor who had trained at Westminster Hospital, London, and who had gone out to India in the 1780s as a surgeon on one of the ships of the East India Company. He thus knew Bengal and convinced the leaders of the Baptist Missionary Society that this needed to be their first field of missionary endeavour. Carey and Thomas sailed to India with their families in 1793.

Among the numerous challenges that Carey faced prior to his six-month voyage to the orient was the fact that his wife Dorothy Plackett (1756–1807) was utterly unwilling at first to go to India, though she was eventually persuaded to do so. But once in India,

---

[35] Carey, *Enquiry*, 108.
[36] Walls, "Missionary Societies," 146.

Dorothy began to lose her grip on reality when one of their sons, their third boy, Peter (1789–94), died at Mudnabati, near Dinajpur (now northern Bangladesh), where William had gone to be the manager of an indigo factory after their money ran out in Calcutta. None of the neighboring Hindus or Muslims would initially help the grieving family by acting as gravediggers, coffin makers or even pallbearers, though eventually four Muslims did dig a grave for their son.[37] Over the next few years Dorothy became completely delusional and believed that her husband was an unrepentant adulterer. She publicly accused him of such in quite vile terms and subsequently made two attempts to kill him. By June 1800, William Ward simply stated in his diary: "Mrs. Carey is stark mad."[38]

Carey spent five years in this remote village of Mudnabati. Three benefits emerged from this time of isolation and great trial. First, given the fact that there were next to no Europeans in the area, Carey was forced to acquire a remarkably extensive knowledge of Bengali. He also had time to begin learning Sanskrit, the classical language of the Indian subcontinent. Although Sanskrit was no longer a spoken language at the time when Carey was in India, Carey soon realized that Indians regarded it as the only language worthy of literary production. It was a classical language that functioned much like Latin did in Europe during the Middle Ages. Carey realized that if the Bible were to be taken seriously by Indian religious leaders, it had to be translated into Sanskrit. Sanskrit was also the basis for many other Indian languages, so Carey hoped that mastery of this language would make the task of translating the Scriptures into other languages easier.

Second, as soon as he had mastered elements of the Bengali language, Carey began work on the translation of the New Testament into Bengali—thus creating the dominant mold for his future ministry, namely, the translation of the Word of God. This Bengali New Testament, completed in 1797, would eventually progress through eight editions, each of them incorporating revisions and sometimes involving a complete retranslation. In time Carey would go on to do translations in five of the great languages of India—Bengali, Sanskrit, Marathi, Hindi, and Oriya—as well as several other languages, like Assamese and Telugu.

---

[37] On the help of these Muslims, see William Carey, Letter to Samuel Pearce, 29 Jan. [1795] (*Periodical Accounts*, I, 127).

[38] Cited in James Beck, *Dorothy Carey: The Tragic and Untold Story of Mrs. William Carey* (Grand Rapids: Baker, 1992; repr. Eugene, OR: Wipf and Stock, 2000), 152. Carey biographers have not been kind to Dorothy, and the way she has been treated in biographies of the Baptist leader are a fascinating study in their own right. Thankfully, James Beck has drawn up a very balanced account of Dorothy's life. For a helpful overview of Dorothy's loss of sanity, see Paul Pease, *Travel with William Carey* (Leominster: Day One Publications, 2005), 83–86.

Finally, Dorothy's illness forced him to develop a deeper trust in God. As Carey told his sisters in December, 1796, "I am very fruitless and almost useless but the Word and the attributes of God are my hope, and my confidence, and my joy, and I trust that his glorious designs will undoubtedly be answered."[39]

THE SERAMPORE TRIO

In late 1799 Carey moved with his family to Serampore, a Danish colony situated on the west bank of the River Hooghly a dozen or so miles from Calcutta. There he linked up with two new missionaries who had just arrived from England. William Ward was a printer whom Carey had met before he left England. He would become the best preacher at Serampore and prove to be all but indispensable as the mission's "printing press manager, cross-cultural pastoral counselor, and peacemaker."[40] During his younger years he had been involved in radical politics—a leaning and inclination he put forever behind him when he went out to India. Joshua Marshman was a man of tremendous diligence and was blessed with an iron constitution. More pugnacious by nature than either Carey or Ward, Marshman easily assumed the role of apologist for the mission. Carey once described Marshman to Ryland as "all eagerness for the work" of making Christ known in India. He had seen him, he told his English correspondent, seek to refute "men of lax conduct or deistical sentiments, and labour the point with them for hours together without fatigue." When it came to zeal, Carey concluded, "He is a Luther and I am Erasmus."[41] Such zeal was needed at Serampore, for two Moravian missionaries had previously labored there from 1777 to 1792 but quit the field with the statement that preaching at Serampore was like plowing up a rock.[42]

So began the Serampore Mission based on the partnership of these three men, a partnership that has few parallels in Christian history, and a work which, in the words of William Wilberforce (1759–1833), became "one of the chief glories of our country."[43]

---

[39] Letter to Mary Carey and Ann Hobson, 22 Dec. 1796 (*The Journal and Selected Letters of William Carey*, ed. Terry G. Carter [Macon, GA: Smyth & Helwys, 2000], 249).

[40] A. Christopher Smith, "Ward, William," in Gerald H. Anderson, *Biographical Dictionary of Christian Missions* (Grand Rapids, MI/Cambridge, UK: Eerdmans, 1998), 717.

[41] Letter to John Ryland, 24 May 1810 (cited in A. Christopher Smith, "Echoes of the Protestant Reformation in Baptist Serampore, 1800–1855," *The Baptist Review of Theology* 6, no. 1 [Spring 1996]: 28–29).

[42] Balasundaran, "Carey, William," 120.

[43] E. Daniel Potts, *British Baptist Missionaries in India, 1793–1837* (Cambridge: Cambridge University Press, 1967), 17.

In all of the extant literature and manuscripts of these three men there is amazingly no trace of mutual jealousy or severe anger. Henry Martyn (1781–1812), an evangelical Anglican and missionary to the Persians, said that never were "such men . . . so suited to one another and to their work."

CAREY THE TRANSLATOR

Carey's principal contribution to the Serampore Mission came through his remarkable linguistic ability. By the time that he moved to Serampore, he had acquired an extensive knowledge of both Bengali and Sanskrit. The Bengali New Testament, though translated by 1797, was not completely published until February 1801. Seven years later the New Testament in Sanskrit was being seen through the press. All told Carey translated or supervised the translation of the Scriptures into 34 Asian languages or dialects. In fact, in these early years of the modern missionary movement, 43 percent of first translations of the Scriptures into new languages anywhere in the world were published at Serampore.

As a grammarian Carey was brilliant. As a translator, though, it must be admitted that he lacked "a keen sensitiveness to the finer shades and nuances of ideas and meaning," a failing which dogged all of his translations.[44] Carey remarked frequently that he knew the translations were not perfect and he hoped that others would build on them. He believed that a translation should be geared as much as possible to the grammatical structure and wording of the original Hebrew or Greek. But in doing so he failed to make the Scriptures communicate in the living language of the people of India. It is not fortuitous that the translation which survived the longest was his translation into Sanskrit. It was 33 years before it was replaced with a new translation. Perhaps it lasted longer because it was a classical, written language and not a spoken, vernacular language. Carey's failure to understand at times the subtleties of translation was, it should be noted, a common failing of the day among translators. A good exception is Adoniram Judson's translation of the Scriptures into Burmese. His Burmese Bible is still in use and has remained readable, whereas none of Carey's translations are still being used.

Driving Carey, though, was the deep conviction that the Word of God had to be available to the people groups that he was trying to reach. He was rightly convinced that

---

[44] Stephen Neill, *A History of Christianity in India 1707–1858* (Cambridge: Cambridge University Press, 1985), 190.

the Word of God is in itself the great instrument for the conversion of unbelievers. Yet, he would have probably achieved more if he had attempted less.

THE CONVERSION OF KRISHNA PAL

Until the move to Serampore, Carey had not seen any lasting spiritual fruit among the Indian people. Within a year of the start of the mission at Serampore, however, people began to respond. The first was Krishna Pal (1764–1822), a Hindu carpenter and long-time seeker after truth. Pal had heard the gospel already from one of the Moravian missionaries, but it had made no lasting impression on his mind. On the morning of November 25, 1800, however, while he was washing in the River Hooghly, not far from the Serampore mission, he fell on the slippery bank and dislocated his shoulder. He sought help from John Thomas, who came to his home with Marshman and Carey. Thomas set his arm and the three missionaries shared some Scripture with Pal. That evening Thomas and Marshman returned and gave Pal this rhyme to ponder along with a full explanation of its meaning (Pal was used to such forms of wording since mantras played a large role in his Hindu convictions):

> Sin confessing, sin forsaking,
> Christ's righteousness embracing,
> The soul is free.[45]

A month or so later, Krishna Pal told Thomas that he believed that "Christ gave his life up for the salvation of sinners" and that he had personally embraced this gospel truth. He subsequently broke caste by eating with the missionaries, and Ward commented rightly: "The door of faith is open to the Gentiles; who shall shut it? The chain of the caste is broken, who shall mend it?"[46] On Sunday, December 28, 1800, a few days after Pal's profession of faith and in the presence of a huge crowd of Europeans, Hindus, and Muslims, Carey baptized Krishna Pal in the Hooghly River.[47]

---

[45] See also the anonymous *The First Hindoo Convert: A Memoir of Krishna Pal* (Philadelphia: American Baptist Publication Society, 1852), 9–11.
[46] Cited in "Memoir of the Rev. William Ward," *New Evangelical Magazine and Theological Review* 10 (1824): 3.
[47] *First Hindoo Convert*, 14–17.

Pal was the first of hundreds who were converted through the witness of the Serampore Mission over the next three decades. By 1821, more than 1,400 believers—half of them Indians—had been baptized, and Krishna Pal, who died the following year, had become one of the finest preachers of the Mission. Carey once described an early sermon of this Indian brother as "fluent, perspicuous, and affectionate, in a very high degree."[48] And in 1811, Carey told John Sutcliff in a letter that Krishna was a "zealous, well-informed, and I may add, eloquent minister of the gospel," who was regularly preaching 12 to 14 times a week in Calcutta or its environs.[49]

Krishna also wrote hymns to express his love, and that of his fellow Bengali believers, for Christ. One of them, translated into English, is still in use in certain evangelical circles. Its first stanza runs thus:

O thou, my soul, forget no more,
The Friend who all thy misery bore;
Let every idol be forgot,
But, O my soul, forget him not.[50]

In its cross-centeredness and description of the power of the cross to deliver from idolatry, this verse is quintessentially evangelical and well captures the heart of why Carey and his colleagues were in India. It is very easy today to view the Serampore Trio and their colleagues primarily as social reformers and educational activists—for they helped abolish such social ills as sati (the self-immolation of a widow on the funeral pyre of her husband) and the prostitution of children in the Hindu temples, and their founding of Serampore College in 1818 was also a remarkable achievement. But this would be to confuse the core of their ministry with its fruit. Sending forth the gospel with its message of the crucified Christ whose death alone delivered from sin and its consequences was the central focus of these men and women. The social and educational impact of that proclamation was a happy by-product of their gospel preaching. To view them as primarily social reformers is to do them a grave injustice.

---

[48] Ibid., 38.
[49] Ibid., 67.
[50] See *Grace Hymns* (London: Grace Publications Trust, 1975), hymn 145, stanza 1. For a study of the hymn, see David W. Music, "Krishna Pal's 'O Thou, My Soul, Forget No More' and 'Global Hymnody' Among Nineteenth-Century Baptists," *American Baptist Quarterly* 28 (2009), 194–207. Music argues that Joshua Marshman, who translated the hymn into English, has reshaped elements of it to reflect a profounder theology.

Final Years and Legacy

In his final years Carey insisted increasingly that his only hope for acceptance with God was the shed blood of Jesus Christ for his sins. In an 1831 letter to his son Jabez, he wrote:

> I am this day seventy years old—a monument of divine mercy and goodness; though, on a review of my life, I find much, very much, for which I ought to be humbled in the dust. My direct and positive sins are innumerable; my negligence in the Lord's work has been great; I have not promoted his cause nor sought his glory and honour as I ought. Notwithstanding all this, I am spared till now and am still retained in his work. I trust for acceptance with him to the blood of Christ alone; and I hope I am received into the divine favour through him. I wish to be more entirely devoted to his service, more completely sanctified, and more habitually exercising all the Christian graces, and bringing forth the fruits of righteousness to the praise and honour of that Saviour who gave his life a sacrifice for sin.[51]

Here are two theological themes that were foundational to Carey's thought and mission. First, the death of Christ for sinners was the Christian's only plea with regard to salvation when he stood in the presence of a holy God at the final judgment. Second, the ultimate goal of the Christian life was the glory of God. Carey felt that he had not made the latter uppermost throughout his life, hence his comfort in the former.

Similar thoughts fill another letter that Carey wrote in 1831, this one to his sisters in England. John Webster Morris, whom Carey had known many years earlier, was hoping to write something about Carey to satisfy a British public clamoring for details about the life of the Baptist missionary. Carey had clearly become something of a celebrity. Carey wanted nothing to do with such "celebrification." As he told his sisters:

> Dear Morris wrote to me for letters and other documents to assist him in writing memoirs of me after my death, but there was a spirit in his letter which I must disapprove. I therefore told him so in my reply, and absolutely refused to send anything. Indeed I have no wish that anyone should write or say anything about me; let my memorial sleep with my body in the dust and at the last great day all

---

[51] Carey, *Memoir of William Carey*, 566–67.

the good or evil which belongs to my character will be fully known. My great concern now is to be found in Christ. His atoning sacrifice is all my hope; and I know that sacrifice to be of such value that God has accepted it as fully vindicating his government in the exercise of mercy to sinners and as that on account of which he will accept the greatest offender who seeks to him for pardon. And the acceptance of that sacrifice of atonement was testified by the resurrection of our Lord from the dead and by the commission to preach the gospel to all nations, with a promise or rather a declaration that whosoever believeth on the Son shall be saved, "shall not come into condemnation but is passed from death unto life" [John 5:24].[52]

Given such sentiments it is not surprising that Carey gave explicit instructions that apart from his date of birth and death, nothing was to be inscribed upon his tombstone but these words from a hymn of Isaac Watts: "A wretched, poor, and helpless worm, On Thy kind arms I fall."[53]

What, then, is Carey's legacy? A number of things could be cited, but two are especially prominent. First, Carey models the vital importance of prayer in the life of God's children. Is prayer—both private and corporate—as great a priority in our lives as it was in Carey's and that of his friends? We gladly confess with Carey that "if a temple is raised for God in the heathen world, it will be by" the Spirit of God. But do we carry our beliefs into action by prayer for His empowering and blessing?

Then, Carey was an activist. Though he often reproached himself for his indolence, his life was focused powerfully on winning the lost for Christ and advancing the kingdom of Christ in this rebellious world. In the words of David Kingdon, Carey and his colleagues knew that they were debtors to grace, and they were thus willing to "hazard health and comfort to bring the gospel to heathen multitudes lost in darkness. They believed in the eternal punishment, not the annihilation, of the impenitent. They entertained no hopeful views of the salvific possibilities of general revelation nor speculated that people could be saved apart from the proclamation of the gospel."[54]

This twofold legacy is well summed up by the two sections of Carey's most famous sermon, which he preached on Wednesday, May 30, 1792, at the annual meeting of the Northamptonshire Association, held that year in Nottingham. Based on Isa 54:2–3,

---

[52] From Ernest A. Payne, "A 'Carey' Letter of 1831," *The Baptist Quarterly* 9 (1938–39): 240–41.
[53] Carey, *Memoir of William Carey*, 572–73.
[54] Kingdon, "William Carey and the Origins of the Modern Missionary Movement," 89. In light of the recent brouhaha over the seeming universalism of Rob Bell, this is an important aspect of Carey's legacy.

the sermon was definitely catalytic in the formation of the Baptist Missionary Society. Although the sermon is not extant, the headings were long remembered and have become something of a motto for Carey's life and thought: "Expect great things [from God]"—"Attempt great things [for God]."[55] The order of these points is important as is the fact that for an evangelical like Carey, the two points are inseparably yoked together: prayer must precede action, but prayer is never alone—it leads to action.

A Link to Judson

The year following Carey's going to India, his close friend Samuel Pearce (1766–99), who shared Carey's missionary zeal to the full, wrote to the American Baptist leader William Rogers (1751–1824) to inform him about what God had been doing in the British Isles in the wake of the momentous events surrounding the formation of the Baptist Missionary Society. Pearce was convinced that a "missionary spirit seems now to prevail among serious Christians of every denomination in Great Britain." But Pearce wanted to do more than inform Rogers. He also longed to see Christians in America heartily involved in the missionary movement as well. Pearce thus added in a postscript that he was hopeful "that whilst the United States are forming societies for the encouragement of arts, liberty, and emigration, there will, ere long, be found a few who will form a society for the transmission of the word of life to the benighted heathen—may not such an event be hoped for?"[56] In due time, 18 or so years later, Pearce's hope, which certainly reflected the desire of Carey and those laboring with him in India, was realized when the American Board of Commissioners for Foreign Missions sent the first American Protestant missionaries to Asia. And among those who were sent out were Adoniram and Ann Judson.

---

[55] On the circumstances surrounding the sermon and its impact, see Haykin, *One Heart and One Soul*, 216–18. The original headings did not include "from God" or "for God," though these phrases were obviously implied. For the date of the sermon, see Thomas J. Budge, "Date of 'Deathless Sermon,'" *The Baptist Quarterly* 33 (1989–90): 335.

[56] Letter to William Rogers, 27 Oct. 1794 ("Original Letters of the Rev. Samuel Pearce," *The Religious Remembrancer* [October 22, 1814]: 29).

Chapter 2

New England's New Divinity and the Age of Judson's Preparation[1]

Robert Caldwell

Contrary to popular historical memory, Adoniram Judson's life did not begin in 1812 when he embarked as a Congregationalist missionary for Southeast Asia, converted to Baptist principles en route, and ultimately became America's first missionary celebrity through his tireless efforts among the people of Burma. Judson had a "past," one that was shaped by the little known New Divinity or Edwardsean movement which characterized many of New England's Congregationalist churches at the turn of the nineteenth century.[2] Members of this movement self-consciously incarnated the theological, revivalistic, and ecclesiological legacy of Jonathan Edwards (1703–58). They saw themselves as a distinct branch of the Calvinist tradition who applied unique features found in Edwards's theology to their own revivalistic context. These features included: (1) Edwards's famous distinction between a sinner's natural ability and moral inability to choose Christ, which the New Divinity exploited in their evangelistic appeals, and (2) Edwards's ethical theory of "disinterested benevolence," which became the basis for an exclusive Edwardsean spirituality that motivated a radical self-denial among America's early missionaries.[3] This mixture of Edwardsean theology with traditional Calvinism resulted in a unique theological school in the Reformed tradition, one that lasted for a century (1760–1860) and found adherents among some Presbyterian and

---

[1] I would like to thank Zachary Bowden and S. Mark Hamilton for comments they provided on an earlier draft of this essay.

[2] In this essay, the terms "New Divinity" and "Edwardsean" will be used synonymously. Two excellent monographs detailing the New Divinity movement are David W. Kling, *A Field of Divine Wonders: The New Divinity and Village Revivals in Northwestern Connecticut 1792–1822* (University Park, PA: Penn State Press, 1993), and Joseph A. Conforti, *Jonathan Edwards, Religious Tradition and American Culture* (Chapel Hill, NC: University of North Carolina Press, 1995).

[3] Later in this essay we will examine these points in greater depth.

Baptist leaders of the Second Great Awakening.[4] In the late 1700s Edwardsean theology spread rapidly through New England due in part to the efficient pastoral mentorship system the New Divinity developed. Together, they presided over a series of spectacular revivals, which graced dozens of New England Congregationalist churches from 1790 to 1820, and they founded numerous missionary societies and educational institutions.[5] Organizations such as the Massachusetts Missionary Society (1799), the American Board of Commissioners for Foreign Missions (1812), Andover Seminary, Williams College, and Mount Holyoke Seminary all had deep ties to Edwardsean leaders, students, and missionaries.[6] Remarkably, the New Divinity movement is largely forgotten today, the sad result of its own theological infighting, the rise of theological liberalism which overtook virtually all of its educational institutions by 1900, and bad press by historians of later generations.[7] What Sydney Ahlstrom termed "the single most brilliant and most continuous indigenous theological tradition that America has produced," today finds no genuine adherents.[8]

This essay examines the New Divinity context of Adoniram Judson's upbringing and ministerial preparation. It will demonstrate that Judson was most likely raised in the parsonage of a New Divinity minister. In addition, the years from his conversion (1808) to the beginning of his missionary work (1812) found him immersed in an Edwardsean

---

[4] For Presbyterian Edwardsians of the early nineteenth century, see George Marsden, *The Evangelical Mind and the New School Presbyterian Experience* (New Haven, CT: Yale University Press, 1970). For a Baptist who articulated a New Divinity theology of the atonement, see Jonathan Maxcy, "A Discourse Designed to Explain the Doctrine of the Atonement," in *The Atonement. Discourses and Treatises by Edwards, Smalley, Maxcy, Emmons, Griffin, Burge, and Weeks* (Boston, MA: Congregational Board of Publication, 1859), 87–110.

[5] These revivals constituted much of the New England phase of the Second Great Awakening, which may be distinguished from the frontier revivals of the Cumberland Valley and the new-measures revivals of western New York. Each of these phases of the Second Great Awakening "had its own unique style and doctrinal accents," as noted by Douglas A. Sweeney, "Evangelical tradition in America," in *The Cambridge Companion to Jonathan Edwards*, ed. Stephen J. Stein (New York: Cambridge University Press, 2007), 220.

[6] Douglas A. Sweeney, *Nathaniel Taylor, New Haven Theology, and the Legacy of Jonathan Edwards* (New York: Oxford University Press, 2003), 40. So significant were they to the region's cultural and ecclesiastical life that Sweeney speaks of an "Edwardsian enculturation of Calvinist New England during the first third of the nineteenth century."

[7] Douglas A. Sweeney and Allen C. Guelzo, eds., "Introduction," in *The New England Theology: From Jonathan Edwards to Edwards Amasa Park* (Grand Rapids: Baker Academic, 2006), 19–20.

[8] Sydney Ahlstrom, *A Religious History of the American People*, 2nd ed. (New Haven, CT: Yale University Press, 2004), 405. While many evangelicals today find in Jonathan Edwards a rich source of theological and spiritual inspiration, no group embodies the Edwardsean tradition that emerged directly from his circle of influence.

context that shaped his convictions and molded his missionary vision. As is the case with any historical movement, the New Divinity cannot be defined merely by referencing its unique theological positions (though theology featured prominently in its identity). With this in mind this essay will examine the cultural context of the New Divinity movement: it origins, leaders, institutions, and ethos. From there this chapter will investigate some of the common theological convictions that animated its revivalism and missionary endeavors. Together these points serve not only to illuminate Judson's background; they also shed light on a largely forgotten story in the history of North American evangelicalism.

The Cultural Context of the New Divinity

Revivals are gifts from God, but unfortunately they tend to foster division. Like a giant prism, the First Great Awakening of the mid-eighteenth century separated numerous groups which had coexisted somewhat amicably within New England Congregationalism for a century.[9] Those who hallowed the names of George Whitefield, Gilbert Tennant, and Jonathan Edwards and welcomed the revivals as wonderful blessings, identified themselves as "New Lights," and generally did what they could to promote the Awakening. Those who viewed the Awakening as emotionalistic, chaotic, rancorous, and divisive for New England's churches adopted the label "Old Lights," for they saw themselves as defending ecclesial tradition.[10] Within these two parties there were various subgroups. Four of them constitute the basic religious landscape of Adoniram Judson's upbringing at the turn of the nineteenth century.

Among the Old Lights there arose a progressive party which rejected not only the revivalism of the New Lights but many tenets of traditional Calvinism as well. They nurtured a vision of religion that underscored morality as the center of Christianity and embraced a broad-mindedness that eschewed the doctrinal conundrums of Reformed theology. Soteriologically, many of these ministers advanced an intellectually respectable

---

[9] While the Great Awakening extended well beyond the boundaries of New England, for the purposes of this essay the focus will be on New England and its established Congregationalist churches, as it comprised the immediate context of Judson's upbringing.

[10] For a recent history of the Great Awakening and its aftermath, see Thomas S. Kidd, *The Great Awakening: The Roots of Evangelical Christianity in Colonial America* (New Haven, CT: Yale University Press, 2007), 94–173.

form of Arminianism.[11] Evidence of their attraction to Enlightenment rationalism can be seen in their rejection of traditional theological beliefs. Charles Chauncy (1705–87) of Boston's First Church, for example, wrote several works toward the end of his life questioning the existence of an eternal hell while attempting to give a biblical defense of universal salvation.[12] Jonathan Mayhew (1720–66) of Boston's West Church challenged the traditional formulations of the divinity of Christ and the doctrine of the Trinity.[13] Toward the end of the century, this group came to be known as the "Liberals." They were the predecessors of the Unitarians of the nineteenth century.

The majority of Old Lights, however, resisted the allure of Enlightenment rationalism and continued to defend a vision of traditional Calvinism they saw exemplified in English and North American Puritanism. In time, this group came to be known as the "Old Calvinists."[14] While they considered the revivalists to be overly emotionalistic, they nonetheless sought spiritual conversions, conversions which were gradual, orderly, and consistent with Christian moral formation. In their minds the partnership their forefathers had forged in the seventeenth century between the church and civil society was central to the proclamation of the gospel. As the theory went, all baptized, morally upstanding citizens had access to the means of grace (preaching, catechizing, and Christian moral formation) through the state church. This access could, if appropriated with earnest prayer and guided by a trained minister of souls, eventuate in the conversion of the sinner.[15] Any theology which might upset the ecclesial-civil balance, such as revivalism with its separatist tendencies, they deemed to be detrimental to the spread

---

[11] E. Brooks Holifield treats the "progressive Old Lights" under the heading of "Arminians" in his *Theology in America: Christian Thought from the Age of the Puritans to the Civil War* (New Haven, CT: Yale University Press, 2003), 128–35. See also Ahlstrom, *Religious History*, 403–4.

[12] Charles Chauncy, *The Mystery Hid from Ages and Generations, Made Manifest by the Gospel-Revelation: or, The Salvation of All Men, the Grand Thing Aimed at in the Scheme of God* (London: Charles Dilly, 1784); and *The Benevolence of the Deity* (Boston, MA: Powars and Willis, 1784).

[13] Mayhew notes that Scripture calls Jesus God not because of His inherent deity but because the Father dwells in the Son and manifests His glory exclusively through Him; see Jonathan Mayhew, *Christian Sobriety: Being Eight Sermons on Titus II.6* (Boston, MA: Richard and Samuel Draper, 1763), 60.

[14] For more on the Old Calvinists and their controversies with the New Divinity, see Holifield, *Theology in America*, 149–56; Mark Noll, *America's God: From Jonathan Edwards to Abraham Lincoln* (New York: Oxford University Press, 2002), 130–37; William Breitenbach, "Unregenerate Doings: Selflessness and Selfishness in New Divinity Theology," *American Quarterly* 34, no. 5 (Winter, 1982): 479–502; and William Breitenbach, "The Consistent Calvinism of the New Divinity Movement," *The William and Mary Quarterly* 41, no. 2 (April 1984): 241–64.

[15] Ezra Stiles, *The Literary Diary of Ezra Stiles, D.D., LL.D, President of Yale College*, ed. Franklin Bowditch Dexter, vol. 1 (New York: Charles Scribner's Sons, 1901), 352.

of the gospel. Consequently, many Old Calvinists engaged in heated polemics against New Light theologians. Ministers like William Hart and James Dana assailed Edwards's theory of true virtue and his treatment of the will.[16] In sum, Old Calvinists united in their opposition to the peculiar tenets of New Light theology which they deemed "uncouth, venomous [and] blasphemous."[17]

Among the New Lights, we can identify two groups who were divided over the issue of ecclesial separatism. At the radical end of the spectrum were New Light Separatists, who embraced regenerate membership and closed communion, positions which prevented them from remaining part of the established Congregationalist churches. True churches, they argued, consisted of covenanting believers who had been radically transformed by the Holy Spirit; in contrast, the established churches, especially those with Old Light sympathies, were not pure churches. New Light Separatism became a significant chapter in New England's ecclesial history.[18] By the revolutionary period many New Light Separatists, like Isaac Backus, pursued pure church principles to their logical conclusions by adopting the practice of believer's baptism, thereby becoming Baptists.[19]

Those New Lights who decided to remain within the orbit of Congregationalism formed what we might call the "moderate" New Light party.[20] Embracing revival yet rejecting separatism, these ministers, like Jonathan Edwards, sought to be agents of change within the standing denominational order. Yet during the 1740s as the Awakening cooled, it became increasingly apparent that moderate New Lights were waging a losing battle within Congregationalism. Many New Lights abandoned the denomination by embracing separatism, and Old Lights prohibited the education and ordination of New Light ministerial candidates. Jonathan Edwards's dismissal from his Northampton congregation in 1750 over his rejection of open communion signaled to many that New Light piety and New England Congregationalism could not coexist. When Edwards took

---

[16] William Hart, *Remarks on President Edwards's Dissertations Concerning the Nature of True Virtue* (New Haven, CT: T. & S. Green, 1771); James Dana, *Examination of the Late Revd. President Edwards's Enquiry on the Freedom of the Will* (Boston, MA: Daniel Kneeland, 1770).

[17] Stiles, *Literary Diary*, 2:115.

[18] The definitive work on New Light Separatism is C. C. Goen, *Revivalism and Separatism in New England, 1740–1800: Strict Congregationalists and Separate Baptists in the Great Awakening* (New Haven, CT: Yale University Press, 1962).

[19] Goen, *Revivalism and Separatism in New England*, 208–57.

[20] For overviews of the New Divinity see Bruce Kuklick, *Churchmen and Philosophers: From Jonathan Edwards to John Dewey* (New Haven, CT: Yale University Press, 1985), 43–65; and Joseph A. Conforti, *Samuel Hopkins and the New Divinity Movement: Calvinism, the Congregational Ministry, and Reform in New England Between the Great Awakenings* (Grand Rapids: Christian University Press, 1981), 76–94.

charge of a small frontier church in Stockbridge, Massachusetts, he was right where the Old Lights wanted him—away from the corridors of influence within New England Congregationalism. Yet surprisingly it was in such frontier towns that the New Divinity movement was birthed.

Enter Joseph Bellamy and Samuel Hopkins, two ministerial protégés of Edwards, who together became the architects of New Divinity theology. Both men were personally mentored by Edwards, both ministered in rural churches, and both vigorously sought to advance their mentor's revivalistic, pietistic, and ecclesiastical vision. Bellamy (1719–90), longtime minister in Bethlehem, Connecticut (1738–90), was a highly regarded preacher and leader in western Connecticut's Litchfield County.[21] *True Religion Delineated* (1750), the first of his 18 books and essays, is generally regarded as the foundational theological text of the New Divinity movement.[22] Edwards himself wrote a glowing preface to the book, and it was instrumental in the conversions of countless individuals in subsequent decades, including Ann Hasseltine, Judson's first wife.[23] *True Religion Delineated* was so widely read by the turn of the century that Harriet Beecher Stowe referenced it in her novel *Oldtown Folks* (1869) in a comment that is only partially fictitious: "My grandmother's blue book [*True Religion Delineated*] was published and recommended to the attention of New England . . . just twenty-six years before the Declaration of Independence. . . . There is not the slightest doubt that it was heedfully and earnestly read in every good family of New England; and its propositions were discussed everywhere and by everybody."[24] Hopkins (1721–1803), minister of Great Barrington, Massachusetts (1743–69), and later Newport, Rhode Island (1770–1803), was less effective in the pulpit but made up for

---

[21] The best study on Bellamy is Mark Valeri, *Law and Providence in Joseph Bellamy's New England: The Origins of the New Divinity in Revolutionary America* (New York: Oxford, 1994).

[22] Joseph Bellamy, *True Religion Delineated; or Experimental Religion, as distinguished from formality on the one hand, and enthusiasm on the other, set in a Scriptural and Rational Light* (Boston, MA: Kneeland, 1750). Edwards wrote in the preface: "I verily believe, from my own Perusal, [that this book] will be found [to be] a Discourse wherein the proper Essence and distinguishing Nature of saving Religion is deduced from the first Principles of the Oracles of God in a Manner tending to a great Increase of Light in this infinitely important Subject." See Bellamy, *True Religion Delineated*, vi–vii.

[23] Courtney Anderson, *To the Golden Shore* (Valley Forge, PA: Judson Press, 1987), 78. One can also note Edwardsean language and themes in Hasseltine's narration of her conversion in James D. Knowles, *The Memoir of Mrs. Ann H. Judson, Late Missionary to Burmah: Including a History of the American Baptist Mission in the Burman Empire* (Boston, MA: Lincoln & Edmands, 1829), 17–30, and Edward Judson, *The Life of Adoniram Judson* (New York: Anson D. F. Randolf & Company), 33–34.

[24] Harriet Beecher Stowe, *Oldtown Folks* (Boston, 1869), 374, as cited in Valeri, *Law and Providence in Joseph Bellamy's New England*, 3.

that deficit with his gifted theological pen.[25] For four decades, he kept New England's presses churning out works which expanded on Edwards's theological vision, including the first biography of Edwards,[26] numerous treatises on ethics, regeneration, theodicy, and the abolition of slavery, and finally the massive *System of Doctrines* (1793) which is considered the first comprehensive systematic divinity text written in the United States.[27] Hopkins left such an imprint on Edwardsians that by 1800 many considered New Divinity theology and "Hopkinsianism" to be synonymous terms. By the end of his life, Hopkins noted that New Divinity theology was "fast increasing" in popularity among ministers and laypersons: "there are now more than one hundred in the ministry who espouse the same sentiments in the United States of America."[28] Others concurred. William Bentley, a Liberal from Salem, noted in 1813 that Hopkins's "System of Divinity is the basis of the popular theology of New England."[29] Later in the nineteenth century Harriet Beecher Stowe described the popularity of the New Divinity theology she experienced in her youth in *The Minister's Wooing* (1859). Edwardsian divinity, she wrote,

> was discussed by every farmer, in intervals of plough and hoe, by every woman and girl, at loom, spinning-wheel, or wash-tub. New England was one vast sea, surging from depths to heights with thought and discussion on the most insoluble mysteries. And it is to be added that no man or woman accepted any theory or speculation simply as theory or speculation; all was profoundly real and vital—a foundation on which actual life was based with intense earnestness.[30]

What accounted for this growth of the New Divinity at the turn of the nineteenth century?

For one thing the New Divinity became very adept at training young men in Edwardsian theology and piety before placing them in churches. By the 1760s word got

---

[25] For the best study of Hopkins, see Conforti, *Samuel Hopkins and the New Divinity Movement*.

[26] Samuel Hopkins, *The Life and Character of the Late Reverend, Learned, and Pious Mr. Jonathan Edwards* (Boston, MA: Kneeland, 1765). Hopkins lived in the Edwards household during much of 1742 as a ministerial apprentice.

[27] Samuel Hopkins, *The System of Doctrines, Contained in Divine Revelation, Explained and Defended*, 2 vols. (Boston: np,1793).

[28] Stephen West, ed., *Sketches of the Life of the Late Rev. Samuel Hopkins, D.D.* (Hartford: Hudson and Goodwin, 1805), 103, as cited in Conforti, *Samuel Hopkins and the New Divinity Movement*, 4–5.

[29] *The Diary of William Bentley*, vol. 4 (Salem, 1905–1914), 302, as cited in Conforti, *Samuel Hopkins and the New Divinity Movement*, 5.

[30] Harriet Beecher Stowe, *The Minister's Wooing* (New York: Derby and Jackson, 1859), 334.

out that if a young man wanted to be a revivalistic Congregationalist minister, he would not only have to obtain a theological degree (usually from Yale), but he also would have to solicit an Edwardsian minister for on-the-job-training before taking a church of his own. Out of this, the New Divinity "schools of the prophets" were born.[31] Newly minted divinity graduates would move into the parsonages of established Edwardsian ministers and for upwards of a year would learn firsthand how to preach, baptize, conduct weddings and funerals, and handle revivals and difficult church situations. In the midst of this, there was usually intense theological education, where students would master the intricate subtleties of New Divinity theology.[32] Some ministers personally mentored dozens of students over their lifetimes, usually one to three at a time. Joseph Bellamy trained 60 students; Charles Backus of Sommers, Connecticut, trained 58; others like John Smalley, Nathan Perkins, Asahel Hooker, and Theophilus Packard trained more than 30 students each. Nathanael Emmons of Franklin, Massachusetts, held the record with almost 90.[33] Many who were mentored in turn became mentors themselves, resulting in a vast ministerial family tree that spread across New England. As William Breitenbach notes, "The educational bloodlines running from Edwards himself through Samuel Hopkins and Joseph Bellamy, and then through Jonathan Edwards Jr., John Smalley, Levi Hart, Stephen West, Samuel Spring, Charles Backus, Timothy Dwight, Asahel Hooker, Nathanael Emmons, and on, resemble nothing so much as one of those interminable series of 'begats' that dishearten readers of the Old Testament."[34]

Students did not just learn about ministry and theology in the schools of the prophets; they often found wives among their mentors' daughters and developed lifetime friendships with other ministerial trainees. After leaving New Hartford, Connecticut, to settle in a New Jersey congregation, Edward Dorr Griffin (1770–1837), one of the leading Edwardsian clergymen of the early nineteenth century, lamented the loss of the

---

[31] See David W. Kling, "New Divinity Schools of the Prophets, 1750–1825: A Case Study in Ministerial Education," *History of Educational Quarterly* 37, no. 2 (Summer 1997): 185–206. Also see Leonard Woods, *History of the Andover Theological Seminary* (Boston, MA: James R. Osgood, 1886), 19–26.

[32] "Dr Bellamy's mode of instruction was to give his students a list of questions on the principal subjects of theology—such as, the existence, attributes and government of God; moral agency, and the law under which we are placed; the sinful state and character of mankind; Divine revelation; the great doctrines of the gospel; the character and offices of Christ; the atonement; regeneration; justification; repentance; love and other Christian graces. . . . He directed his pupils to read the ablest treatises on the subject before them, and generally spent his evenings in examining their views, and in solving difficulties" (Woods, *History of Andover Seminary*, 19–20).

[33] Kling, "New Divinity Schools of the Prophets," 195.

[34] Breitenbach, "The Consistent Calvinism of the New Divinity Movement," 243.

"dear circle of ministers" he left behind in a letter to one of them. "You know not how much I miss that precious and united brotherhood of ministers. The ministers here are agreeable, friendly, and pious, but I have not prayed and wept, and triumphed with them. I shall never see such another circle. They were my first love."[35] These schools helped form an identifiable New Divinity movement replete with its own theology, approach to ministry, and extended brotherhood.[36]

Members of Judson's family were part of this brotherhood. Adoniram's uncle, Ephraim Judson (1737–1813), studied with Joseph Bellamy after graduating from Yale in 1763 before taking churches in Connecticut and later Sheffield, Massachusetts.[37] Like his mentor, he opened up his parsonage for training future New Divinity "prophets" and eventually trained eight students for gospel ministry.[38] Ezra Stiles, Yale's Old Calvinist president from 1778 to 1795 who kept a watchful eye on the state of New England's ministers, complained in his *Diary* that "Mr. [Ephraim] Judson is full in [sic] the New Divinity."[39]

His younger brother, Adoniram Judson (1750–1826), father of the famed missionary, followed a similar path to the pulpit. After graduating from Yale in 1775, Judson trained for the ministry under Bellamy before settling at Malden, Massachusetts, where Adoniram Jr. was born.[40] The elder Adoniram experienced friction at the Malden church in 1787 because a few community leaders voiced concerns about his theological views. Captain John Dexter formally protested that Judson was "a minister of Bade [sic] Hopkintonian Principels [sic]" who would probably prevent an envisioned merger of Malden's First and South churches.[41] Several years later when Judson was unanimously

---

[35] Edward Dorr Griffin to Jeremiah Hallock, 3 March 1810, as cited in Kling, *Field of Divine Wonders*, 34.
[36] David W. Kling, "The New Divinity and the Origins of the American Board of Commissioners for Foreign Missions," *Church History* 72, no. 4 (December 2003): 809.
[37] Conforti, *Samuel Hopkins and the New Divinity Movement*, 230.
[38] Kling, "New Divinity Schools of the Prophets," 195.
[39] Stiles, *Literary Diary*, 1:171.
[40] Conforti, *Samuel Hopkins and the New Divinity Movement*, 230; Anderson, *To the Golden Shore*, 5.
[41] Joshua W. Wellman, D.D., "The Ecclesiastical History of Malden," in D. Hamilton Hurd, ed., *History of Middlesex County, Massachusetts*, vol. 3 (Philadelphia, PA: J. W. Lewis, 1890), 498. Wellman continues by commenting that "what Capt. Dexter and his party called 'Bade' principles were the Christian beliefs which, at a later day, made the son of that pastor-elect a self-sacrificing and apostolic missionary—'The apostle of Burmah,' as he was called, whose name is immortal. What that objector and his part found fault with were those interpretations of the Scriptures which inspired the men who founded the Andover Theological Seminary, who organized the American Board for Foreign Missions, and nearly all our great missionary and benevolent societies; which inspired in the churches that evangelistic spirit that, under God, has brought on the great revivals of religion, for which New England has been distinguished during the present century."

called to serve in Wenham, Massachusetts, the church simultaneously voted to do away with its adherence to the "Half-Way Covenant," an action that revealed its willingness to part with its Old Calvinist heritage in order to secure a New Divinity minister who would have had strong objections to Half-Way principles.[42] These snapshots of the elder Judson's ministry provide us with fairly clear evidence that the future missionary grew up in a New Divinity context. Later, when he was converted as a young adult, his associations with Edwardsian leaders and institutions continued.

Andover Theological Seminary was founded in 1808 as a response to the increase of Unitarianism in New England. In 1805 the Unitarian Henry Ware was installed in the Hollis Chair of Theology at Harvard, an event that produced such alarm among Trinitarian Congregationalists that Old Calvinists and the New Divinity united in the founding of a postgraduate institution for divinity students in Andover, the first Protestant seminary established in North America. Edwardsian theologians of differing stripes occupied its early faculty positions. Leonard Woods (1774–1854), a Newbury, Massachusetts, minister who was trained by Charles Backus and Nathanael Emmons, held the Abbot Professorship of Christian Theology for almost four decades. Moses Stuart (1780–1852), student of Yale's Edwardsian president Timothy Dwight, taught "sacred literature" at Andover from its early years to 1848 where he revolutionized North American biblical studies. Edward Dorr Griffin, already mentioned, became professor of pulpit eloquence in the early years of the seminary as well as the first pastor of Park Street Congregational Church in nearby Boston. The Seminary's doctrinal guidelines included the Westminster Shorter Catechism as well as the Hopkinsian nuanced Associate Creed.[43] As the seminary prepared to launch its inaugural semester, Drs. Stuart and Griffin visited the Reverend Adoniram Judson, now pastor of Plymouth, Massachusetts, to encourage his gifted son to enter Andover for theological studies.[44] Young Adoniram had recently graduated valedictorian of Providence College (later Brown University), yet was confused as to the future direction of his life.[45] Leonard Woods later recalled that Judson was a "young man of excellent talents and scholarship"

---

[42] Anderson, *To the Golden Shore*, 16. The Half-Way Covenant was an agreement that allowed people to become church members without being converted to faith in Christ.

[43] See *The Constitution and Associate Statues of the Theological Seminary in Andover* (Andover, MA: Flagg and Gould, 1817), 28–31.

[44] Francis Wayland, *A Memoir of the Life and Labors of the Rev. Adoniram Judson, D.D.*, vol. 1 (Boston, MA: Phillips, Sampson, and Company, 1853), 25–26.

[45] In the next chapter Jason G. Duesing shall revisit this and subsequent comments about Judson in greater depth. My task here is merely to illustrate how connected Judson was to the New Divinity movement.

but could not be admitted as a "member" of the institution because he had not yet been converted. "He was, indeed, unsettled in his opinions, and tending to a habit of skepticism, but he still retained the impressions of an early religious education, and wished for a better state of mind. . . . We gave him permission to pursue his studies here for a limited time. During that time he became the subject of deep convictions of sin, and at length gave evidence of a renewed heart."[46]

Judson undoubtedly studied under these men during his years at Andover, imbibing not only their theology but also their piety. The faculty encouraged reading that aimed at nourishing the devotional life, like "Owen on Spiritual-mindedness, and on the 130th Psalm, Baxter's Saints' [Everlasting] Rest, Edwards On the Affections, Doddridge's Rise and Progress [of Religion in the Soul], The Life of [David] Brainerd, and the works of Howe and Leighton."[47] As Judson was wrapping up his studies at Andover in 1810, he apparently impressed Griffin enough that the latter approached Judson regarding the possibility of him becoming Griffin's ministerial colleague at Park Street Church in Boston, a position that would have given him personal training under one of the best preachers in America.[48] To the shock of his family (and Griffin), Adoniram respectfully declined the offer, for by this time his heart was being drawn in a different direction.

The modern missionary movement in North America was beginning, and Edwardsian leaders, institutions, and ideals were central to it.[49] Home missionary societies like the Connecticut Missionary Society (1798) and the Massachusetts Missionary Society (1799) were founded by New Divinity leaders, and they published periodicals providing readers with accounts of local revivals and New Divinity theology. Regional Colleges such as Williams, Dartmouth, Union, Amherst, Middlebury, and Hamilton, along with Yale, were populated by Edwardsian faculty members and presidents who inspired hundreds of students to embrace the call of foreign missions.[50] These schools alone provided the American Board of Commissioners for Foreign Missions with 75 percent of its missionaries by 1840.[51] Williams College, nestled in the Berkshire Mountains of northwest Massachusetts, is noteworthy among these schools in that it was the location

---

[46] Woods, *History of Andover*, 136.

[47] Ibid., 169.

[48] Wayland, *Memoir*, 1:38.

[49] See the extensive footnotes in Kling, "The New Divinity and the Origins of the ABCFM," 791–819.

[50] David W. Kling, "The New Divinity and Williams College, 1793–1836," *Religion and American Culture* 6, no. 2 (Summer 1996): 195–97.

[51] Clifton Jackson Phillips, *Protestant American and the Pagan World: The First Half Century of the American Board of Commissioners for Foreign Missions, 1810–1860* (Cambridge, MA: Harvard University Press, 1969), 29; and Kling, "The New Divinity and the Origins of the ABCFM," 811.

of the famed "Haystack Prayer Meeting" where a group of about a half dozen undergraduates gathered for prayer in 1806 under a haystack to avoid a drenching summer thunderstorm. Before they emerged, they solemnly dedicated themselves to foreign missions. Samuel J. Mills Jr. (1783–1818), sometimes known as the "father" of American foreign missions, was among them. The son of a New Divinity minister, Samuel Sr. of Torringford, Connecticut, Mills was converted in 1801 following a long struggle with sin that ended in a typical Edwardsian conversion narrative.[52] He took degrees at Williams College and later at Andover Seminary where he helped establish societies to create interest in missions as well as a theological society for debating Edwardsian theology.[53] Two of his Haystack colleagues, Gordon Hall and Harvey Loomis, later trained in Ebenezer Porter's New Divinity "school" at his parsonage in Washington, Connecticut.[54] Judson joined this group at Andover. Together Judson, Mills, and fellow students Samuel Nott and Samuel Newell formally petitioned the Massachusetts Association of Ministers regarding support for their missionary vocation.[55] Their request led to the formation of the American Board of Commissioners for Foreign Missions. In time, Judson married Ann Hasseltine and was ordained (Griffin, Woods, and Samuel Spring were on his ordaining council) before embarking on a ship bound for Calcutta.[56] It was the last time he would set foot again in North America as a Congregationalist.

This brief overview of the New Divinity movement in New England Congregationalism reveals how central it was to Adoniram Judson's upbringing and ministerial training. Judson was a pastor's son raised in a New Divinity parsonage, received theological training at the premier New Divinity institution, and launched missions endeavors with fellow students who had deep ties to the Edwardsian tradition. In short, he was riding a wave generated in part by the winds of an Edwardsian theology that had been bearing much fruit in the early revivals of the Second Great Awakening and that was just beginning to bear fruit in modern missions. What was this theology, and how did it inspire so many to such self-sacrificing service for Christ?

---

[52] Gardiner Spring, *Memoir of Samuel John Mills*, 2nd ed. (Boston, MA: Perkins & Marvin, 1829), 5–8.

[53] Ibid., 23–24, 29–30; Kling, "The New Divinity and the Origins of the ABCFM," 816–17.

[54] Kling, "New Divinity School of the Prophets," 196. Leonard Woods also noted that Hall studied under Asahel Hooker, a New Divinity minister from Goshen, Connecticut, who trained 33 ministers; see Woods, *History of Andover*, 25–26.

[55] *Memoirs of American Missionaries Formerly Connected with the Society of Inquiry Respecting Missions, in the Andover Theological Seminary* (Boston, MA: Pierce and Parker, 1833), 15–16.

[56] Wayland, *Memoir*, 1:79–80, 93.

Prominent Features of New Divinity Theology

New Divinity theology was not a monolithic entity. Like any school of thought, there were numerous sub-schools within it which evolved over time, adapting their messages as new questions emerged. There were, however, features of the Edwardsians that remained fairly constant throughout their century-long existence (1760–1860). For one, their staunch commitment to the sovereignty of God in salvation placed them within the Calvinist tradition, as did their adherence to various versions of the Westminster standards. Consequently, most of the New Divinity looked back fondly on both the Reformed tradition and its English and New England heirs, the Puritans. In addition, the Great Awakening left an indelible stamp on the New Divinity's spiritual DNA, which led it to hallow the writings of Jonathan Edwards, who championed a version of Calvinism that underscored revival and missions. As they appropriated Edwards's theological vision, they modified aspects of the Calvinist tradition they had inherited, modifications which they believed cleared up many of the conundrums that plagued traditional Calvinism.[57] As a result, they called themselves "Consistent Calvinists."[58] Their Old Calvinist critics repeatedly identified these modifications as defections from the Reformed tradition, dubbing their theology a *"new"* divinity that should be resisted.

The remainder of this essay will explore two prominent features of New Divinity theology. First it examines the theology of natural ability and moral inability, a theological distinction which concerns the capacity of the human will. Second, it explores the New Divinity's concept of disinterested benevolence, a doctrine that generated a great surge of social and evangelistic activism.

Natural Ability, Moral Inability, and the Possibility of Salvation

No writing, save Scripture, exerted such a profound influence on the New Divinity as Jonathan Edwards's *Freedom of the Will*.[59] Published in 1754 to counter Arminian

---

[57] For an overview of how the New Divinity saw Edwards make "improvements" to Calvinism, see the essay by his son, Jonathan Edwards Jr., *Remarks on the Improvements Made in Theology by His Father, President Edwards*, in *The Works of Jonathan Edwards, D. D.*, vol. 1 (New York: Dayton and Newman, 1842), 481–92.
[58] For explanations of this term and others that were used to identify the New Divinity, see Breitenbach, "The Consistent Calvinism of the New Divinity Movement," 241–44.
[59] Jonathan Edwards, *Freedom of the Will*, vol. 1, *The Works of Jonathan Edwards*, ed. Paul Ramsey (New Haven, CT: Yale University Press, 1957). After initial citing of Edwards's writings from Yale's critical edition, the work will be cited as *WJE* (for *Works of Jonathan Edwards*) followed by the volume and then page numbers.

arguments against Calvinism, Edwards's work inaugurated a century of theological discussion on the role of human volition in salvation. Many of the peculiar features of New Divinity theology can be traced to the zeal with which they embraced the themes of this work.

Edwards's goal in *Freedom of the Will* was to demonstrate that divine sovereignty over human actions and meaningful freedom of the will are not mutually exclusive.[60] In other words, salvation is entirely God's work, yet the decision to repent and believe is rightly called a free choice. Edwards's argument is complex, so this essay will limit its discussion to an important distinction he made in the course of his argument: that between natural and moral ability.[61] In response to critics who demonized the Calvinist notion of sinners' "inability" to repent of sin by their own power, Edwards and the New Divinity argued that sinful human beings do indeed possess a *natural ability* to repent and trust Christ for salvation.[62] "[M]an," wrote Hopkins, "has not lost any of his natural powers of understanding and will, etc. by becoming sinful."[63] Similarly, Edward Dorr Griffin preached, "It is not true that they *cannot* love and submit to Him. They have ample power, and nothing prevents [them] but their desperate wickedness."[64] The problem lies not in what one *can* do but in what one *wants* to do.

While having a natural ability to repent and believe, humans' inclinations are so warped by sin that they never seek Christ and His gospel. This inability has nothing to do with an individual's natural capacities but everything to do with a volitional bias against submitting to God. Sinners fail to repent and believe simply because they do not want to. Edwards called this the *moral inability* of a sinner.[65] No external power holds sinners back against their wills. Rather, their own sinful wills despise God, making faith in Christ an impossibility. In short, though they *could* repent and trust in Christ (natural ability), they *will not* do so (moral inability) because of sin.

Edwards offered a helpful illustration.[66] Imagine two prisoners; both were approached by the king and offered freedom, if they would come out of their cells and humbly beg him for a royal pardon. The first prisoner was willing and heartily repented

---

[60] The key lies in how one defines "freedom" as seen below.

[61] See Edwards, *Freedom of the Will*, in *WJE* 1:156–62 for his definition of these terms.

[62] Holifield, *Theology in America*, 142–43.

[63] Hopkins, *System of Doctrines*, 1:341.

[64] Edward Dorr Griffin, *A Series of Lectures, Delivered in Park Street Church* (Boston: 1813), 246.

[65] "[M]oral inability," Edwards wrote, "consists in the opposition of want of inclination." Edwards, *Freedom of the Will*, in *WJE* 1:159.

[66] Edwards, *Freedom of the Will*, in *WJE* 1:362–63. Griffin employs a similar illustration to portray the doctrine of election in *A Series of Lectures*, 223–26.

of his crimes, but was prevented from exiting his cell because no one unlocked the bars. This prisoner had a natural inability to be freed; he *could not* leave his cell even though he wanted to. The second prisoner "possessed with an extreme and inveterate enmity to his lawful sovereign" was so disgusted by the king and his offer of pardon that even though his chains were removed and the cell unlocked, he refused the offer and stubbornly remained in his cell. This prisoner had a moral inability to be freed; he *would not* leave even though he could. Because his will caused the inability, he was fully blameworthy. No one would hold the first prisoner responsible for remaining in his cell; everyone would blame the second.

This second prisoner, Edwards and the New Divinity held, illustrates the situation of unbelievers. The sinful will, possessed of a selfish disinclination to holiness, opposes God and the gospel. Arminians may counter that this nullifies freedom, for it subjects the will completely to the prevailing disposition of the heart. Resulting choices would not be morally accountable because they are not freely willed. In answering this objection Edwards affirmed that the will is completely subject to the prevailing inclinations of the heart, but denied that this nullifies freedom. Freedom, he argued, is not defined as a power to counter the prevailing inclinations of the soul (which would be a logical impossibility).[67] Rather, freedom is merely the power to do as one pleases.[68] If individuals choose certain actions based upon their preferences (willing "as they please," i.e., freely), they are completely responsible—even if the choices were determined by the disposition of their souls. The second prisoner is still responsible for his refusal to seek the king's pardon even though he is seized by a hateful spite of the king. In contrast, a husband may possess such a love for his wife that he may have a moral inability to murder her, an "inability" that most would agree is a completely praiseworthy virtue.

In sum, Edwards and the New Divinity held that moral necessity (the fact that the will necessarily chooses according to the heart's prevailing inclination), freedom (the power to do as one pleases), and moral accountability (being held responsible for one's freely willed actions) are perfectly consistent with each other.[69] Individuals do what they

---

[67] Edwards argued that the will, by definition, is determined by "that motive, which, as it stands in the view of the mind, is the strongest." It thus is logically impossible for the will to counter the strongest motives of the mind for they are essentially the same thing. See Edwards, *Freedom of the Will*, in *WJE* 1:141.

[68] Edwards, *Freedom of the Will*, in *WJE* 1:163.

[69] While this is an admittedly brief and abstract overview of these concepts, New Divinity theologians were careful to note their biblical foundations. See, for example, Nathanael Emmons, "Man's Activity and Dependence Illustrated and Reconciled," in *The Works of Nathanael Emmons, D.D.*, vol. 2 (Boston, MA: Congregational Board, 1860), 405–10.

want. But they have a sinful disposition and will not "will" their way to God unless He miraculously reorients the prevailing disposition of their souls. The priority of divine sovereignty is thus preserved.[70]

The New Divinity applied these distinctions as they made evangelistic appeals.[71] First, because everyone had a natural ability to repent and believe, New Divinity ministers called all sinners to repent and believe the gospel immediately. No one needed to wait for a season of conviction before getting serious about the claims of Christ. For generations New Englanders had grown accustomed to more of a gradualist view of salvation, popularized in many Puritan devotionals and sermons, where individuals were converted only after lengthy spiritual crises.[72] According to the Puritan model, an individual would come under conviction of sin, perhaps upon hearing a sermon or reading the Scriptures. Then an enormous spiritual struggle would ensue, involving guilt, sin, moral resolutions, and a deep perception of God's wrath. Pastors who oversaw these struggles would direct the convicted individuals to use the means of grace (prayer, seeking God, reading Scripture, attending sermons) with the hopes that God might, in His sovereignty, regenerate them.[73] Only then, when a person discerned within himself faith and a heart that loved Christ, was he encouraged to repent and "close" with Christ. The problem New Divinity ministers saw with this approach is that it sometimes became an excuse for spiritual lethargy (i.e., "I'm not ready; God has not begun His work in me yet"). They reacted strongly against such an attitude. "You indeed are ready; you *can* if you *will*," they said. "You possess the natural capacity to comply with the claims of the gospel. The only thing keeping you from Christ is your stubborn, sinful will! Repent immediately!" The practice of immediate repentance drew sharp criticism from Old Calvinists because of its potential to bypass what they saw as prerequisites to receiving Christ. Yet practically, the advice New Divinity ministers gave to seekers was not much different from that of Old Calvinists. For when it was asked "How do I repent?" the response was the same: seek God by using the means of grace. In due time, He might

---

[70] Nathanael Emmons gives an instance of how the New Divinity envisioned the compatibility between freedom and divine "influence" in the following quote: "It is their own free, voluntary agency, which alone constitutes their virtue or vice, and which renders them worthy of either praise or blame. Though they always act under a divine influence, yet that influence neither increases their virtue nor diminishes their guilt." Nathanael Emmons, "Human and Divine Agency Inseparably Connected," *Works*, 2:439.

[71] For a summary of New Divinity homiletics, see Kling, *Field of Divine Wonders*, 95–103, 110–43.

[72] For the Old Calvinist view on these issues, see Breitenbach, "Unregenerate Doings: Selflessness and Selfishness in New Divinity Theology," 482–87; and Holifield, *Theology in America*, 149–56.

[73] The means of grace never were the cause of regeneration. They were, however, its occasion, for it was argued that God usually regenerates a sinner in the midst of a prayerful appropriation of the means.

create in the heart a new set of affections which would incline the individual toward Christ. In spite of this similarity, the New Divinity's focus on the will's capacity shifted the discourse of revivalism toward a preoccupation with motives, loves, hatreds, and decisions made for or against Christ.

Disinterested Benevolence and the Nature of True Piety

The New Divinity's theology of religious experience arose from Edwards's *Treatise Concerning Religious Affections* and his dissertation on *The Nature of True Virtue*.[74] True Christians, the New Divinity argued, possess a benevolent principle of the heart which seeks the good or happiness of all things, including God and neighbors. Benevolence is essentially other-centered, and the benevolent Christian soul suspends its own needs and desires in order to obtain good for others. The Christian thus is "disinterested" in his own good because of his complete preoccupation with the good of God and others.

In his *Dissertation on the Nature of True Virtue*, Edwards argued that true Christian morality requires benevolence toward all things, or "Being in general." "True virtue most essentially consists in benevolence to Being in general. Or . . . that consent, propensity and union of heart to Being in general, that is immediately exercised in a general good will."[75] The Christian thus has a "propensity" to manifest good will to all things. The unconverted, in contrast, is benevolent toward a private, limited sphere related to the self.[76]

Universal benevolence originates at conversion when the Holy Spirit graces the heart with a new set of holy desires, enabling it to "see" and love the beauty of God's glory. Whereas before conversion persons did not appreciate the gospel, they now through new hearts see the glory of Christ, desire to unite with Him through faith, and lovingly embrace the way of the cross. Subsequently, the principle of self-love is broken, and the converted seek their happiness in God and all that He has made. This benevolent disposition was central to Edwardsian piety.

---

[74] Jonathan Edwards, *A Treatise Concerning Religious Affections*, in *The Works of Jonathan Edwards*, vol. 2, ed. John E. Smith (New Haven, CT: Yale University Press, 1959); and Jonathan Edwards, *The Nature of True Virtue*, in *The Works of Jonathan Edwards*, vol. 8: *Ethical Writings*, ed. Paul Ramsey (New Haven, CT: Yale University Press, 1989), 539–627.
[75] Edwards, *True Virtue*, in *WJE* 8:540.
[76] Ibid., 8:555–56.

To Edwards, being disinterested in self indicated the work of the Spirit in an individual. When individuals became so joyously preoccupied with God's moral excellence that they stopped noticing themselves, then Edwards concluded that they most likely had been regenerated. He wrote of this phenomenon in his narrative of the revival at his Northampton church:

> It has more frequently been so amongst us, that when persons have first had the gospel ground of relief for lost sinners discovered to them, and have been entertaining their minds with the sweet prospect, *they have thought nothing at that time of their being converted.* . . . There is wrought in them a holy repose of soul in God through Christ, and a secret disposition to fear and love him, and to hope for blessing from him in this way. *And yet they have no imagination that they are now converted, it don't so much as come in their minds.*[77]

In short, Edwards observed that in new Christians a disinterested love for God generally eclipses the desire for assurance of salvation because they are lost in contemplation of God's glories, not fixed upon the status of their own souls.[78]

Samuel Hopkins amplified the theme of disinterested benevolence to radical proportions.[79] First, he popularized the peculiar notion that true conversion must be preceded by a willingness to be damned for the sake of God and all of creation.[80] Second, and even more idiosyncratic, was Hopkins's explanation of evil in the world. Moral evil in a portion of the universe, he argued, magnifies justice, goodness, and holiness in the created order. Though God hates moral evil in itself, He allows it out of disinterested

---

[77] Jonathan Edwards, *A Faithful Narrative*, in *The Works of Jonathan Edwards*, vol. 4: *The Great Awakening*, ed. C. C. Goen (New Haven, CT: Yale University Press, 1970), 173, emphasis added. Edwards's own conversion followed a similar pattern; see Jonathan Edwards, *Personal Narrative*, in *The Works of Jonathan Edwards*, volume 16: *Letters and Personal Writings*, ed. George S. Claghorn (New Haven, CT: Yale University Press, 1998), 792–93.

[78] This was a central point Joseph Bellamy made against antinomianism; see Dialogue 1 in Joseph Bellamy, *Theron, Paulinus, and Aspasio: or, Letters and Dialogues upon the Nature of Love to God, Faith in Christ, Assurance of a Title to Eternal Life, containing some Remarks on the Sentiments of the Rev. Messrs. Hervey and Marshall, on these Subjects* (1759), in *The Works of Joseph Bellamy, D. D.*, vol. 2 (Boston, MA: Doctrinal Tract and Book Society, 1853), 165–85.

[79] For a summary of Hopkins's theological views on these subjects, see Conforti, *Samuel Hopkins and the New Divinity Movement*, 59–75, 109–24.

[80] Samuel Hopkins, *A Dialogue between a Calvinist and a Semi-Calvinist*, in *Works*, 3:143–57.

benevolence in order to promote the greater good.[81] This point is well-summarized by Gordon Hall, an early missionary associate of Judson's. "Benevolence desires the greatest good of the whole. And if, on survey of the several parts, it be found that this good of the whole will be augmented by the misery of a part, benevolence demands suffering. It demands this misery, not as in itself desirable, but because by it greater good will be promoted."[82] Lastly, and more positively, Hopkins applied the idea of disinterested benevolence to slavery in North America.[83] As a minister in the port city of Newport, Rhode Island, Hopkins saw the evils of the institution firsthand as traders brought in slaves for sale to New Englanders. Disinterested benevolence in this setting meant publically countering this accepted and lucrative institution for the good of the enslaved. In the 1770s Hopkins penned several lengthy treatises on the subject decades before a vigorous anti-slavery movement got underway in America.[84]

Perhaps no one exemplified the ideal of disinterested benevolence in ministry more than David Brainerd (1718–47), the tireless missionary to Native American Indians whose diary became the most reprinted of all of Edwards's works.[85] While Bellamy and Hopkins wrote about disinterested benevolence, Brainerd lived it. Converted during the First Great Awakening as a student at Yale, Brainerd ministered to Native Americans in western Massachusetts, New York, Pennsylvania, and New Jersey throughout the 1740s before dying from tuberculosis in Edwards's parsonage at age 29. As Brainerd's life ebbed away, Edwards recognized in him the type of Christlike piety he had written about in *Religious Affections*, and he secured Brainerd's permission to publish the spiritual diary he had kept during his years as a missionary. Published in 1749, *The Life of David Brainerd* is a first-person account of an incredibly difficult ministry, one fraught with loneliness, failing health, fruitlessness, and despondency yet punctuated with times of close communion with God that energized him to press on:

---

[81] See his three sermons on this subject in Samuel Hopkins, *Sin, Through Divine Interposition, an Advantage to the Universe*, in *Works*, 2:493–545.

[82] Gordon Hall, untitled essay fragment found in *Memoir of Nathanael Emmons; with Sketches of His Friends and Pupils*, ed. Edwards Amasa Park, in *Works of Nathanael Emmons*, 1:189.

[83] David S. Lovejoy, "Samuel Hopkins: Religion, Slavery, and the Revolution," *New England Quarterly* 40 (June 1967): 227–43; Conforti, *Samuel Hopkins and the New Divinity Movement*, 125–41.

[84] Samuel Hopkins's *A Dialogue Concerning the Slavery of the Africans*, in *Works*, 2:547–88, is one of five separate works devoted to the subject in this volume.

[85] Jonathan Edwards, ed., *The Life of David Brainerd*, in *The Works of Jonathan Edwards*, vol. 7, ed. Norman Pettit (New Haven, CT: Yale University Press, 1985).

Monday, March 7. This morning when I arose, I found my heart go forth after God in longing desires of conformity to him, and in secret prayer found myself sweetly quickened and drawn out in praises to God for all he had done to and for me, and for all my inward trials and distresses of late; my heart ascribed glory, glory, glory to the blessed God! And bid welcome all inward distress again, if God saw meet to exercise me with it; time appeared but an inch long, and eternity at hand; and I thought I could with patience and cheerfulness bear anything for the cause of God: For I saw that a moment would bring me to a world of peace and blessedness; and my soul, by the strength of the Lord, rose far above this lower world, and all the vain amusements and frightful disappointments of it.[86]

For the next century, *The Life of David Brainerd* was one of the most reprinted works in evangelical literature.[87] Joseph Conforti has argued that among the New Divinity, Brainerd's life was the quintessential example of disinterested benevolence, a point illustrated by the overwhelming number of Brainerd references in evangelical and missionary diaries from the period.[88] "Much refreshed this day by perusing the life of Brainerd," Levi Parsons wrote in his diary in 1815 as an Andover student. "How completely devoted to God, how ardent his affections. What thirst after holiness, what love for souls. . . . Counting pain and distress and every bodily infirmity as dross, he patiently encountered difficulties and dangers, and at last sweetly resigned his all to his savior. Multitudes have reason to call him blessed."[89]

By Judson's day disinterested benevolence had become a standard theme of New Divinity preaching and piety. It helped draw young Ann Hasseltine, Judson's future wife, to the gospel as she meditated upon Bellamy's *True Religion Delineated*.[90] It shaped the conversion experience of Judson's early missionary associate, Samuel Mills.[91] It moti-

---

[86] *Life of David Brainerd*, in *WJE* 7:199.

[87] Conforti, *Jonathan Edwards, Religious Tradition, and American Culture*, 68.

[88] See his essay, "David Brainerd and Disinterested Benevolence in Antebellum Evangelical Culture," in Conforti, *Jonathan Edwards, Religious Tradition, and American Culture*, 62–86.

[89] Daniel O. Morton, ed., *Memoir of Levi Parsons, First Missionary to Palestine from the United States* (Burlington, VT: 1830), 42, as quoted in Conforti, *Jonathan Edwards, Religious Tradition, and American Culture*, 75.

[90] Anderson, *To the Golden Shore*, 78. One can also note Edwardsian language and themes in Hasseltine's narration of her conversion in Edward Judson, *The Life*, 33–34.

[91] See Spring, *Memoirs of Samuel Mills*, 8. An unidentified acquaintance of Mills noted that "the conversion of the youthful Samuel J. Mills was, in a peculiar degree, coincident with the Hopkinsian standard of

vated Christians to take great risks for the sake of the gospel, risks that might end in the death of a loved one. In fact, Judson called for disinterested benevolence in a fascinating letter to Ann Hasseltine's father asking for permission to marry his daughter: "I have now to ask," he wrote, "whether you can consent to part with your daughter early next spring, to see her no more in this world; whether you can consent to her departure, and her subjection to the hardships and sufferings of a missionary life; . . . to degradation, insult, persecution, and perhaps a violent death. Can you consent to all this?"[92] Lastly, disinterested benevolence factored into the enormous self-sacrifice undertaken by the early ABCFM missionaries, many of whom went to an early grave like Brainerd. Citing Brainerd's example in his farewell address before leaving for Palestine, Levi Parsons noted that it is "Better, my brethren, [to] wear out and die within three years than live forty in slothfulness."[93] Disinterested benevolence, in short, was more than merely an Edwardsian ethical theory; it represented the New Divinity's codification of radical self-denial that unleashed a torrent of missionary activism.

Final Observations

Did Adoniram Judson embrace New Divinity theology as a young student, and if so, to what extent? Unfortunately, no long-lost stash of theological essays from Judson's Andover days have surfaced, so the exact details of his early theological convictions are not known. There is, however, a fairly reliable witness, a paragraph from an anonymous acquaintance tucked away in the memoir of Nathanael Emmons. The writer seeks to show the importance of Emmons's theology to the early missionary movement and appears to have firsthand knowledge of the basic theological orientation of the early Andover missionaries. He notes that Judson's father "loved the character and imbibed the theories of Emmons." Judson himself studied under a "Hopkinsian professor, and a pupil of Emmons" at Brown and came to "defend [these positions] after he became a devoted Christian in the Theological Seminary at Andover." Later he "was approbated to preach as a Hopkinsian and an Emmonite."[94] These remarks suggest that Judson embraced at

---

practical religion." See *Works of Nathanael Emmons*, 1:188.
[92] Cited in Anderson, *To the Golden Shore*, 83.
[93] Levi Parsons, "Farewell Address," as cited in Conforti, *Jonathan Edwards, Religious Tradition, and American Culture*, 76.
[94] Anonymous "sketch" found in Park, *Memoir of Nathanael Emmons; with Sketches of His Friends and Pupils*, in *Works of Nathanael Emmons*, 1:188.

least some New Divinity theology. It would make sense that he picked up at least some of his theology from that context. He boarded the ship bound for Calcutta in 1812 as a recent seminary graduate of the Edwardsian tradition, poised to embark on a life of selfless gospel ministry.

Biographical Presentation

Chapter 3

Ambition Overthrown

The Conversion, Consecration, and Commission of Adoniram Judson, 1788–1812

Jason G. Duesing[1]

Resting 165 feet above Plymouth Rock is a forgotten cemetery. Burial Hill in Plymouth, Massachusetts, dates to the arrival of the Pilgrims, and the panoramic view of both ocean and land once made for a fitting location for a fort and watchtower. After the need for vigilant defense of the area subsided, Burial Hill became the cemetery for many local families. By the end of the nineteenth century, a memorial slab near the site of the old watchtower commemorated one of Plymouth's notable families. Surrounded by a small white fence and elevated on short pillars, the six-foot stone lists the names of the Judsons. Among the inscriptions one finds:

ADONIRAM JUDSON.D.D.
Missionary of the American Baptist
Missionary Union to the Burman
Empire, who died at Sea
April 12, 1850, Æ. 62 years.[2]

Though he gained the type of national notoriety generally reserved for public officials and dignitaries, Judson would not have wanted even this obscure and hidden tribute. However, this was not always the case. During his formative years, he sought fame and the praise of men. By the end of his life, this ambition had been overthrown and redirected. The 62-year-old Judson delighted in obscurity and sought no recognition for himself. Burial at sea was ideal, and he likely would have rejected the suggestion of a

---

[1] My thanks to Zachary Bowden and Candi Finch for their review and comments on drafts of this chapter. Thanks also to Matthew Queen and Tommy Kiker.
[2] Frank H. Perkins, *Handbook of Old Burial Hill* (Plymouth, MA: A. S. Burbank, 1896), 5–13, 31–35.

memorial stone of any kind. Nevertheless, the family slab at Burial Hill marks the life of America's first commissioned pioneer missionary. On the bicentennial of Judson's departure for missionary service in the East, this essay, too, marks his life. Specifically, it details his preparation for the mission field and the rise, fall, and redirecting of his ambition.

Conversion

The story of Adoniram Judson's formative years (1788–1812) is the story of the work of the Spirit of God on a man's life by the sharp instrument of the Word of God. As one biographer noted, Judson's earnest ambition would serve him his entire life.[3] Yet, prior to his conversion at age 20, Judson's unregenerate ambition opposed the Spirit and the Word at every turn.

The eldest son of a Congregationalist pastor, Judson was born August 9, 1788, in Malden, Massachusetts. In his early years, he showed remarkable intellectual ability, learning to read by the age of three. His first encounter with the Word of God came when his mother trained him to read a chapter of the Bible as a surprise gift to his preacher-father. Indeed, the Book that he later translated into the Burmese language was never far from him. But he drifted far from it. Judson's remarkable abilities were fanned into a competitive ambition by his father, who sought for his son a life of great achievement.[4]

The Judson family relocated to Wenham, Massachusetts, in January 1793, where they remained until Adoniram was 11. From science experiments to advanced arithmetic to nautical navigation, Judson excelled, and his ambition drove him to make a significant impression on many outside his own family. However, in language study and reading he enjoyed unique proficiency, setting himself apart in grammar school in the study of Greek. The majority of the books to which Judson had access were his father's theology books. Though he read them, he had little genuine interest in the subject matter. On one occasion, he overheard his father speak of a new volume on the biblical book Revelation, which had garnered the attention of many in the community. Adoniram, nearly 12 and eager to join the discussion and show off his intellectual abilities, sought permission from his father to borrow the new book from a neighbor. His father refused—much to

---

[3] H. C. Conant, *The Earnest Man* (Boston, MA: Philips, Samson and Company, 1856).
[4] Edward Judson, *The Life of Adoniram Judson* (New York: Ansom D. F. Randolph, 1883), 2.

Judson's disappointment.[5] While the Word of God was near the young Judson, he studied it only out of self-seeking ambition.

Leaving Wenham in May 1800, the Judsons spent two years in Braintree, Massachusetts, before settling in Plymouth on May 11, 1802. At the age of 14, Judson contracted a debilitating illness that effectively suspended his life for an entire year. During that time, he realized that his well-conceived plans for personal greatness as an orator, poet, or statesman were in danger of failing. He began to think that the attainment of all his worldly goals might not satisfy him in the end. Attributing such thinking to his illness, Judson attempted to return his thoughts to future greatness only to find himself faced with the words of Psalm 115:1, "Not unto us, O LORD not unto us, but unto thy name give glory." The Holy Spirit's conviction did not sit well with Judson, for becoming a Christian would threaten his ambition.[6]

After recovering from the illness, Judson enrolled at Providence College in August 1804. Just 16 years old, he gained admittance a year early due to his intellectual accomplishments. Why the Congregationalist family selected a Baptist College—Providence would later become known as Brown University—is not clear. Brumberg notes that Judson's hometown was equidistant from both Harvard and Brown. But the recent theological drift toward liberalism at Harvard likely influenced Judson's parents to send him to Brown.[7] Biographer Stacy Warburton explains that

> Brown was popular with Congregationalists, even though a Baptist institution. Up to the time Adoniram Judson entered, one hundred and three Brown graduates had become ministers, and of these at least sixty-six were Congregationalists. . . . And indeed, the latter had had a considerable share in the founding of the college, almost as much as Baptists.[8]

Even though Brown aimed to produce orthodox and committed evangelicals, Judson found avenues there to satisfy both his ambitions and his skeptical intellect. At a school that promoted the study of the Word of God, Judson's ambition continued to oppose the Spirit and the Word. One early biographer of Judson observes that

---

[5] Ibid., 6.
[6] Ibid., 9–10.
[7] Joan Jacobs Brumberg, *Mission for Life* (New York: The Free Press, 1980), 33, n62.
[8] Stacy R. Warburton, *Eastward! The Story of Adoniram Judson* (New York: Round Table, 1937), 5.

in the years which Mr. Judson spent at Providence, French infidelity was extremely popular. It is no wonder that with the general tendencies of young men to favor novel and extreme views, and when leading minds were entangled in its sophistical mazes, that it found many to welcome it in the colleges of the land. Not a few soon learned contempt for the Bible. Mr. Judson was of their number.[9]

Deistical philosophy, sometimes called French infidelity, made inroads in New England following the Revolutionary War. Timothy Dwight, president of Yale College, observed that prior to the war,

> the same reverence for God, the same justice, truth, and benevolence, the same opposition to inordinate indulgences of passion and appetite, prevailed without any material exceptions. A universal veneration for the Sabbath, a sacred respect for government, an undoubting belief in Divine revelation, and an unconditional acknowledgement and performance of the common social duties, constituted everywhere a prominent character.[10]

However, when Americans welcomed the French,

> foreigners, for the first time, mingled extensively with the inhabitants of New-England. . . . Most of their American companions had never heard the Divine origin of the Scriptures questioned, and their minds were, of course, unprovided with answers even to the most common objections . . . . These gentlemen were at the same time possessed of engaging manner; and practised all those genteel vices, which, when recommended by such manners, generally fascinate young men of gay, ambitious minds; and are naturally considered as conferring an enviable distinction on those, who adopt them. Many of the Americans were far from being dull proficients in this school. The vices they loved; and soon found the principles necessary to quiet their consciences.[11]

---

[9] E. H. Fletcher, *Records of the Life, Character, and Achievements of Adoniram Judson* (New York, NY: Edward H. Fletcher, 1854), 15; Brumberg, *Mission for Life*, 33.

[10] Timothy Dwight, *Travels in New-England and New-York*, vol. 4 (London: William Baynes & Son, 1823), 353. Published posthumously by the former president of Yale, Timothy Dwight had long incorporated regular travels into his duties as college president. The four volumes represent his observations.

[11] Ibid., 354.

Thus, by the time Judson went to Brown, skeptical philosophy was not only readily available but was seen as intellectually superior and sought by those with "ambitious minds."

While at Brown, Judson befriended Jacob Eames. Eames, a year older, embodied the attributes to which Judson aspired, including the rejection of Christianity in favor of deism. The two became close friends and encouraged one another in their pursuit of greatness. At one time they considered entering the practice of law to open the door for later political opportunities. On another occasion they marveled at their own dramatic prowess and planned to climb the ranks of society as playwrights.[12] The friendship stoked Judson's ego and, consequently, his rejection of Christianity.

Judson met every challenge his worldly ambition set for him at Brown. Fearful of a health-related setback, he never took a break from his studies, pushing himself to excel through academic rivalries. One contemporary had "no recollection of his ever failing, or even hesitating, in recitation."[13] The president of Brown even wrote Judson's father after his first year to report that "a uniform propriety of conduct, as well as an intense application to study, distinguishes his character."[14] Judson set his heart on achieving the highest marks in his class and anticipated the day when he would be chosen to give the valedictory address at his commencement. In 1807, upon receiving the news that his strivings would be rewarded at commencement, he immediately wrote home to his father a one-line letter stating, "Dear father, I have got it."[15]

Graduating at age 19, Judson returned home to Plymouth to operate a private academy and publish two textbooks. However, his newfound philosophy did not fit with the Congregationalist commitments of his family. In August 1808 Judson closed his academy, and much like the Prodigal Son, left town on an undisciplined tour of the surrounding states. Before leaving, he informed his parents of his religious views and plans, much to their disappointment. His father provided him with a horse, and after spending time with an uncle in Connecticut, Judson went to New York, traveling down the Hudson River on a steamer. Embracing the anonymity of the journey, he referred to himself as Mr. Johnson, and upon arrival in New York, he sought to become a playwright.[16] Later in life, he would recount to a friend that

---

[12] Francis Wayland, *A Memoir of the Life and Labors of the Rev. Adoniram Judson, D.D.* (Boston, MA: Phillips, Sampson, and Company, 1853), 1:22–23.
[13] Edward Judson, *The Life*, 7.
[14] Asa Messer to Adoniram Judson Sr., 30 April 1805, quoted in Edward Judson, *The Life*, 7.
[15] Edward Judson, *The Life*, 7.
[16] Ibid., 11.

in my early days of wildness, I joined a band of strolling players. We lived a reckless, vagabond life, finding lodgings where we could, and bilking the landlord where we found opportunity—in other words, running up a score, and then decamping without paying the reckoning.[17]

Following his New York experience, Judson returned to his uncle's house to retrieve his horse before heading west in search of further adventure.

The next evening, Judson found lodging in a small inn. The caretaker explained that he had to place Judson in a room next to a young man who was very ill and possibly dying. Such circumstances led to a sleepless night. Sounds of visitors and the groans of the ill man continued unabated. However, the prospect that a man in an adjacent room might die disturbed the prodigal wanderer more than the noise. Was Judson ready to die? His philosophy could not calm his fears or answer his questions. Embarrassed over his weak moment, he considered how Jacob Eames surely would chide him in that hour. Yet, the thoughts of his and the neighboring man's eternal state would not leave him.[18]

When the morning arrived, Judson dismissed his nightmares with the light of dawn and asked the caretaker about the ill man.

"He is dead," came the reply.

"Dead!"

"Yes, he is gone, poor fellow! The doctor said he would probably not survive the night."

"Do you know who he was?"

"O, yes; it was a young man from the Providence College—a very fine fellow; his name was Eames."

Judson was completely stunned. After hours had passed, he knew not how, he attempted to pursue his journey. But one single thought occupied his mind, and the words, Dead! lost! lost! were continually ringing in his ears. He knew the religion of the Bible to be true; he felt its truth; and he was in despair.[19]

---

[17] Henry Gougher, *A Personal Narrative of Two Years' Imprisonment in Burmah, 1824–26* (London: John Murray, 1860), 179.

[18] Edward Judson, *The Life*, 12.

[19] Ibid., 12–13. Brumberg, *Mission for Life*, 35, contends that this story recounted by many biographers "is probably apocryphal" since Judson never mentioned it. However, both Wayland and Edward Judson cite the account as the recollection of close family members. Since Judson did not speak much about his preconversion days, one should not be surprised that he never mentioned the incident.

For the first time, Judson suspended his ambition in the face of a growing conviction from the Spirit and the Word of God. He discarded his plans to travel west and in September 1808 headed toward Plymouth. His future wife, Ann, provided the following account:

> His mind became so deeply impressed with the probability of the Divine authenticity of the Scriptures, that he could no longer continue his journey; but returned to his father's house, for the express purpose of examining thoroughly the foundation of the Christian religion. After continuing his investigations for some time, he became convinced that the Scriptures were of Divine origin, and that he himself was in a lost situation by nature, and needed renovation previous to an admittance into heaven. It now became his sole enquiry, "What shall I do to be saved?"[20]

Having returned home to his parents, Judson still could not find spiritual relief. After delving for so long into intellectual pursuits, he could not bring his mind to trust what he knew to be true from the Word of God. Two professors from the new Andover Theological Seminary, after visiting with Judson's father, suggested that Judson should enter the seminary to aid in his search for truth.[21] The seminary, formed in reaction to the drift toward Unitarianism at Harvard, was a bastion of orthodoxy at which Judson could work through his difficulties. To guard against theological error, one historian of the school explains that

> among the regulations which the Trustees thus accepted was one to the effect that every professor in the Seminary must "be a man of sound and orthodox principles in divinity according to that form of sound words or system of evangelical doctrines, drawn from the Scriptures, and denominated by the Westminster Assembly's Shorter Catechism, and more concisely delineated in the Constitution of Phillips Academy." In further regulations it was provided that every professor must at the time of his inauguration solemnly promise to maintain and inculcate the Christian faith as summarily expressed in the Shorter Catechism "in opposition not only to Atheists and Infidels, but to Jews, Mahommetans, Arians, Pelagians, Antinomians, Arminians, Socinians,

---

[20] Ann Judson, *An Account of the American Baptist Mission to the Burman Empire* (London: J. Butterworth & Son, 1823), 6.
[21] Wayland, *Memoir*, 1:26.

Unitarians, and Universalists, and to all other heresies and errors, ancient or modern, which may be opposed to the Gospel of Christ, or hazardous to the souls of men," and that every professor must repeat this declaration in the presence of the Trustees once in five years.[22]

Should Judson enroll, the seminary also had clear expectations for the education its students would receive. Armed with an allegiance to the Word of God,

> the purpose of the Founders, according to their constitution, was to increase "the number of learned and able defenders of the Gospel of Christ, as well as of orthodox, pious, and zealous ministers of the New Testament; being moved, as we hope, by a principle of gratitude to God and benevolence to man." A similar purpose motivated the Associate Founders. . . . "To the Spirit of Truth, to the divine Author of our faith, to the only wise God, we desire in sincerity to present this our humble offering, devoutly imploring the Father of Lights, richly to endue. . . . with spiritual understanding the professors therein, that, being illuminated by the Holy Spirit their doctrine may drop as the rain; and that their pupils may become trees of renown in the courts of our God, whereby He may be glorified."[23]

While Judson considered seminary, he accepted a position as an assistant to a teacher in Boston.[24]

While in Boston, perhaps to help provide answers to his questions, Judson was given a copy of Thomas Boston's *Human Nature in Its Fourfold State*.[25] Boston, a minister in the Church of Scotland in the early eighteenth century, began the volume with the following explanation of the positions in which man has or can find himself before God:

> There are four things very necessary to be known by all that would see heaven: First, what Man was in the state of innocence, as God made him. Secondly, what he is in the state of corrupt nature, as he hath unmade himself. Thirdly, what he must be in the state of grace, as created in Christ Jesus unto good

---

[22] Henry K. Rowe, *History of Andover Theological Seminary* (Newton, MA: Thomas Todd, 1933), 13–14; Brumberg, *Mission for Life*, 27.
[23] Ibid., 14.
[24] Wayland, *Memoir*, 1:26.
[25] Thomas Boston, *Human Nature in Its Fourfold State* (Edinburgh: Bockfellers, 1794).

works, if ever he be made a partaker of the inheritance of the saints in light. And, lastly, what he shall be in his eternal state, as made by the Judge of all, either perfectly happy, or completely miserable, and that for ever. These are weighty points, that touch the vitals of practical godliness, from which most men, and even many professors, in these dregs of time, are quite estranged. I design therefore, under the divine conduct, to open up these things, and apply them.[26]

Something in Boston's work must have resonated with Judson because it motivated him to enroll at Andover.[27]

Since Judson was not a Christian, he entered Andover Theological Seminary on October 12, 1808, as a special student. Professor Leonard Woods later recalled:

When Mr. Judson came to Andover, he was not a professor of religion, and gave no evidence of being a Christian. We consented to his staying in the Seminary for a time, but did not then admit him as a member.[28]

In the years ahead, Judson stated that he knew at the time of his admittance that he was still "a wretched infidel,"[29] and Professor Woods observed that he "was naturally the subject of manifest pride and ambition."[30] Still only 20 years of age, Judson had self-reliance and ambition that prevented him from turning to Christ. However, at Andover Seminary, Judson would have regular exposure to the Word of God and the fellowship of those directed by the Spirit.

As a part of the regular curriculum, students were required to read Psalm 130.[31] Perhaps it was the reading of these verses of desperation that the Spirit used to overcome Judson's ambition and underscore his need for forgiveness:

---

[26] Ibid., 17.
[27] Warburton, *Eastward!* 14; Brumberg, *Mission for Life*, 35–36.
[28] Leonard Woods to Daniel C. Eddy, 25 November 1850, quoted in Eddy, *A Sketch of Adoniram Judson* (Lowell: Nathaniel L. Dayton, 1851), v; Brumberg, *Mission for Life*, 33.
[29] Leonard Woods, *History of the Andover Theological Seminary*, 136–37; Brumberg, *Mission for Life*, 35.
[30] Woods to Eddy, *A Sketch of Adoniram Judson*, v.
[31] Woods, *History*, 168–69.

Psalm 130

Out of the depths have I cried unto thee, O Lord.
Lord, hear my voice: let thine ears be attentive to the voice of my supplications.
If thou, Lord, shouldest mark iniquities, O Lord, who shall stand?
But there is forgiveness with thee, that thou mayest be feared.
I wait for the Lord, my soul doth wait, and in his word do I hope.
My soul waiteth for the Lord more than they that watch for the morning: I say, more than they that watch for the morning.
Let Israel hope in the Lord: for with the Lord there is mercy, and with him is plenteous redemption.
And he shall redeem Israel from all his iniquities.

In the weeks following Judson's arrival, a professor observed that he "became thoughtful and anxious; and after a time he showed signs of a change, which we hoped was the saving work of the Holy Spirit."[32] In November, Judson recorded that he began "to entertain hope of having received the regenerating influences of the Holy Spirit."[33] This admission, though subtle and without fanfare, represented the beginning of the destruction of his self-fashioned idols of ambition and autonomy. Judson confessed that all he had obtained in life and much of what he had regarded as truth was without value. The Spirit of God, through the Word of God, had worked to overcome his ambition. Speaking from what must have been first-hand experience, Judson would later write to his wife, Ann, on the eve of their wedding, "God is waiting to be gracious, and is willing to make us happy in religion, if we would not run away from Him."[34]

On December 2, 1808, Judson dedicated himself to God, and on May 28, 1809, he joined the Third Congregational Church in Plymouth as a public profession of his new faith. He continued as a regular student at Andover and became known for his devotion to the Bible. His son would later recount,

> He found the Bible wiser than any of the books he had hitherto encountered. It revealed his waywardness and sinfulness and at the same time the mercy and lovingkindness of God. He gave his heart to the Saviour and perceived that the

---

[32] Woods to Eddy, *A Sketch of Adoniram Judson*, v.
[33] Edward Judson, *The Life*, 562.
[34] Adoniram Judson to Ann Hasseltine, 31 December 1810, quoted in Wayland, *Memoir*, 1:14.

ambition to please God was more delightful than all the other forms of ambition which had beset him.[35]

According to one biographer, Judson's new outlook on life was expressed by Eph 3:14–19:

> For this cause I bow my knees unto the Father of our Lord Jesus Christ, Of whom the whole family in heaven and earth is named, That he would grant you, according to the riches of his glory, to be strengthened with might by his Spirit in the inner man; That Christ may dwell in your hearts by faith; that ye, being rooted and grounded in love, May be able to comprehend with all saints what is the breadth, and length, and depth, and height; And to know the love of Christ, which passeth knowledge, that ye might be filled with all the fulness of God.[36]

CONSECRATION

In the years that followed, God harnessed Judson's ambition for His glory. At the start of his second year at Andover, Judson began to "reflect on the personal duty of devoting his life to the cause of missions."[37] The idea of consecrating his life to go to the ends of the earth, though perhaps an abrupt concept for his family, was not a novel development in 1809 New England. As one historian relates, "To get through Andover without reading Brainerd was virtually unthinkable."[38] Jonathan Edwards's *Diary and Journal of David Brainerd* appeared on the reading list for all students because "theological students could not neglect this kind of reading, without experiencing an essential loss both as

---

[35] Adoniram B. Judson, *How Judson Became a Baptist Missionary* (Philadelphia, PA: Griffith & Rowland, 1913), 6.

[36] F. W. Boreham, *A Temple of Topaz* (Philadelphia, PA: Judson, 1928), available from http://fwboreham.blogspot.com/2007/02/boreham-on-adoniram-judson.html, states, "Here, on my desk, are three separate accounts of his conversion. In summing up the situation, each writer refers to this factor in the case. 'The love of Christ displaced selfish ambition as the ruling motive of his life,' says the First. 'He became a man of one idea—the love of Christ—and he desired to spend his whole life demonstrating it' says the Second. 'Having been forgiven much, he loved much,' says the Third. To comprehend the breadth and length and depth and height and to know the love of Christ which passeth knowledge—this became, at the dawn of his manhood, his one supreme and passionate aspiration. It is the climax of all that has gone before; it is the key of all that follows."

[37] Wayland, *Memoir*, 1:29.

[38] Brumberg, *Mission for Life*, 25.

to their present advancement in holiness, and their future usefulness in the ministry."[39] Edwards's work told the story of the sacrificial life of the young New England minister, David Brainerd, spent reaching Native Americans with the gospel.[40] The volume, published in 1749, found wide reading as the first full missionary biography ever published. As the modern missionary movement advanced, Brainerd's *Diary and Journal* could be found in various missionary settings, often consulted as a field manual.[41]

Also, in New England, especially among evangelicals, there existed a wide following of William Carey. Motivated by the Great Commission in Matt 28:18–20, Carey, with the publication of his *Enquiry* in 1792, led British Baptists to support an effort to take the gospel to "those who have no Bibles, no preachers, nor many other common advantages which are taken for granted at home."[42] By the early nineteenth-century, many in America were also sought to support Carey's work. In an evangelical publication, *The Panoplist*, in March 1806 a notice was posted "to all who love the prosperity of Zion, and are disposed to aid in propagating the Gospel among the Heathen," seeking aid "for the purpose of printing the sacred scriptures in one of the languages" of India. It referenced the missionaries to whom such support would go including, "the laborious, learned, and pious Mr. Carey, Professor of Oriental languages, in the college of Fort William, at Calcutta."[43]

Judson's reading of Brainerd and awareness of Carey prepared him to respond to a sermon he read in September 1809 on Matt 2:2, "For we have seen his star in the East, and are come to worship him." On February 26, 1809, Claudius Buchanan preached the sermon "The Star in the East" in Bristol, England.[44] Buchanan, an Anglican priest and chaplain in the East India Company, took the account of Jesus' birth and emphasized the uniqueness of the Gentile visitors, the wise men following a star, as "representatives of the whole heathen world."[45] The star's eastern location, Buchanan noted, is significant because "millions of the human race inhabit that portion of the globe." Therefore, just as in the day of the arrival of God's Son, the East once again was bearing witness to the Messiah, "not indeed by the shining of a Star, but by affording luminous evidence of the

---

[39] Woods, *History*, 168–69.

[40] Jonathan Edwards, *Diary and Journal of David Brainerd with Preface and Reflections by Jonathan Edwards* (Edinburgh: Banner of Truth Trust, 2007).

[41] Iain Murray, *Jonathan Edwards: A New Biography* (Edinburgh: Banner of Truth Trust, 1987), 307, 470.

[42] William Carey, *An Enquiry into the Obligations of Christians, to Use Means for the Conversion of the Heathens* (1792 ed.; repr., Didcot, Oxfordshire: The Baptist Missionary Society, 1991), 40–41. E.8.

[43] *The Panoplist* 1 (March 1806): 462–63; Brumberg, *Mission for Life*, 25.

[44] Claudius Buchanan, *The Star in the East* (New York, NY: Williams & Whiting, 1809).

[45] Ibid., 4.

divine origin of the Christian Faith."[46] Buchanan then proceeded to give evidence for the spread of Christianity in the East and the need for men to take the gospel to that region of the world. Brumberg notes that "The Star in the East" appeared in the *Massachusetts Baptist Missionary Magazine* right at the time Judson indicated he read it.[47] What might have caught Judson's attention was Buchanan's description of the need to translate Scripture into various languages:

> When the gospel was first to be preached to all nations, it was necessary to give a diversity of *tongues*; a *tongue* for each *nation*; and this was done by the Divine Power. But in this second promulgation, as it were, of the Gospel, the work will probably be carried on by a diversity of *translations*, a diversity of Scriptures; a *translation* for each *nation*. Instead of the gift of tongues, God, by his providence, is giving to mankind the gift of Scriptures.[48]

The emphasis on the translation of Scripture as an essential part of missions represents the predominate methodology employed during the early years of the modern missions movement. Buchanan was a friend of William Carey, and Carey's approach as a linguist and translator resonated with Judson.[49] Indeed, one biographer says that Judson's reverence for the Word of God fueled his desire to translate the Bible:

> A third peculiarity of his character—and one that tinged his whole life—was his reverence for the Bible. This habit is significant in connexion with his work as a translator, and it often influenced his plans, himself unconscious of its power. Judson's name is to be added to the names of Waldo and Lefevre, of Wickliffe and Tyndale, of Luther, Bedell, and Carey. He did the same work, and had the same history. France, England, Germany, Ireland, India, and Burmah, are largely indebted for their Bible to men who themselves learnt their religion from the devout study of its pages. Their *message*, and their convictions, as well as their office, they received from God.[50]

---

[46] Ibid., 5–6.
[47] Brumberg, *Mission for Life*, 36 n72. See *Massachusetts Baptist Missionary Magazine* (Sept 1809): 202–6.
[48] Buchanan, *Star*, 22.
[49] See "The Star in the East" available from http://www.wmcarey.edu/carey/buchanan/star.htm.
[50] Joseph Angus, "Introduction," in H. C. Conant, *The Earnest Man: A Memoir of Adoniram Judson* (London: J. Heaton, 1861), viii.

Judson said that the reading of Buchanan's sermon had two effects on him. First, it enabled him to "break the strong attachment I felt to home and country, and to endure the thought of abandoning all my wonted pursuits and animating prospects."[51] Although the excitement faded, the sermon led him to the woods to contemplate and pray about becoming a missionary. In February 1810, while walking alone, he arrived at a moment of decision: "The command of Christ, 'Go into all the world, and preach the gospel to every creature,' was presented to my mind with such clearness and power, that I came to a full decision, and though great difficulties appeared in my way, resolved to obey the command at all events."[52] Thus, the Word of God, brought to his mind by the Spirit, solidified Judson's future course when he was 21.

Second, Buchanan's sermon focused Judson's gaze on the East. His future wife, Ann, writing in 1823, recounted that "the subject harassed his mind from day to day, and he felt deeply impressed with the importance of making some attempt to rescue the perishing millions of the East."[53] Judson began to read all that he could regarding countries in the East. He soon discovered Michael Symes's, *An Account of an Embassy to the Kingdom of Ava*, and within its pages found his future home.[54] Symes, a British army officer, was sent to Burma in 1795; and in the two-volume work that detailed his experiences, he described the country: "There are no countries on the habitable globe, where the arts of civilized life are understood, of which we have so limited a knowledge, as of those that lie between the British possessions in India and the Empire of China."[55] Of their religion, Symes explained, "The Birmans are Hindoos: not votaries of Brahma, but sectaries of Boodh."[56] As Anderson concludes, a civilized society in the East that

---

[51] Adoniram Judson to Stephen Chapin, 18 December 1837, quoted in Wayland, *Memoir*, 1:51–52. Judson continues, "Though I do not now consider that sermon as peculiarly excellent, it produced a very powerful effect on my mind. For days I was unable to attend to the studies of my class, and spent my time wondering at my past stupidity, depicting the most romantic scenes in missionary life, and roving about the college rooms, declaiming on the subject of missions. My views were very incorrect, and my feelings extravagant; but yet I have always felt thankful to God for bringing me into that state of excitement."

[52] Ibid.

[53] Ann Judson, *An Account*, 7–8.

[54] Courtney Anderson, *To the Golden Shore: The Life of Adoniram Judson* (New York: Little, Brown and Company, 1956), 54.

[55] Michael Symes, *An Account of an Embassy to the Kingdom of Ava, in the Year 1795*, vol. 1 (Ediburgh: Constable & Co., 1827), 7.

[56] Ibid., 33.

was completely pagan and without the Word of God held forth a great opportunity in the mind of Judson.[57]

With newfound clarity regarding his life and ministry, Judson searched for like-minded compatriots among the students and professors at Andover. Perhaps due to the lack of an organized missionary society, Judson "found none among the students who viewed the subject as I did, and no minister in the place or neighborhood who gave me any encouragement."[58] As a result, Judson felt he had no choice but to make application to the London Missionary Society in England to see if they would accept his services and appoint him as a missionary.[59] However, five students from Williams College arrived at Andover, whom Judson found not only to be supporters of his vision but also colaborers in the task.

In 1856, on the fiftieth anniversary of what became known as the Haystack Prayer Meeting at Williams College, Rufus Anderson, secretary of the American Board of Commissioners for Foreign Missions (ABCFM), acknowledged that the college grounds served as "the *Antioch* of our western hemisphere."[60] Often cited as the birthplace of American foreign missions, a nondescript field beyond the campus in Williamstown, Massachusetts, served as the setting for a meeting of the Brethren, a student missionary society, in August 1806. Thomas Kiker recounts,

> The prayer meeting was a consistent gathering, but it seems the extremely hot conditions kept the attendance low on this particular day. The Haystack took place during a normally scheduled time of prayer in August of 1806. As the men had gathered to pray in the grove a dark cloud came up, and it began to thunder and lightning, so the men left the grove and went under the haystack to gain some protection from the coming storm. As they say, the conversation turned to the subject

---

[57] Anderson, *To the Golden Shore*, 56.
[58] Adoniram Judson to Stephen Chapin, Wayland, *Memoir*, 1:52; The Baptists had formed the Massachusetts Baptist Missionary Society in Boston on May 26, 1802, "to furnish occasional preaching and to promote a knowledge of evangelistic truth in the new settlements within these United States, or farther, if circumstances should render it proper," but had not yet organized for foreign work in 1810. Cited in George H. Tooze, ed., *The Life and Letters of Emily Chubbuck Judson*, vol. 1 (Macon, GA: Mercer University Press, 2009), 139.
[59] Wayland, *Memoir*, 1:52; Ann Judson, *An Account*, 7–8.
[60] *Proceedings of the Missionary Jubilee Held at Williams College* (Boston, MA: T. Marvin & Son, 1856), 54.

of a recent geography class, Asia . . . . Samuel Mills saw an opportunity and suggested that they commit to pray for the sending of the gospel to heathen lands.[61]

As the Brethren continued to meet, led by Mills, they drafted a constitution in September 1808 and focused on missions to the West. Joined by Luther Rice, James Richards, and Gordon Hall, the Brethren migrated at different times to Andover Seminary during 1809–10. There they befriended Samuel Nott Jr. and continued to meet both at Williams and also informally at Andover.[62] By December 1809 circumstances led Mills to consider missionary activity beyond America. Writing to Hall, Mills, who had yet to arrive at Andover, stated,

> I trust that we shall be able to establish more than one mission in a short time, at least in a few years. I mean that God will enable us to extend our views and labors farther than we have before contemplated. We ought not look only to the heathen on our own continent. We ought to direct our attention to that place where we may, to human appearance, do the most good, and where the difficulties are the least . . . . The field is almost boundless; in every part of which there ought to be missionaries.[63]

Furthermore, by this time Mills had learned of Judson and his recent commitment to missions. He wrote to Hall,

> I heard previously of Mr. Judson. You say he thinks of offering himself as a missionary to the London Society for the East Indies. What! is England to support her own missionaries and ours likewise? O, for shame! If he is prepared to go, I would fain press him forward with the arm of Hercules, if I had the strength; but I do not like this dependence on another nation, especially when they have already done so much, and we nothing.[64]

---

[61] Thomas H. Kiker, "The Relationship Between Samuel J. Mills Jr. and the Influence of the Second Great Awakening on Missions and Evangelism," unpublished PhD dissertation (Wake Forest, NC: Southeastern Baptist Theological Seminary, 2009), 102.
[62] Wayland, *Memoir*, 1:41.
[63] Ibid., 1:42.
[64] Ibid., 1:43.

Upon Mills's arrival at Andover, the Brethren gathered,[65] Judson joined their society, and the others came to have his sanctified ambition for the East.[66] Still without an organization to send them, the Brethren agreed to contact England. Judson, writing on their behalf in April 1810 to the president of the seminary in Gosport, inquired about such a venture.[67] While they waited for a response, the students met with their professors and local pastors at Andover on June 25, 1810. The professors encouraged them to make their desires known to the representative body for Congregationalist churches, the General Association, who were to meet in Bradford.[68]

On June 27, Judson, Nott, Mills, and Newell asked the General Association in a letter whether they should seek missionary support from a missionary society in America or from a European society.[69] In response, the General Association voted to form a Board of Commissioners for Foreign Missions "for the purpose of devising ways and means, and adopting and prosecuting measures, for promoting the spread of the Gospel in heathen lands." They counseled Judson and the others to pursue prayer and continued studies until such openings presented themselves.[70] Though thankful that their request brought attention to the missionary task in America, Judson and the others still expected to join with the English.[71] In the meantime, Judson completed his studies at Andover

---

[65] John H. Hewitt, *Williams College and Foreign Missions* (Boston, MA: The Pilgrim Press, 1914), 75, describes the commitment of the Brethren, "One of the articles of the Constitution [of the Brethren] enjoined the exercise of utmost care in admitting new members, and no one was to be admitted who was under any engagement of any kind which should be incompatible with going on a mission to the heathen. Mills seems to have been particularly strenuous about this requirement, and after he went to Andover, wrote an urgent letter about it. . . . The letter is dated Divinity College, Andover, March 20, 1810. Mills had quoted one of the commands of the Society of Illuminati, and then continued: 'Let us be more cautious in the admission of members than eve[n] the Illuminati. We shall do well to examine their every look, their every action, above all see that they are possessed of ardent piety. Let them take hold, as it were, of the Angel of the Covenant. Let their souls go out to God in fervent supplications that the heathen might be given to Jesus Christ as an inheritance.'"

[66] Ibid., 1:41–43. Wayland believes that Nott already had aspirations for the East, but clearly Judson's leadership helped to solidify the vision. Judson, *A Letter to the Rev. Adoniram Judson, Sen.*, 4–5, gives a one-sided recounting of the events that emphasizes his solitary vision for the East first and apart from that of the Brethren from Williams College.

[67] Adoniram Judson to Dr. Bogue, April 1810, quoted in Edward Judson, *The Life*, 22.

[68] Edward Judson, *The Life*, 23.

[69] Ibid., 23–24. The names of Rice and Richards were omitted so as not to present too large of a number.

[70] Ibid., 24–25; *First Ten Annual Reports of the American Board of Commissioners for Foreign Missions* (Boston, MA: Crocker & Brewster, 1834), 2–14. Wayland, *Memoir*, 1:44–48, explains that the formation of the ABCFM was not as spontaneous as it might appear. The sentiment for such an organization had been present since 1799 and subsequently discussed. Thus, the Brethren's request did occasion the organization's official start. Brumberg, *Mission for Life*, 39, suspects that there was tinge of nationalism at play as well.

[71] Wayland, *Memoir*, 1:56–57.

in September 1810. Now 22 years old, he had recently received a license to preach and began to pursue that task. During the visit to Bradford in June, he met Ann Hasseltine, the daughter of one of his hosts, and had pursued his acquaintance with her since July.[72]

In the letter to the General Association, the Brethren indicated that they considered themselves "devoted to this work for life, whenever God, in His providence, shall open the way."[73] Judson's surrender and consecration to missionary service reveals the depths to which the Spirit of God had worked to harness his ambition and set him on a course to take the gospel into all the world.

COMMISSION

One chronicler of Judson's life compared Judson's willingness to go, regardless of cost or circumstances, to Abraham who "obeyed when he was called to go out to a place.... And he went out, not knowing where he was going" (Heb 11:8 NKJV). Judson's ambition, now sanctified, led him to obey the Spirit of God and the Word of God. However, there was some debate as to whether Judson was following the Spirit or his old ambition when he departed America in February 1812.

The ABCFM held its first meeting on September 5, 1810, and adopted rules for proceeding. A Prudential Committee, consisting of William Bartlet, Samuel Spring, and Samuel Worcester, who also served as corresponding secretary, was appointed to obtain "the best information in their power respecting the state of unevangelized nations on the western and eastern continents."[74] The board grew concerned that the churches in America might not be up to supporting missionaries financially, so it made an official inquiry to the London Missionary Society. The Prudential Committee selected Judson as its representative and sent him, along with a letter from Worcester, to London on January 11, 1811.[75]

Worcester's letter explained that the board was discouraged by its failure to reach the Native Americans as well as the dim prospects for success in South America. He stated,

---

[72] For further study on the life of Ann Judson see Candi Finch's chapter.
[73] Edward Judson, *The Life*, 24; *First Ten Annual Reports of the American Board of Commissioners for Foreign Missions* (Boston, MA: Crocker & Brewster, 1834), 9.
[74] Wayland, *Memoir*, 1:62; *First Ten Annual Reports of the American Board of Commissioners for Foreign Missions*, 13.
[75] Wayland, *Memoir*, 1:63.

On our own continent, indeed, there are many millions of men "sitting in darkness and in the region and shadow of death," and our brethren in England may wonder what that, while such is the fact, we should turn our views to any other part of the world. But the attempts which have been made to evangelize the aboriginal tribes of the North American wilderness, have been attended with so many discouragements, and South America is yet in so unpromising a state, that the opinion very generally prevalent is, that for the Pagans on this continent but little can immediately be done. Hence, though the hope is entertained, that the time is coming when the benevolent exertions of the Redeemer's friends here, for spreading the knowledge of his name, may be successfully employed nearer home; yet at present the Eastern world is thought to offer a more promising field.[76]

However, Judson did not arrive in England until May. On the way, his ship was captured by the French. First he was arrested and detained in Spain for some time and then transferred to France. He was released after receiving aid from an American woman who had lived in France for most of her life.[77] Judson stayed in London for six weeks visiting London Missionary Society personnel and delivering the letter from Worcester. The LMS gave him its support and said it would appoint Judson and the four others. In addition, he made contact with the seminary in Gosport, where he was welcomed. He returned to America in August 1811 in time for the second annual meeting of the ABCFM in September.[78]

At the annual meeting, the ABCFM received Judson's report but determined to support the missionaries itself rather than depend on England. On September 19, 1811, the board voted to appoint Judson, Samuel Nott, Samuel Newell, and Gordon Hall as missionaries "to labor under the direction of this Board in Asia, either in the Birman Empire, or in Surat, or in the Prince of Wales Island or elsewhere, as in the view of the Prudential Committee, Providence shall open the most favorable door."[79] In addition to this appointment, the board also admonished Judson for not returning from London with a written report or a letter indicating what action the LMS was willing to take. Instead, he returned with an LMS appointment, which the ABCFM felt necessitated its

---

[76] Samuel Worcester to George Burder, 3 January 1811, quoted in *First Ten Annual Reports of the American Board of Commissioners for Foreign Missions*, 18.
[77] Wayland, *Memoir*, 1:68–74.
[78] Ibid., 1:74, 77.
[79] Wayland, *Memoir*, 1:79; *The Panoplist* 4, no. 4 (September 1811): 186.

immediate action lest the missionaries go with England. Was Judson's old sinful ambition affecting his behavior? In his zeal to depart as soon as possible, did he manipulate circumstances to force the ABCFM's hand? These questions were addressed in 1811 but continued to arise well into the 1830s. Indeed, for years Judson denied that he was ever reprimanded by the board.[80] But, as Wayland explained, Judson likely did not interpret the admonition as a reprimand. When Judson resigned from the ABCFM to join the Baptists, the controversy escalated. Likely, Judson was at least somewhat manipulative,[81] but his motive was not selfish gain or acclimation. Rather he wanted to depart for the East as soon as possible.[82]

Once the ABCFM determined to appoint the Brethren, funds needed to be secured to send them. Worcester described the ensuing days:

> Letters were sent in various directions. Some pastors of churches moved at once to arouse their people. The professors at Andover dispatched a portion of the students, to visit different towns and churches, soliciting contributions. They returned with cheering reports of success. . . . And considering the poverty or very limited resources of most of the members of orthodox churches, in Massachusetts and other States, it would be impossible otherwise to account for the sudden contribution of so large an amount of funds, in less than four weeks, from the announcement of the designs of the Prudential Committee. . . . There was incomparably more of missionary spirit in the churches, than had ever been imagined to exist. The occasion had now come, as never before, when it could so be seen, to the glory of the Lord of all.[83]

---

[80] See Judson, *Letter to the Rev. Adoniram Judson, Sen.*, 4, for his 1820 denial. Wayland, *Memoir*, 1:83, 88–89, for his acknowledgment of the admonishment.

[81] David B. Raymond, "The Controversy over Adoniram Judson's Famous 'Change of Sentiments,' 1813–1820," in *Baptist History and Heritage* (Spring 2010): 59–71, and "Judson's 'Famous Change of Sentiments' Reconsidered," in *American Baptist Quarterly* 28, no. 2 (Summer 2009): 208–22, assumes the worst regarding Judson's motives, allowing for no nuance of understanding and intimating that Judson not only lied about what he recalled but, prior to his departure, made arrangements to depart the ABCFM and join the Baptists because he was offended that they would correct him. These conclusions appear unwarranted and ill conceived.

[82] Wayland, *Memoir*, 1:89–90.

[83] Samuel M. Worcester, *The Life and Labors of Rev. Samuel Worcester*, vol. 2 (Boston, MA: Crocker and Brewster, 1852), 123–24; Brumberg, *Mission for Life*, 39.

According to biographer Stacy Warburton, "The days of 1812 were great days—full of achievement, full of daring, full of imagination, full of high purpose. The time was ripe for a challenging enterprise."[84] The advent of the year in which Judson turned 24 brought a flurry of events. On February 3, he bid farewell to his parents in Plymouth. On February 5, he and Ann Hasseltine were wed. On February 6, he was ordained in Salem, along with Nott, Newell, Hall, and Rice. Their professor from Andover, Leonard Woods, preached their ordination sermon from Psalm 67, a prayer to God that "Thy way may be known upon the earth, thy saving health among all nations."[85] Woods explained the missionary task and the sufficiency of Christ's death for those they would serve:

> The *second motive* by which I urge you to seek the conversion of all mankind is the plenteousness of the provision which Christ has made for their salvation. . . . But my brethren, the word of eternal truth has taught us that Jesus tasted death for every man; that he is the propitiation for our sins, and not for ours only, but also for the sins of the *whole world*; that a rich feast is prepared, and all things ready; that whosoever will may come and take of the water of life freely. This great atonement is sufficient for Asiatics and Africans, as for us. The door of Christ's kingdom is equally open to them and to us.[86]

He concluded with a lengthy address to the missionaries followed by a stirring appeal to the congregation:

> Brethren and friends, these dear young men are going to preach to the heathen that religion, which is your comfort in life, your hope in death, your guide to heaven. Consider yourselves now looking upon them for the last time, before you shall meet them at the tribunal of Christ. . . . The Lord of the universe, in these last days, is about to do a marvelous work; a work of astonishing power and grace. . . . My hearers, God offers you the privilege of aiding in this great

---

[84] Stacy R. Warburton, *Eastward! The Story of Adoniram Judson* (New York: Round Table, 1937), 1.
[85] Leonard Woods, *A Sermon Delivered at the Tabernacle in Salem, Feb. 6, 1812* (Boston, MA: Samuel T. Armstrong, 1812), 13–14; David W. Kling, "The New Divinity and the Origins of the American Board of Commissioners for Foreign Missions," in *Church History* 72, no. 4 (December 2003): 804.
[86] Woods, *A Sermon Delivered*, 13–14; Kling, "The New Divinity," 804.

work of *converting the nations*. . . . Nothing else is worth living for. But who would not live, labor, and die for this?[87]

On February 19, 1812, Adoniram and Ann Judson departed for the East.

Conclusion

The ambition that first opposed God's work met His Spirit and Word and was overthrown in Judson's conversion. This is evidenced by his continued repentance from his life of waywardness. Judson recounted how, before his departure, "when the enormity of this vicious course rested with a depressing weight upon my mind, I made a second tour over the same ground, carefully making amends to all whom I had injured."[88] With his zeal overhauled and harnessed, Judson pursued a life consecrated to God. Along with Samuel Mills, Judson pioneered the American missionary movement. The June 1913 issue of the *Foreign Mission Journal* recounts the presentation of the Judson Centennial fundraising movement at the Southern Baptist Convention's annual meeting in St. Louis. One statement recorded from that convention summarizes well the life of Adoniram Judson, guided by the Spirit and the Word:

> The mighty significance of the Judson spirit is not the fact that when a missionary is left alone with his Bible he becomes a Baptist, but the significant thing is that when a Baptist is left alone with his Bible he becomes a missionary.[89]

---

[87] Ibid., 28–29. The Judsons' departure and service overseas would not receive universal support from some sectors in America. John Taylor, a pastor in Virginia, would lead a movement discouraging the support of organized missionary societies. The "anti-missions" movement had as a key document one of Taylor's works, *Thoughts on Missions*. There, Taylor critiques both Judson and Luther Rice for their devoted efforts to raise funds to support missionary activity. See John Taylor, *Thoughts on Missions* (Franklin County, KY: 1820); Thomas J. Nettles, "Baptists and the Great Commission," in Martin I. Klauber and Scott M. Manetsch, eds., *The Great Commission: Evangelicals and the History of World Missions* (Nashville, TN: B&H, 2008), 100–102.

[88] Henry Gougher, *A Personal Narrative of Two Years' Imprisonment in Burmah, 1824–26* (London: John Murray, 1860), 179.

[89] *The Foreign Mission Journal* 63, no. 12 (June 1913): 355.

Chapter 4

"Until All Burma Worships the Eternal God"

Adoniram Judson, the Missionary, 1812–50

Nathan A. Finn

NEW LANDS AND NEW CONVICTIONS

Adoniram and Ann Judson embarked from Salem, Massachusetts, for India on February 19, 1812. The young couple had married only two weeks earlier, the day before Adoniram's ordination to the gospel ministry. The previous fall, Adoniram had been appointed by the American Board of Commissioners for Foreign Missions (ABCFM) to serve as a missionary to the Far East. After a brief delay, the day had finally arrived for the Judsons and their friends Samuel and Harriett Newell to board the *Caravan* and depart for Calcutta. Their fellow missionaries Luther Rice, Gordon Hall, and Samuel and Roxanna Nott set sail from Philadelphia a few days later on board the *Harmony*. Though circumstances had compelled a handful of earlier American Christians to preach the gospel overseas, these two ships carried the first officially commissioned foreign missionaries in American history.[1]

The voyage from Salem to Calcutta lasted four months. After some initial seasickness, especially among the women, the passage was fairly pleasant. During these months at sea, Adoniram devoted most of his time to theological study. He focused much of his attention on the doctrine of baptism. According to Francis Wayland, Adoniram's most famous nineteenth-century biographer, there were two reasons for this focus on baptism. First, Adoniram was driven by evangelistic considerations. As a Congregationalist, he

---

[1] Some African American Baptists had already served as "informal" foreign missionaries when the threat of forced servitude occasioned their relocation to other countries. The most notable example is George Leile (alt. Liele; Lisle), a freed slave who was forced to relocate to Jamaica in 1782 to avoid capture and enslavement. Leile spent almost four decades evangelizing and church planting in Jamaica. See Edward A. Holmes, "George Leile: Negro Slavery's Prophet of Deliverance," *Baptist History and Heritage* (August 1965): 27–36.

77

held to covenant theology and infant baptism. He was hopeful that a multitude of heathen would convert to Christianity and become baptized church members. But should he also baptize the children and servants of converts? The second reason he studied baptism was polemical. He knew that, upon arrival, he and his colleagues would be hosted for several weeks by British Baptist missionaries, including the famous William Carey. Adoniram wanted to be certain he could adequately argue his covenantal pedobaptist views among his British Baptist colleagues.[2]

The Judsons' famous rejection of infant baptism in favor of believer's baptism is addressed in detail in Greg Wills's chapter in this volume. For present purposes, it is enough to note that Adoniram's study led him to the conviction that the full immersion of professed believers was the New Testament practice and thus the only proper form of baptism:

> In a word, I could not find a single intimation in the New Testament, that the children and domestics of believers were members of the church, or entitled to any church ordinance, in consequence of the profession of the head of their family. Every thing discountenanced this idea. When baptism was spoken of, it was always in connection with believing. None but believers were commanded to be baptized; and it did not appear to my mind that any others were baptized.[3]

Ann, whom Adoniram affectionately called "Nancy," subsequently became convinced of believer's baptism, though only after considerable reluctance.[4] Upon arrival in Calcutta, both Judsons were baptized as believers by Carey's colleague William Ward on September 6, 1812. Three weeks later, Adoniram preached a sermon advocating his new baptismal convictions. The sermon was later published and became a sensation among the Baptists, though Congregationalist observers were less enthused.[5]

---

[2] Francis Wayland, *A Memoir of the Life and Labors of the Rev. Adoniram Judson, D.D.* (Boston, MA: Phillips, Sampson, and Company, 1853), 1:95.

[3] See, "A Letter to the Third Church in Plymouth, Mass.," in Adoniram Judson, *Christian Baptism. A Sermon on Christian Baptism, with Many Quotations from Pedobaptist Authors*, 5th American ed. (Boston, MA: Gould, Kendall & Lincoln, 1846), 100. The document states the letter was written on August 20, 1817.

[4] Letters from Ann Judson to an unnamed friend and her parents, respectively, quoted in ibid., 105–9.

[5] See Adoniram Judson, *Christian Baptism: A Sermon Preached in the Lal Bazaar Chapel, Calcutta, On Lord's Day, September 27, 1812, Previous to the Administration of the Ordinance of Baptism: With Many Quotations from Pedobaptist Authors* (Boston, MA: Lincoln & Edmands, 1817). For more information about the controversy Judson's baptism and sermon occasioned among Congregationalists, see David Raymond, "Judson's 'Famous Change of Sentiments' Reconsidered," *American Baptist Quarterly* (Summer 2009):

In consultation with the Newells, who remained unpersuaded of Baptist views, Adoniram reached the conclusion he could no longer serve as a Congregationalist missionary. Judson and his colleagues had been instructed to baptize professing believers and their households, but he could no longer fulfill this obligation with a clear conscience. Just prior to his baptism Adoniram wrote a letter to the ABCFM resigning his appointment. In that letter, he also expressed his hopes that American Baptists might support his missionary work.[6]

Shortly after the Judsons' baptisms, the *Harmony* arrived in Calcutta with the other missionaries. Luther Rice had also been struggling with the baptismal question, though he initially kept it to himself and argued with Adoniram over the ordinance. After reading the latter's sermon and conversing with William Carey, Rice finally conceded his agreement and received believer's baptism by immersion on November 1, 1812.[7] He also resigned from the ABCFM. Adoniram and his British Baptist colleagues wrote letters back to American Baptists requesting financial support for the freshly minted Baptist missionaries. The following spring, the men decided Rice would return to America to recuperate from ailing health and elicit financial support for their mission work from the Baptists. By the time Rice arrived in America, Baptists were already beginning to organize for foreign missions, in part because of Judson's correspondence concerning his baptism. Rice, who never returned to Asia, helped unify these efforts through his work with the Triennial Convention.[8]

Together, Rice and Judson played a key role in uniting American Baptists and mobilizing them for foreign missions. Rice was commissioned by the Triennial Convention to raise funds for the Judsons and, once some were appointed, other American Baptist foreign missionaries.[9] He also became involved in a number of other ministry initiatives under

---

208–22, and idem, "The Controversy over Adoniram Judson's Famous 'Change of Sentiments,' 1813–1820," *Baptist History and Heritage* (Spring 2010): 59–71.

[6] Letter from Adoniram Judson to Samuel Worchester, September 1, 1812, quoted in Wayland, *Memoir*, 1:110.

[7] Courtney Anderson, *To the Golden Shore: The Life of Adoniram Judson* (New York: Little, Brown, 1956), 148. See also Evelyn Wingo Thompson, *Luther Rice: Believer in Tomorrow* (Nashville, TN: Broadman, 1967), 76–77.

[8] The official name of the Triennial Convention was the General Missionary Convention of the Baptist Denomination in the United States of America for Foreign Missions.

[9] For a brief account of the role Rice played in mobilizing American Baptists for foreign missions, see Robert G. Torbet, *Venture of Faith: The Story of the American Baptist Foreign Mission Society and the Woman's American Baptist Foreign Mission Society, 1814–1954* (Philadelphia, PA: Judson, 1955), 26–30.

taken by the Triennial Convention during its first dozen years of existence.[10] For his part, Adoniram's mission work became a rallying point for Baptists in America. According to William Brackney, Judson "gave them [American Baptists] not only an overseas missionary program but also a sense of national denominational identity and purpose."[11]

Following their baptisms, the Judsons had to decide where they wished to serve. They had been instructed by the Indian government, under the control of the anti-missions British East India Company, to leave the country. After considering a number of options, Adoniram decided they would relocate to Burma, a nation that had long captivated his interests. British Baptist missionaries had attempted to establish a mission in Burma, but these efforts proved unsuccessful. William Carey's son Felix was serving as a governmental official in Burma and laboring in his spare time on Bible translation. Once Adoniram met Felix, it solidified his desire to relocate to the Burmese city of Rangoon.[12] After several false starts and a couple of sea voyages that required more than a little subterfuge to avoid government detection, the Judsons arrived in Rangoon in July 1813. This marked the beginning of their missionary work in Burma.

ESTABLISHING A BURMESE MISSION

Nineteenth-century Burma was not a pleasant setting for American missionaries. As Richard Pierard notes, "For the new arrivals, existence in Rangoon—a hot, steamy, dirty city with no European society and untouched by Western influence—was extremely difficult. The community was firmly Buddhist and controlled by officials who had no understanding of religious diversity."[13] The Judsons moved into the mission compound founded by Felix Carey, which was located about a half mile outside the city. Carey had

---

[10] In 1826, the Triennial Convention abandoned most of its ministries besides foreign missions and censured Rice for mismanaging funds and involving himself in ministries beyond the purview of his role as a foreign missions fundraiser. The architect of this decision was Francis Wayland, who would later write a two-volume biography of Adoniram Judson. See G. Thomas Halbrooks, "Francis Wayland and 'the Great Reversal,'" *Foundations* (July–September 1977): 196–214.

[11] William H. Brackney, "The Legacy of Adoniram Judson," *International Bulletin of Missionary Research* (July 1998): 124.

[12] Both *Burmese* and *Burman* were commonly used in describing the language and culture of nineteenth-century Myanmar. This chapter uses these terms interchangeably.

[13] Richard V. Pierard, "The Man Who Gave the Bible to the Burmese," *Christian History & Biography* 90 (April 2006), accessed June 24, 2011, available online at http://www.ctlibrary.com/ch/2006/issue90/6.16.html.

decided to relocate to the capitol city of Ava, which was more conducive to his work for the Burmese government. Like his more famous father, Felix was using secular employment as a platform to open the door for missions work. After losing his family in a boating accident en route to Ava, Felix moved to Calcutta as the Burmese emperor's ambassador to India. William Carey complained that his son had been demoted from a missionary to an ambassador, though in later life, after a period of spiritual wandering, Felix joined his father's mission work in Serampore.[14]

The Judsons immediately set about learning the Burmese language. Understanding Burmese was crucial for personal evangelism and Bible translation, both of which were necessary if the gospel was to gain a foothold in Burma. It was not enough to learn the language; the Judsons also had to learn how to live and minister in a Burmese context. Phyllis Rodgerson Pleasants describes the centrality of this learning for the Judsons' mission:

> The Judsons recognized that they had to be learners before they would be able to teach anything. They were persistent in learning from the Burmese [sic], their entire lives in order to communicate the gospel authentically in ways natural to the Burmese instead of trying to make the Burmese American so they could understand the gospel. More than learning the language from their teachers, the Judsons learned what it meant to be Burmese.[15]

Learning the Burmese language and being immersed in Burman culture were critical components in providing a contextually appropriate Christian witness. The Judsons eventually excelled at both.[16]

Both Adoniram and Ann struggled with language learning; early on, the only way to learn a word was through Adoniram pointing to an object and his language teacher giving him the corresponding Burmese word.[17] Through a combination of persistence and being totally immersed in a Burmese-speaking culture, the Judsons gradually

---

[14] Erroll Hulse, "Adoniram Judson: Devoted for Life," in *Building on a Sure Foundation: Papers Read at the 1994 Westminster Conference* (Mirfield, West Yorkshire, UK: Westminster Conference, 1994), 132; Vinita Hampton Wright, "William Carey: A Gallery of Carey's Companions and Converts," *Christian History & Biography* 36 (October 1992), accessed June 24, 2011, available online at http://www.ctlibrary.com/ch/1992/issue36/3632.html.

[15] Phyllis Rodgerson Pleasants, "Beyond Translation: The Work of the Judsons in Burma," *Baptist History and Heritage* 42, no. 2 (Spring 2007): 22.

[16] For a helpful treatment of this and other facets of the Judsons' strategy, see Keith Eitel's chapter in this book.

[17] Anderson, *To the Golden Shore*, 172.

improved their language skills. Adoniram better understood the grammar and syntax of the language, but Ann spoke it with greater ease, in part because she interacted regularly with Burmans in the marketplace as she managed the affairs of the house.[18] In addition to Burmese, Adoniram also studied Pali, which was an older language still spoken among the learned classes, including Buddhist teachers.

As their language skills improved, the Judsons began evangelizing the Burmans. Adoniram adopted a contextual approach to evangelism by dressing and acting like the Buddhist teachers in Rangoon. Following the latter's habit, Adoniram erected a *zayat*—a small, open air awning built upon four posts. Like the Buddhist teachers, he would sit on the front porch of the *zayat* and call out, "Ho! Everyone that thirsteth for knowledge!" He would then talk about the Christian faith with any interested seekers. Later missionaries to Burma adopted the same approach.[19] For her part, Ann concentrated on private conversations with Burmese women, a weekly prayer meeting with interested women, and, after their relocation to Ava in 1824, operating a school for children. This became the paradigm for many missionary wives during the nineteenth century.[20]

Unlike the Careys, Adoniram never took on permanent secular employment but rather worked openly as a missionary. Everyone knew why he was in Burma. Adoniram thus sought to gain the approval of the ruling authorities. The viceroy in Rangoon was known to be a harsh man who severely punished thieves and troublemakers. Early efforts to win his favor were unsuccessful. But once the Judsons discovered that the viceroy's wife was fascinated by Ann, the latter spent a great deal of time cultivating a relationship between the two women. Ann often presented her new friend with gifts, which she hoped would help gain her approval. The viceroy's wife became an advocate for the Judsons, which likely played a role in their ability to minister early on without much interference from the viceroy.[21]

After six years in Burma, Adoniram finally baptized his first convert. Moung Nau was a common laborer who visited Adoniram's *zayat*. The missionary sensed immediately that his new friend was a sincere spiritual seeker. Moung subsequently moved in with the Judsons, in part so he could assist them with household tasks, but more importantly so Adoniram could continue to instruct him about Christianity. In early June

---

[18] Ann Judson, journal entry from 16 April 1815, quoted in Wayland, *Memoir*, 1:171.
[19] Pierard, "The Man Who Gave the Bible to the Burmese."
[20] Dana L. Robert, *American Women in Mission: A Social History of Their Thought and Practice*, The Modern Mission Era, 1792–1992: An Appraisal, series ed. Wilbert R. Shenk (Macon, GA: Mercer University Press, 1997), 44–46.
[21] Anderson, *To the Golden Shore*, 175–76, 189; Wayland, *Memoir*, 1:164–65.

1819, Moung wrote a letter to Adoniram explaining his conversion to faith in Christ and requesting baptism. Adoniram recounted Moung Nau's baptism in a journal entry:

> June 27, Lord's day. There were several strangers present at worship. After the usual course, I called Moung Nau before me, read and commented on an appropriate portion of Scripture, asked him several questions concerning his *faith, hope,* and *love,* and made the baptismal prayer, having concluded to have all the preparatory exercises done in the zayat. We then proceeded to a large pond in the vicinity, the bank of which is graced with an enormous image of Gaudama, and there administered baptism to the first Burman convert. O, may it prove the beginning of a series of baptisms in the Burman empire which shall continue in uninterrupted succession to the end of time![22]

After the conversion of Moung Nau, the Buddhist priests began to oppose the Judsons. One teacher in particular convinced the viceroy to pass a law that forbade anyone who practiced a variety of Western customs from coming within a half mile of Burma's holiest Buddhist temple, the Shwe Dagon, which was located in Rangoon. This effectively precluded Adoniram from teaching in his *zayat*. The only recourse was for him and an associate, James Colman, to take their case before the Burmese emperor in Ava. When they arrived in the capital, the missionaries were granted an audience with the emperor, whom the Burmese called "The Golden Feet." They presented their petition to him, formally requesting the right to propagate the Christian religion in Burma. The emperor had little interest in the missionaries, so he dismissed their request outright.[23] They returned to Rangoon without the emperor's endorsement, though in 1822 a new opportunity arose to return to Ava.

That year, a new missionary named Jonathan Price joined the Judsons, a physician specializing in cataract surgery. The emperor was impressed with this medical skill, so he commanded Price to relocate to Ava. Adoniram accompanied Price, leading to a second audience with the emperor. This time, Adoniram received a somewhat better reception. While the emperor showed no interest in Christianity and forbade Burmese conversions to it, he did grant Adoniram permission to share his religious beliefs with other foreigners.

---

[22] Quoted in Wayland, *Memoir,* 1:224.

[23] The elaborate pomp and ritual involved in the missionaries making their formal petition to the emperor is recounted in Anderson, *To the Golden Shore,* 246–51. Francis Wayland ardently disagreed with Adoniram's strategy of seeking an imperial endorsement, spending several pages making a biblical case against the practice. See Wayland, *Memoir,* 1:247–49.

He also decided to leave any persecution of Burmese believers in the hands of local officials.[24] Though this by no means constituted imperial endorsement, Adoniram believed it was beneficial to the mission. Because other missionaries had joined the Judsons in Rangoon, which by that time had a church of 18 baptized members, Adoniram felt comfortable entrusting his associates with that work.[25] The Judsons relocated to Ava.

Translating the Goods News

Bible translation has been a central component of missionary work since the earliest days of cross-cultural evangelism and church planting.[26] Though Adoniram was a successful evangelist and helped establish a number of churches, like his older contemporary William Carey, his lasting missions legacy is as a Bible translator. As Phyllis Rodgerson Pleasants notes, the Judsons "were translators *par excellence* for their intended audience, the Burmese Buddhists."[27] Upon arriving in Burma, Adoniram had planned to focus his attention on evangelism, with translation as a secondary (though necessary) ministry. But early on, the Judsons recognized the vast gulf between American and Burmese language and culture. According to William Brackney, "This led [Adoniram] to make the first priority of his work of translation of Scripture and suitable tracts for evangelical purposes."[28]

Adoniram had given attention to language studies since his days in New England, but his interest grew when he met the Serampore Trio and learned of their long-term efforts to translate the Bible into various Indian languages.[29] Adoniram inherited a translation Felix Carey had made of the Gospel of Matthew, and in the earliest days of the Judsons' language learning, this was the only Burmese Scripture available. But as Adoniram gained greater ability in the language, he began to translate more and more of the Bible, despite the paucity of language tools at his disposal.[30] Adoniram's son and biographer, Edward Judson, recounts that

---

[24] Pleasants, "Beyond Translation," 29–30.
[25] Hulse, "Adoniram Judson—Devoted for Life," 134.
[26] For a helpful history of missionary Bible translation, see William A Smalley, *Translation as Mission*, The Modern Mission Era, 1792–1992: An Appraisal, series ed. Wilbert R. Shenk (Macon, GA: Mercer University Press, 1991).
[27] Pleasants, "Beyond Translation," 22.
[28] Brackney, "The Legacy of Adoniram Judson," 124.
[29] Ibid. The Serampore Trio was the name given to William Carey, William Ward, and Joshua Marshman for their pioneer work in Serampore, India.
[30] Wayland, *Memoir*, 1:157.

from that time on [the earliest days of the mission], beneath all his toils and sufferings and afflictions, there moved the steady undercurrent of this great purpose and labor of Bible translation. It was a task for which he had little relish. He much preferred dealing with the Burmans individually, and persuading them, one by one, of the truth of the Gospel. . . . But the translation of the Bible was essentially necessary to the permanent establishment of Christianity in Burmah, and no other living man was qualified for the work.[31]

Adoniram was fortunate to have a skilled language teacher. Despite their early struggles to understand each other, Adoniram learned a great deal from his teacher, including not only Burmese but also Pali. This relationship helped Adoniram and Ann see the value of utilizing indigenous language experts to double-check the accuracy of their translation work. As Pleasants notes, "The Judsons remained learners using educated Burmese . . . to review and revise what they translated. No matter how the Judsons progressed in the language, they did everything possible to avoid miscommunication through translation mistakes by having everything reviewed by Burmese assistants."[32]

This humble approach to translation paid rich dividends. In 1823, Adoniram published the first edition of his Burmese New Testament. Three years later, he published his *Dictionary of the Burman Language*. By 1834, the full Bible was translated into Burmese; a one-volume Burmese Bible was published in 1840. Adoniram also wrote or translated into the Burman language numerous tracts, including catechetical, liturgical, evangelistic, and apologetic works. At the end of his life, Adoniram worked on a comprehensive *Burman and English Dictionary*, though he died before completing it. The dictionary was finished by his associate Jonathan Wade and published in 1852, two years after Adoniram's death. His works, especially the Burmese Bible, had a lasting influence among Burman Christians. According to the Judsons' most recent biographer, Rosalie Hall Hunt, a committee of Burmese biblical scholars met several years ago to consider translating and publishing a new edition of the Bible. The committee ultimately disbanded after opting to leave Adoniram's translation unchanged, claiming it was "so beautiful and so compellingly rendered" that it could not be improved upon.[33]

---

[31] Edward Judson, *The Life of Adoniram Judson* (New York: Anson D. F. Randolph, 1883), 404–5. In the nineteenth century, both *Burma* and *Burmah* were appropriate spellings.

[32] Pleasants, "Beyond Translation," 23.

[33] Rosalie Hall Hunt, *Bless God and Take Courage* (Valley Forge, PA: Judson, 2005), 254–55. Unfortunately, Hunt does not provide the year the translation committee met.

A key element of Adoniram's translation strategy was his use of the Pali language. By the time the Judsons arrived in Burma, Pali was for all practical purposes a dead language. But it remained the preferred language of the Buddhist teachers, similar to the way Latin continues to occupy a key place in Roman Catholic theology and liturgy. Elements of Pali were incorporated into Adoniram's Burmese Bible and many of his evangelistic tracts. His hope was to appeal to educated Buddhists. Ironically, the use of the sacred language of Burmese Buddhism led to what one scholar has called a "conflicted legacy"—using Buddhist vocabulary and worldview elements in the service of Christian missions.[34]

Adoniram's leadership in translation reached beyond his own work. In 1839, he developed the rules for translation used by other Baptist missionaries appointed by the Triennial Convention. At his encouragement, the convention appointed George Hough as the first missionary printer from America. Hough subsequently set up the American Baptist Missionary Press in Rangoon, which for many years was the principle publisher of Christian works in the indigenous languages of South Asia.[35] Hough became one of Adoniram's key associates, much like the printer William Ward labored beside William Carey for many years.[36] Adoniram once claimed he "could not translate as fast as brother Hough" could print.[37]

Adoniram's translation skills also encouraged the Triennial Convention, known later as the American Baptist Foreign Mission Society, to develop stringent language requirements for foreign missionaries. According to Brackney, American Baptists were among the first mission agencies to develop clear language training policies for missionary personnel. As he notes, "The fruits of their labors were seen in the unusually high number of published dictionaries, language study aids, and Scripture portions from their [American Baptist] presses in the nineteenth century."[38] Richard Pierard helpfully summarizes Adoniram's legacy as a translator: "Adoniram Judson became a symbol of the preeminence of Bible translation for the Protestant missionary. He was, above all else, the man 'who gave the Bible to the Burmese.'"[39]

---

[34] See La Seng Dingrin, "The Conflicting Legacy of Adoniram Judson," *Missiology* 37, no. 4 (October 2009): 485–97.

[35] Brackney, "The Legacy of Adoniram Judson," 125.

[36] Thomas W. Hill, "A Brief History of Publication Work on Southern Baptist Foreign Mission Fields," *Baptist History and Heritage* (October 1977): 219. For more on Hough, see Eugene Dinsmore Dolloff, "George H. Hough, Co-worker of Judson," *Foundations* (July 1961): 231–40.

[37] Letter from Adoniram Judson to Thomas Baldwin, 10 February 1817, quoted in Wayland, *Memoir*, 1:187.

[38] Brackney, "The Legacy of Adoniram Judson," 125.

[39] Pierard, "The Man Who Gave the Bible to the Burmese."

SICKNESS, SORROW, PAIN, AND DEATH

"The story of Adoniram Judson's losses is almost overwhelming. Just when you think the last one was the worst, and he could endure no more, another comes. In fact, it would be overwhelming if we could not see it all from God's long historical view."[40] These words, written by John Piper, describe a central part of Adoniram's life on the mission field. During his almost 40 years overseas, he suffered the loss of most of his children and his first two wives. He battled constant sicknesses and physical ailments. He was imprisoned for almost two years and endured daily torture because of the erroneous assumption he was a British spy. Through all his struggles, he remained committed to the missionary task to which the Lord had called him.

Death haunted the Judsons from their earliest days on the mission field. Harriet Newell and her infant daughter died while the Newells were en route to the Isle of France (Mauritanius), where they were forced to relocate following eviction from India by the East India Company. Though the Newells and Judsons had parted ways because of their divergent views of baptism, they remained close friends. According to Wayland, the loss of Harriet "affected the whole company very deeply, and taught them, more emphatically than their wandering loneliness, that here they had no continuing city."[41] After the loss of Harriet and their child, Samuel Newell established a mission in Ceylon (modern-day Sri Lanka). He later relocated to Bombay, where he spent the remainder of his life.[42]

As tragic as the loss of Harriet Newell was to Adoniram and Ann, it paled in comparison to the loss of their first two children. Their first was stillborn shortly before the Judsons began their mission in Rangoon. The baby died on board the *Georgiana*, which at the time was anchored in the Rangoon River within sight of the city.[43] Ann gave birth without the aid of physicians or midwives. Though a Burmese servant girl had intended to travel with them and attend to Ann and the baby, the young woman died as the *Georgiana* set sail for Rangoon. The labor was very difficult, and for a time Adoniram and the ship's crew feared that Ann would die as well. Fortunately, she recovered, and a few days later the Judsons started their life in Rangoon.

---

[40] John Piper, "'How Few There Are Who Die So Hard': The Cost of Bringing Christ to Burma," in *Filling up the Afflictions of Christ: The Cost of Bringing the Gospel to the Nations in the Lives of William Tyndale, Adoniram Judson, and John Paton*, The Swans Are Not Silent, vol. 5 (Wheaton, IL: Crossway, 2007), 85.

[41] Wayland, *Memoir*, 1:117.

[42] See Gerald H. Anderson, ed., *Biographical Dictionary of Christian Missions* (Grand Rapids: Eerdmans, 1999), s.v. "Newell, Samuel (1784–1821) and Harriet (Atwood) (1793–1812)."

[43] Hunt, *Bless God and Take Courage*, 49, identifies the child as a boy.

The loss of their second child was even worse. Roger Williams Judson was born in 1815 and lived for eight months. Both parents were consumed with grief at his loss. In a letter to one of the Serampore missionaries, Adoniram expressed his struggles with mourning a dead son and trying to remain focused on his missionary work:

> Our little Roger died last Saturday morning. We looked at him through the day, and on the approach of night we laid him in the grave. This is the fourth day, and we just begin [sic] to think, What can we do for the heathen? But yet it seems hard to forget little Roger so soon, to force off our thoughts from the attractive, painful subject, and to return to our usual employments. O may we not suffer in vain! May this bereavement be sanctified to our souls! and for this I hope we have your prayers.[44]

Ann experienced the same struggle. In a letter to her parents, she expressed her confidence in God's sovereign goodness, even in the death of a child:

> We do not feel a disposition to murmur, or inquire of our Sovereign why he has done this. We wish rather to sit down submissively under the rod and bear the smart, till the end for which the affliction was sent shall be accomplished. Our hearts were bound up in this child; we felt he was our earthly all, our only source of innocent recreation in this heathen land. But God saw it was necessary to remind us of our error and strip us of our little all. Oh may it not be in vain that he has done it. May we so improve it that he will stay his hand and say, "It is enough."[45]

Another great struggle was sickness. As Westerners in a foreign context, the Judsons and their missionary colleagues frequently battled illness. In the summer of 1821, both Adoniram and Ann became very sick. Though Adoniram eventually recovered, Ann grew increasingly ill. He became convinced her condition "preclude[d] all hope of her

---

[44] Letter from Adoniram Judson to Rev. Mr. Lawson, 7 May 1816, quoted in Judson, *The Life of Adoniram Judson*, 97.

[45] Letter from Ann Judson to her parents, 7 May 1816, quoted in Arabella W. Stuart, *Lives of the Three Mrs. Judsons: Mrs. Ann H. Judson, Mrs. Sarah B. Judson, Mrs. Emily C. Judson, Missionaries to Burmah* (Boston: Lee and Shepard, 1855), 69–70. While John Piper helpfully emphasizes this same point, he mistakenly claims Roger was 17 months old at his death and he cites an incomplete excerpt of Ann's letter from *To the Golden Shore*. See Piper, "How Few There Are Who Die So Hard," 88.

recovery in this part of the world."⁴⁶ On August 21, Ann departed for America to convalesce—she would remain separated from Adoniram for almost two and a half years.

Though gravely ill, she returned to America to great fanfare. Now a famous missionary, she used her fame to advocate the cause of foreign missions among American Baptists and other evangelicals. In a letter to Francis Wayland, she provided a glimpse into the missionary zeal that inspired so many American believers:

> I want the Baptists throughout the United States to feel, that Burmah *must be converted* through their instrumentality. They must do more than they have ever yet done. They must *pray* more, they must *give* more, and make greater efforts to prevent the Missionary flame from becoming extinct. Every Christian in the United States should feel as deeply impressed with the importance of making continual efforts for the salvation of the heathen, as though their conversion depended solely on himself. Every individual Christian should feel himself guilty if he has not done and does not continue to do *all* in his power for the spread of the gospel and the enlightening of the heathen world. But I need not write thus to you. You see, you feel the misery of the heathen world. Try to awaken Christians around you. Preach frequently on the subject of Missions. I have remarked it to be the case, when a minister feels *much* engaged for the heathen, his people generally partake of his spirit.⁴⁷

She also authored a book titled *An Account of the American Baptist Mission in the Burman Empire*, which became a best seller and further helped to promote the cause of foreign missions among American evangelicals. In this case, sickness and separation bore much fruit for the Judsons' missionary work.

Ann recovered her health and returned to Burma in December 1823. Shortly thereafter, the Judsons relocated to Ava with their new colleague, Price. Unfortunately, they never had the chance to establish a strong Christian presence in the capital city. In May 1824, the British fleet bombarded Rangoon, which quickly surrendered to an occupying force of 5,000 British troops. The Burmese were a proud people who could not understand

---

⁴⁶ Edward Judson, *The Life*, 192.

⁴⁷ Letter from Ann Judson to Francis Wayland, 22 January 1823, quoted in James Knowles, *Memoir of Mrs. Ann H. Judson, Late Missionary to Burmah, Including a History of the American Baptist Mission in the Burman Empire*, 3rd ed. (Boston, MA: Lincoln & Edmands, 1829), 194–95. Emphasis in original. Though this chapter necessarily deals with Ann's important contributions, as well as those of Adoniram's other wives, Candi Finch's chapter addresses the lives of the "three Mrs. Judsons" in greater detail.

how they lost Rangoon. The emperor became convinced British spies had contributed to the loss, so in June 1824 virtually all Western men in Burma were arrested on the presumption they were spies. Though Adoniram was American, he was violently arrested on June 8. Ann was the only foreigner in Ava not imprisoned as a suspected spy.[48]

Adoniram spent the next 19 months imprisoned.[49] At first, he was taken to a Burmese "death prison" and crammed into a dark room with about one hundred other prisoners.[50] Each of them were placed in fetters. At night, a bamboo pole was used to raise up the prisoners by their chains so that only their heads and shoulders touched the ground. The camp's guards were called "Spotted Faces"—convicted murderers who were spared the death sentence for agreeing to serve as jailers. Under the brutal treatment of the Spotted Faces, many of the prisoners died. Adoniram came close to death on several occasions, sometimes by fever and other times via execution. Only Ann's devotion prevented Adoniram from dying during his months of confinement.

She became a constant advocate for him and, when she could, other Western prisoners. She regularly petitioned the authorities to release her husband. When those requests were denied, she requested that his accommodations be improved; her success in these requests varied. Ann provided food for Adoniram, often after bribing government and prison officials. She also managed to give him his personal pillow, into which was sewn his translation of the Burmese Bible. During this time, she was also nursing an infant, Maria, and was caring for two orphaned Burmese girls.

In the spring of 1825, the Pakan Wun became the general of the Burmese army and the de facto military governor of the nation. He hated all foreigners and had previously been confined in the death prison—he was eager to kill all the Westerners, including Adoniram. At his command, the prisoners were forced to march to a new prison at Oung-pen-la.[51] The march was so grueling that one prisoner died of exhaustion. Adoniram was very sick at the time and might have died also had not another prisoner's servant wrapped his wounded feet and assisted him in walking. Fortunately, the prisoners were allowed to ride in the back of a cart for the final few miles of the trek.

---

[48] Wayland, *Memoir*, 1:329.

[49] The experiences discussed in the next several paragraphs were recounted by Ann in a lengthy letter to her brother, 26 May 1826, quoted in ibid., 334–73. An extensive narrative account can be found in Anderson, *To the Golden Shore*, 302–64. See also Piper, "How Few There Are Who Die So Hard," 97–99; Hulse, "Adoniram Judson—Devoted for Life," 134–38.

[50] The Burmese called the prison "Let Ma Yoon." For a firsthand account see Henry Gouger, *A Personal Narration of Two Years' Imprisonment in Burmah* (London: John Murray, 1860).

[51] Oung-pen-la is alternately spelled Aungbinle.

"Until All Burma Worships the Eternal God"

The new prison camp was more spacious than the death prison. Furthermore, the prisoners were granted a bit more freedom to walk around the camp during daylight hours. Ann relocated to Oung-pen-la and rented a room from one of the jailers. By this time, her own health had deteriorated to such a degree that she could no longer nurse Maria. She bribed the jailers to release Adoniram each day to take Maria to the village and beg nursing mothers to share some of their milk with the infant. Thankfully, the Pakan Wun was executed for treason shortly after the prisoners arrived in Oung-pen-la. The Westerners later learned they had been relocated to the new prison so that the Pakan Wun could offer them as sacrifices.

In November 1825, Adoniram was suddenly released from prison and summoned to Ava. The emperor needed the missionary to act as a translator in his negotiations with the advancing British. By early February 1826, the British army was closing in on Ava, and the Burmese emperor entered into treaty talks with them. Adoniram worked hard to represent fairly the Burmese government. The war officially ended on February 24. All prisoners of war were released, including the missionaries, so Adoniram and Ann decided to return to Rangoon.

The lowest point of Adoniram's life occurred shortly after his release from prison. The Rangoon mission was in shambles; the other missionaries had fled to India and the Burmese believers had been scattered. The Judsons relocated to Amherst and began a new mission. Shortly after their relocation, Adoniram reluctantly accepted a part-time translator position with the East India Company with the promises that he could continue his mission work and that the company would guarantee full religious freedom in the areas of Burma under its control. While engaging in diplomatic work in Ava, Adoniram learned that Ann had died of fever on October 24, 1826, despite the fact that she seemed healthy when he left Amherst a month earlier. Six months later, little Maria died at age 2. Her health had been declining since the death of her mother. Three months later, he received word his father had died in America.[52]

In his grief, Adoniram developed a morbid fascination with death and an unhealthy tendency toward introspection regarding his own spiritual condition. For several years

---

[52] Anderson, *To the Golden Shore*, 202, states that Adoniram Judson Sr., resigned from the Third Congregational Church in Plymouth due to a change in convictions regarding believer's baptism by immersion and was baptized on 31 August 1817 at age 67. In a 1 June 1819 letter from son to father, Adoniram Jr. states, "You will readily conceive, conceive that your change of sentiments on the subject of baptism, was particularly gratifying to my feelings" in *A Letter to the Rev. Adoniram Judson, Sen., Relative to the "Formal and Solemn Reprimand": To Which Is Added, a Letter to the Third Church in Plymouth, Mass., on the Subject of Baptism* (Boston, MA: Lincoln & Edmands, 1820), 3.

he grew increasingly interested in Roman Catholic mysticism, especially the writings of Thomas á Kempis and the French mystic Madame Guyon.[53] He wrestled with whether his missionary work was motivated by a yearning for the salvation of the nations or whether it was the fruit of his prideful ambition to be the first American Protestant missionary. In an effort to mortify his pride, he destroyed every letter of commendation he owned and renounced his honorary doctorate from Brown University in a letter to the *American Baptist Magazine*.[54] He wrote his sister, asking her to burn all of his letters home, even those to his parents. He donated all his savings to missions and asked the Triennial Convention to reduce his salary by one-quarter.[55]

Adoniram then retreated into seclusion. After Ann's death, he relocated to Moulmein, a city where George and Sarah Boardman were working as missionaries to the Karen people. Then he built a hut in the jungle bordering Moulmein. He named his hut "the Hermitage" and moved into it on October 24, 1828—the second anniversary of Ann's death. He spent 40 days at the Hermitage, eating little besides minimal rice rations. His obsessions with mysticism and death coalesced into an unfortunate condition described by Courtney Anderson:

> [H]e had a grave dug near the Hermitage and for days sat beside it, deliberately considering the stages of the body's decay in all its gruesome detail, in hopes that he might thus rise above fleshly considerations and through solitary reflection bring himself close to some intimation of Divinity. . . .
>
> But this grave-watching period did not last long, for in addition to his doubts about such self-inflicted austerities some remaining sense of the ridiculous must have come to his rescue. After all, the grave was not a real grave. There was no more sense in sitting beside it, staring into it, than in sitting beside and staring into any other excavation.[56]

Adoniram was not as alone as he assumed. A deacon in the Moulmein church, Ko Dwah, followed him into the jungle and erected a small shelter so he could watch out for his safety. The jungle was tiger infested, and many feared he would be eaten. For his

---

[53] Madame Guyon helped popularize the Quietist movement, which downplayed the intellectual elements of the faith in favor of a passive, inward submission to God's will that was thought to lead to total sanctification in this life. See Hulse, "Adoniram Judson—Devoted for Life," 149–50.

[54] A. Judson, "Renunciation of the Title D. D.," in *The American Baptist Magazine* 9, no. 3 (March 1829): 89.

[55] Piper, "How Few There Are Who Die So Hard," 100; Anderson, *To the Golden Shore*, 387, 390.

[56] Anderson, *To the Golden Shore*, 388.

part, Adoniram knew he was being watched, but he was never able to determine who was spying on him. When he returned safely from his self-exile, everyone was surprised he had survived. Over the course of 1830, he emerged from his spiritual darkness with new resolve to reach the Burmese for Christ. John Piper argues that his gradual recovery from personal loss and subsequent return to his spiritual senses paved the way for fruitfulness over the next several years.[57]

A Finished Bible and a New Wife

Now that Adoniram was a childless widower, he focused on translation work, revising his New Testament and translating the Old Testament. The Old Testament translation was finished in 1834, making the entire Bible available in Burmese for the first time. During this period, he also ordained the first Burmese pastor, Ko-Thah-a, one of the earliest Burmese converts to Christianity. After his ordination, Ko-Thah-a became pastor of the reestablished Baptist church in Rangoon.[58]

Adoniram did not remain unmarried. In February 1834, Sarah Hall Boardman wrote a letter commending him for the finished Burmese translation, and two months later they married.[59] Three years earlier, Sarah's husband George had died after the Boardmans came to Burma in 1827. Shortly after their arrival, the Karen people, an ethnic minority in South Burma, requested missionaries to work among them. The Karens were a traditionally animistic group that had previously been exposed to Anglicanism, which piqued their interest in Christianity. So the Boardmans focused their ministry on the Karens.[60]

The Boardmans and Judsons had been friends. The former had cared for little Maria after Ann's death, and Adoniram lived with them prior to his retreat in the jungle. Adoniram had been pleasantly surprised when Sarah did not return to America after George's death, for most missionary widows were unwilling to remain in Burma.[61] In light of their friendship and the scarcity of potential spouses, it is not surprising Adoniram and Sarah decided to marry. In their 11 years of marriage, they were blessed with a close relationship and significant ministry success. Sarah gave birth to eight

---

[57] Piper, "How Few Are Those Who Die So Hard," 101.
[58] Pierard, "The Man Who Gave the Bible to the Burmese."
[59] See the letter from Sarah H. Boardman to Adoniram Judson, 1 February 1834, quoted in Anderson, *To the Golden Shore*, 412.
[60] Pleasants, "Beyond Translation," 31.
[61] Anderson, *To the Golden Shore*, 401–2.

children, five of whom lived beyond childhood.[62] Adoniram continued to translate material into Burmese and to encourage the growth of the struggling Burman Baptist churches in Rangoon and Ava. Sarah also proved to be a skilled linguist, translating *Pilgrim's Progress* into Burmese; her translation is still used to this day.[63]

Sarah no longer ministered regularly among the Karens after her marriage to Adoniram, but the Boardmans' labors among them helped establish a thriving Baptist movement. Though Adoniram focused his work on the Burmese, he aided the Karen mission by creating an alphabet for their language and training Karen believers to work as translators and evangelists. In present-day Myanmar there are 26 million Burmese, approximately 50,000 of whom profess Christianity. But about 40 percent of the nearly 4 million Karens claim faith in Christ. The Karen Baptist Convention is the largest member group within the Myanmar Baptist Convention, which is the largest Protestant denomination in the country. The Karens also operate the Karen Baptist Theological Seminary, which was established by American Baptist missionaries in 1845.[64]

After the birth of a son named Henry Hall Judson in 1842, Sarah's health began to decline. By late 1844, she was seriously ill, and Adoniram made a decision he resolved previously never to make—he asked the Triennial Convention for a furlough.[65] Plans were laid for Adoniram, Sarah, and their three oldest children to return to America. The intention was for Sarah to recover her health and for the children to be left in America under the care of relatives.[66] On April 26, 1845, the Judsons set sail for their homeland.

Though Sarah's health initially improved, within a few weeks she began to decline again. She died on September 1, 1845, as the ship was making its way around the Cape of Good Hope off the coast of South Africa. In an obituary published in the *American Baptist Missionary Magazine,* Adoniram later recounted the final moments of Sarah's life:

---

[62] Piper, "How Few Are Those Who Die So Hard," 103.

[63] Hunt, *Bless God and Take Courage*, 183.

[64] For general statistical information about the Karen Baptist Convention and other Baptist groups in present-day Myanmar, see the entries related to Myanmar at the following websites: Operation World (http://www.operationworld.org/myan); The Joshua Project (http://www.joshuaproject.net/countries.php?rog3=bm); The World Council of Churches (http://www.oikoumene.org/en/member-churches/regions/asia/myanmar-burma/myanmar-baptist-convention.html). All websites accessed June 29, 2011. See also Hunt, *Bless God and Take Courage*, 353, and Robert E. Johnson, *A Global Introduction to Baptist Churches* (New York: Cambridge University Press, 2010), 206–7.

[65] Anderson, *To the Golden Shore*, 436.

[66] Sarah's oldest child, George Boardman Jr., had been living in America since 1834.

On our passage homeward, as the strength of Mrs. J. gradually declined, I expected to be under the painful necessity of burying her in the sea. But it was so ordered in Divine Providence, that when the indications of approaching death had become strongly marked, the ship came to anchor in the port of St. Helena. For three days she continued to sink rapidly, though her bodily sufferings were not very severe. Her mind became liable to wander, but a single word was sufficient to recall and steady her recollections. On the evening of the 31st of August, she appeared to be drawing near to the end of her pilgrimage. The children took leave of her and retired to rest. I sat alone by the side of her bed during the hours of the night, endeavoring to administer relief to the distressed body and consolation to the departing soul. At 2 o'clock in the morning, wishing to obtain one more token, of recognition, I roused her attention and said, "Do you still love the Savior?" "O yes," she replied, "I ever love the Lord Jesus Christ." I said again, "Do you still love me?" She replied in the affirmative, by a peculiar expression of her own. "Then give me one more kiss;" and we exchanged that token of love for the last time. Another hour passed,—life continued to recede,—and she ceased to breathe. For a moment I traced her upward flight, and thought of the wonders which were opening to her view. I then closed her sightless eyes, dressed her, for the last time, in the drapery of death; and being quite exhausted with many sleepless nights, I threw myself down and slept. On awaking in the morning, I saw the children standing and weeping around the body of their dear mother, then, for the first time, inattentive to their cries.[67]

Sarah's body was taken to shore, where a funeral ceremony was held. A few hours after the memorial service, Adoniram and his children returned to the ship, which continued its journey to America.

AN AMERICAN CELEBRITY

After a six-week voyage, Adoniram and his children landed in Boston Harbor on October 15, 1845. He intended to stay in America just long enough to visit his sister Abigail, his only surviving sibling, and to help his children get settled. But he did not account for his

---

[67] Adoniram Judson, "Obituary—Mrs. Sarah B. Judson," *American Baptist Missionary Magazine* 26, no. 2 (February 1846): 43–44.

fame. Ann Judson had been similarly surprised during her time in America more than two decades earlier. Ann's book *An Account of the American Baptist Mission to the Burman Empire*, published in 1823, played a key role in increasing Adoniram's renown. Likewise, James Knowles's 1829 book *Memoir of Mrs. Ann Judson* had cemented Ann's popularity in the American imagination. As John Piper notes, "Adoniram Judson was a celebrity. Countless parents had named their children after him. He had been the topic of thousands of sermons. His homecoming was a sensation."[68]

Almost as soon as he landed, Adoniram was virtually forced to begin a goodwill tour of churches, colleges, and civic groups in the Northeast. Despite persistent throat problems that caused him to speak frequently in a whisper, he drew large crowds wherever he went. Both Baptists and Congregationalists seemed eager to claim him.[69] Though there had been hard feelings in the past over Adoniram's conversion to Baptist views and a debate over whether or not he should be considered the father of the foreign missions movement in America, by 1845–46 virtually all evangelicals revered him as their own.[70]

The famous missionary found himself at the center of one controversy while he was in America—surrounding his marriage to Emily Chubbuck, a much younger woman. Adoniram was first introduced to Emily through her novels, which were written under the pen name Fanny Forrester. He was impressed with her writing, and once he discovered she was a Baptist, he asked to meet her. Their first meeting was a bit tense.

---

[68] Piper, "How Few Are Those Who Die So Hard," 105.

[69] This included the newly formed Southern Baptist Convention. Separating from their Northern brethren on May 8, 1845, Southern Baptists sought to secure a visit with Judson as well as claim a connection with his work in Burma. See "James B. Taylor to Rev. Adoniram Judson, Jan 22, 1845." During the meeting of the Foreign Mission Board (SBC) on December 1, 1845, the board voted to "invite in behalf of the Board Brethren A. Judson, Abbot and Dean to visit this city as early as their engagements may allow," in Minutes of the Foreign Mission Board, Archives of the International Mission Board, Richmond, Virginia. In his address as president of the Convention on May 12, 1845, W. B. Johnson stated, "The Constitution we adopt is precisely that of the original union; that in connection with which throughout his missionary life, Adoniram Judson has lived, and under which Ann Judson and Boardman have died." See *Proceedings of the Southern Baptist Convention* (Richmond, 1845), 19. On February 8, 1846, Jeremiah Jeter, a Southern Baptist pastor in Richmond, addressed Judson at a meeting held to welcome him home. After reviewing Judson's personal pilgrimage to join the Baptists and the start of the Triennial Convention, Jeter stated, "Henceforth, my brother, you and we shall labor in connection with different boards. Events which neither you nor we could control produced the separation; and God, we trust, will overrule it for good. One thing is certain: the southern Baptists have no thought of abandoning the missionary field. . . . Welcome, thrice welcome are you, my brother, to our city, our churches, our bosoms. I speak as the representative of Southern Baptists. We love you for the truth's sake, and for your labors in the cause of Christ. We honor you as the father of American missions." See Wayland, *Memoir*, 2:243–48.

[70] Anderson, *To the Golden Shore*, 447.

Upon being introduced, Adoniram asked Emily, "How can you reconcile it with your conscience to employ such noble talents in writing so little useful and spiritual as those sketches I read?"[71] Fortunately, she was not permanently offended. Adoniram asked her to consider writing a biography of his late wife Sarah, which Emily readily agreed to do.

The two struck up a friendship as Adoniram tried to provide Emily with the information she needed to write the biography. Very quickly, Adoniram was smitten. Less than a month after their first meeting, he proposed to her. She had actually considered becoming a missionary as a young girl, a desire first sparked by reading James Knowles's biography of Ann Judson. Even after she embarked on a literary career, Emily closely followed news about the Baptist missionaries in Burma. Nevertheless, she confessed to Adoniram she felt no distinct calling to be a missionary. He argued that their compatibility and affection, which were clear, were more important than a sense of calling. Persuaded, she accepted his proposal and resigned her position as a teacher at Utica Female Seminary.[72]

Many evangelical observers were upset that Adoniram intended to marry such a young woman—he was twice her age. Worse, Emily was a novelist at a time when many Christians treated nonreligious fiction with great suspicion. In the words of Edward Judson, many Christians "feared the moral grandeur of the missionary cause was compromised by an alliance between its venerable founder and a writer of fiction."[73] The literary world was also upset—one of the most promising young novelists in America was throwing away her career to marry a foreign missionary. But the couple was undeterred by their critics. They were married in June 1846; three weeks later, they set sail for Burma.

FINAL YEARS

The Judsons arrived in Rangoon in November 1846, where Adoniram resumed his work on a comprehensive English-Burmese dictionary and Emily began writing Sarah Judson's biography. They lived in a house Emily dubbed "the Bat Castle" because of the various types of vermin, particularly the aforementioned flying rodents. Bats aside, it was a happy time for both Judsons. Emily adjusted to the rigors of missionary life very quickly, especially for a woman who had not intended to be a foreign missionary a year

---

[71] Ibid., 454.
[72] Ibid., 455–57.
[73] Edward Judson, *The Life*, 485.

earlier. Their marriage was a happy one, as Emily recounted in a letter to her sister on their first wedding anniversary:

> Just one year to-day since I stood before good old Doctor Kendrick, and said the irrevocable "love, honor, and obey." It was on many accounts a day of darkness, but it has dragged three hundred and sixty-five *very* light ones at its heels. It has been far the happiest year of my life; and, what is in my eyes still more important, my husband says it has been among the happiest of his. We have been in circumstances to be almost constantly together; and I never met with any man who could talk so well, day after day, on every subject, religious, literary, scientific, political, and—and nice baby-talk. He has a mind which seems exhaustless, and so, even here in Rangoon, where all the English I hear, from week's end to week's end, is from him, I never think of wanting more society. I have been ill a great deal, but not in a way to hinder him; and he treats me as gently and tenderly as though I were an infant.[74]

Though she had been a spinster of almost 30 at the time of her marriage, Emily quickly adapted to motherhood and tenderly cared for all of her stepchildren as if they were her own. In December 1847, she gave birth to a daughter; she was the last of Adoniram's children born during his lifetime.

Though they were happy, the Judsons were not free from the struggles that had always plagued Adoniram and his wives. The local government in Rangoon was intolerant of all non-Buddhists, forcing the Judsons to allow Burmese believers to meet secretly at the Bat Castle for worship. There were food shortages, and the food that was available was of poor quality. All of the Judsons experienced periodic illness. By early 1849, Emily's health declined to such an extent that Adoniram feared for her life. He even wrote to one of Emily's friends,

> A crushing weight is upon me. I can not resist the dreadful conviction that dear Emily is in a settled and rapid decline. For nearly a year after the birth of baby, she enjoyed pretty good health, and I flattered myself that she would be spared for many years. But three or four months ago her appetite almost entirely failed her. Soon after, baby was taken very ill, and in the midst of it our usual help left

---

[74] Letter from Emily Judson to Katy Chubbuck, 30 May 1847, quoted in A. C. Kendrick, *The Life and Letters of Mrs. Emily C. Judson* (New York: Sheldon & Co., 1860), 275–76. Though the letter was dated May 30, Emily wrote it over several days. The section cited herein was written on June 2, 1847.

us, and she was obliged to undergo a great deal of severe fatigue; and I see now that she has been declining ever since.[75]

Emily slowly recovered and was soon pregnant with their second child, but around the same time in fall 1849, Adoniram contracted his final illness.

He grew weak in the coming months, though he also felt a peace about his standing with Christ, his love of others, and future prospects for the Burmese mission.[76] By the spring, Adoniram was so sick that it seemed his only hope was a sea passage to the Isle of France. *The Aristide Marie* departed on April 3, 1850. Her passengers included Adoniram and a friend named Thomas Ranney, who was his caretaker. This was Adoniram's final voyage. On April 12, he passed into the next life and was buried at sea during a quiet ceremony.[77] Ten days later, Emily gave birth to a boy named Charles, who died at birth. Four months later, she learned of her husband's death. She remained in Burma six more months before returning to New England.[78] Upon her return, she shared numerous anecdotes with American Baptist leader Francis Wayland, who was preparing Adoniram's memoir.[79] Emily died three and a half years later, in June 1854.

A Missionary's Legacy

In a brief article titled "The Legacy of Adoniram Judson," historian William Brackney demonstrates the influence of Adoniram and his wives on American Baptists in particular and missions-minded evangelicals in general.[80] The famous missionary was the subject of numerous biographies, the most notable written by Wayland (1853), Robert Middlemarch (1854), and Edward Judson (1883).[81] Adoniram's wives were also the

---

[75] Letter from Adoniram Judson to "Miss Anable," no date, quoted in Judson, *The Life of Adoniram Judson*, 525. Based upon context, it seems likely this letter was written in the early months of 1849.

[76] Anderson, *To the Golden Shore*, 495–96.

[77] While Judson was buried at sea, there exists a memorial gravestone for Adoniram Judson Sr., Elnathan Judson, Ann Judson, Sarah B. Judson, Adoniram Judson Jr., Emily C. Judson, and Abigail Brown Judson in the Burial Hill cemetery, Plymouth, Massachusetts.

[78] For a detailed description of Adoniram's final days, see ibid., 501–6. Cf. Piper, "How Few Are Those Who Die So Hard," 105–6.

[79] Kendrick, *Life and Letters*, 347.

[80] Brackney, "The Legacy of Adoniram Judson," 126.

[81] The Wayland and Judson biographies have been frequently referenced in this chapter. For the Middlemarch biography, see Robert Middlemarch, *Burmah's Great Missionary: Records of the Life of Adoniram Judson* (New York: E. H. Fletcher, 1854).

subjects of biographies, perhaps the most famous of which was Arabella Stuart's *The Lives of the Three Mrs. Judsons* (1855).[82]

Dozens of Baptist churches in America are named for Adoniram Judson; the most famous is probably the Judson Memorial Church in New York City, founded by Edward Judson in 1890.[83] Several Baptist associations, retreat centers, retirement communities, missionary houses, and even Sunday school classes are named for Adoniram. The official publication ministry of the American Baptist Churches USA is named Judson Press. Two Baptist schools own the Judson name: Judson College in Marion, Alabama, and Judson University in Elgin, Illinois.[84] Andover-Newton Theological Seminary has endowed a Judson Chair of World Missions, and several other Baptist schools have buildings, rooms, or streets named for Adoniram.[85] An endowed scholarship at Southern Baptist Theological Seminary is named in honor of both Adoniram Judson and Luther Rice.[86] Hundreds of parents have named their sons after Adoniram Judson, some of whom were Christian leaders in their own right.[87] These are just some of the ways that the Judson legacy endures among those inspired by the sacrificial service of the father of American foreign missions and his three remarkable wives.

---

[82] For more on this important book and other biographies of the Judson wives, see Candi Finch's chapter.

[83] Edward Judson was a son of Adoniram and Sarah who became a prominent pastor and professor among American Baptists. Judson Memorial Church became one of the leading "institutional churches" at the turn of the twentieth century. The institutional church movement centered around large urban congregations that combined evangelism with social uplift programs designed to minister to the poor and uneducated, especially immigrants. See Charles Hatch Sears, *Edward Judson: Interpreter of God* (Philadelphia: Griffith and Rowland, 1917), and Edward Judson, *The Institutional Church* (New York: Lentilhon & Co., 1899).

[84] Judson College in Alabama is a historically women's college named for Ann Judson.

[85] My own institution, Southeastern Baptist Theological Seminary, has a street named Judson Circle. The street is home to a number of student apartments, including one reserved for students and alumni who are serving as Southern Baptist missionaries on stateside assignment (furlough).

[86] For information about the Rice-Judson Scholarship, accessed June 30, 2011, see http://www.sbts.edu/current-students/financial-aid/sbts-scholarships/rice-judson.

[87] The most famous is Adoniram Judson Gordon, who was a missions advocate and leading promoter of premillennial theology. See Scott M. Gibson, *A. J. Gordon: American Premillennialist* (Lanham, MD: University Press of America, 2001).

Chapter 5

So That the World May Know
The Legacy of Adoniram Judson's Wives

Candi Finch

Edward Judson, one of the sons of Adoniram and Sarah Judson, remarked about his father in the biography he penned, "There are very few of those who have gone out from this country as missionaries who are not indebted to Mr. Judson for his methods and inspiration."[1] Indeed, Judson's life and ministry has left an indelible mark not only on Burma but also on many missionaries who have surrendered to God's call to go to the uttermost parts of the earth. However, Judson's story is incomplete without a look at the three incredible women who shared the journey with him at different points along the way.

On June 25, 1832, Adoniram Judson wrote a letter from Moulmein to the Foreign Missionary Association of the Hamilton Literary and Theological Institution in New York. His purpose was to give advice to prospective missionary candidates. The letter begins,

Dear Brethren,

Yours of November last, from the pen of your Corresponding Secretary, Mr. William Dean, is before me. It is one of the few letters that I feel called upon to answer, for you ask my advice on several important points. There is, also, in the sentiments you express, something so congenial to my own, that I feel my heart knit to the members of your association, and instead of commonplace reply, am desirous of setting down a few items which may be profitable to you in your future course. Brief items they must be, for want of time forbids my expatiating.

In commencing my remarks, I take you as you are. You are contemplating a missionary life.

---

[1] Edward Judson, *The Life of Adoniram Judson* (New York: Anson D. F. Randolph, 1883), 559.

> *First*, then, let it be a missionary *life*; that is, come out for life, and not for a limited term. Do not fancy that you have a true missionary spirit, while you are intending all along to leave the heathen soon after acquiring their language. Leave them! for what? To spend the rest of your days in enjoying the ease and plenty of your native land?
>
> *Secondly.* In choosing a companion for life, have particular regard to a good constitution, and not wantonly, or without good cause, bring a burden on yourselves and the mission.[2]

One cannot help but wonder if he had in mind his first wife Ann, who died almost six years before he wrote this letter. She had suffered considerably from health issues while overseas and gave her life in service to her husband and the people of Burma. Her story is a remarkable account of heroism, and Judson felt her loss deeply for many years after her death. In fact, aside from his imprisonment, the period after her death was perhaps the most difficult time in his ministry.[3] Judson knew how important Ann's contribution had been to the work in Burma, and his letter to the missionary candidates illustrates how important one's life companion is in the consideration of pursuing missionary work. Judson's story cannot be told without also telling the stories of Ann, Sarah, and Emily.[4]

Each of Judson's wives made unique contributions to the missionary endeavors in Burma. Ann was gifted with languages and displayed incredible heroism during her husband's imprisonment. Sarah, who bore 11 children on the field, attacked the missionary task with an unrelenting zeal and passion. Emily, a gifted writer, used her talents to immortalize Sarah and to assist Adoniram in his final days. These ladies endured incredible hardships on the field. Their faith in God and His calling and their love for the people of Burma sustained them in their most difficult moments.

---

[2] Ibid., 577–78.

[3] Ibid., 293–307, see especially the poem he composed to his wife Ann after her death titled "The Solitary's Lament," 305–7.

[4] Ann recognized the invaluable contribution that women could have on the mission field shortly after she arrived overseas. She observed the work of Hannah Marshman and remarked in a letter home: "Good female schools are everywhere needed in this country. I hope no Missionary will ever come out here, without a wife, as she, in her sphere, can be equally useful with her husband. I presume Mrs. Marshman does more good in her school than half the ministers in America," recorded in James Knowles, *The Memoir of Mrs. Ann H. Judson, Late Missionary to Burmah, Including a History of the American Baptist Mission in the Burman Empire*, 3rd ed. (Boston, MA: Lincoln & Edmands, 1829), 72.

ANN HASSELTINE JUDSON, "NANCY" (1789–1826)

Show us the situation of our tawny sisters the other side of the world, and though the disgusting picture break our hearts, it will fill us with gratitude to Him who has made us to differ, and excite us to stronger exertion in their behalf . . . let us make a united effort; let us call on all, old and young, in the circle of our acquaintance, to join us in attempting to meliorate the situation, to instruct, to enlighten, and save females in the Eastern world; and though time and circumstances should prove that our united exertions have been ineffectual, we shall escape at death that bitter thought, that Burman females have been lost, without an effort of ours to prevent their ruin.[5]

Early Years: Surrender to the Lord

Born in Bradford, Massachusetts, on December 22, 1789, to parents John and Rebecca, Ann Hasseltine (sometimes called "Nancy") grew up to be one of the first and most heroic female missionaries to the Far East. Her father was a minister in a Congregational church, and she was involved in religious activities from a young age, though she was not converted to faith in Christ until her teen years. James Knowles remarked in her biography, "She loved learning, and a book could allure her from her favorite walks, and from the gayest social circle."[6] She was also a very beautiful girl with a cheerful disposition: "A clear olive skin, glowing with the rich hues of healthful youth, harmonized well with the jetty hair, which fell in natural ringlets around her face, and with the sparking intelligent black eye; while the movements of her fine figure were full of native dignity and grace."[7]

Several incidents during her mid-teens caused her to consider her eternal state and question whether just being "good" was enough to obtain salvation. One morning the following words by Hannah Moore in *Strictures on Female Education* pricked her heart,

---

[5] Portion of Ann Judson's address "To Females in America, Relative to the Situation of Females in the East," written from Boston, 19 November 1822, in Knowles *The Memoir of Mrs. Ann H. Judson*, 402, 406.

[6] Knowles, *The Memoir of Mrs. Ann H. Judson*, 12.

[7] Mrs. H. C. Conant, *The Ernest Man: A Sketch of the Character and Labor of Adoniram Judson, First Missionary to Burmah* (Boston, MA: Phillips, Sampson, and Company, 1856), 77. One of Ann's classmates said of her, "Where Ann is, no one can be gloomy or unhappy. Her cheerful countenance, her sweet smile, her happy disposition, her keen wit, her lively conduct, never rude nor boisterous, will dispel the shades of care and hang the smiles of summer upon the sorrows of the coldest heart," Daniel C. Eddy, *Heroines of the Missionary Enterprise* (Boston, MA: Ticknor, Reed, and Fields, 1850), 35.

"She that liveth in pleasure is dead while she liveth." Ann remarked, "They struck me to the heart. I stood for a few moments amazed at the incident, and half inclined to think that some invisible agency had directed my eye to those words."[8] Several months later she read Bunyan's *Pilgrim's Progress*, and it convinced her to "begin a religious life." Unfortunately, this life was based on her own good works and not the work of Christ on the cross. Attending religious conferences in the spring of 1806, Ann became convinced of her need for a "new heart" and realized that her "soul was lost."[9] However, she struggled for several weeks before finally surrendering to the Lord:

> I began to discover a beauty in the way of salvation by Christ. He appeared to be just such a Saviour as I needed. I saw how God could be just, in saving sinners through him. I committed my soul into his hands, and besought him to do with me what seemed good in his sight. When I was thus enabled to commit myself into the hands of Christ, my mind was relieved from that distressing weight which had borne it down for so long a time.[10]

After her conversion, she approached her studies with a fresh zeal. She graduated from the Bradford Academy and began teaching at age 18. However, a meeting three years later forever changed the course of her life.

Courtship: Hearts United for Christ and His Mission

In June 1810, a group of men gathered in Bradford for the Massachusetts General Association of Congregational Churches Associational meeting. Among the group was a young seminary graduate, Adoniram Judson, with a heart set on forming a missionary society "to awaken the American churches to combined action for the support of foreign Missions."[11] Judson was described by one author as

> small and exceedingly delicate in figure, with a round, rosy face, which gave him the appearance of extreme youthfulness. . . . His voice, however, was far from what would be expected of such a person, and usually took the listeners by surprise. An instance of this occurred in London. He sat in the pulpit with a

---

[8] Knowles, *The Memoir of Mrs. Ann H. Judson*, 14.
[9] Ibid., 18.
[10] Ibid., 19.
[11] Ibid., 38.

clergyman somewhat distinguished for his eccentricity, and at the close of the sermon was requested to read a hymn. When he had finished, the clergyman arose, and introduced his young brother to the congregation as a person who purposed devoting himself to the conversation of the heathen, adding, "And if his faith is proportioned to his voice, he will drive the devil from all India."[12]

During the meeting in Bradford, attendees were invited to the home of John Hasseltine for a meal, and Ann helped serve them. Edward Judson described Adoniram and Ann's first meeting:

During the sessions the ministers gathered for a dinner beneath Mr. Hasseltine's hospitable roof. His youngest daughter, Ann, was waiting on the table. Her attention was attracted to the young student whose bold missionary projects were making such a stir. But what was her surprise to observe, as she moved about the table, that he seemed completely absorbed in his plate! Little did she dream that she had already woven her spell about his young heart, and that he was, at that very time, composing a graceful stanza in her praise![13]

Soon after this encounter, Adoniram asked Ann to marry him, but she did not give her answer immediately; she wanted to consider fully whether God had called her to a missionary life. Indeed, no woman from America had ever gone overseas as a missionary; moreover, no American missionary had ever been to India.[14] There was no precedent for her to consider or experienced person for her to consult for guidance. Aside from two or three counselors, most people were not in favor of her marriage to Judson

---

[12] Francis Wayland, *A Memoir of the Life and Labors of the Rev. Adoniram Judson, D.D.*, vol. 1 (Boston, MA: Phillips, Sampson, and Company, 1853), 1:74.
[13] Edward Judson, *The Life*, 32–33.
[14] Several years after the Judsons left for the mission field, the picture of mission work in India became clearer as reports from the Serampore mission made it back to London. On the plight of women in India, see "On the Burning of Widows" in *The Friend of India* no. 12 (Serampore: Printed at the Mission Press, May 1825): 449–477. Though the Judsons did not end up in India, it was to that country that they initially set their course. Women in India had a very difficult life. Knowles, *The Memoir of Mrs. Ann H. Judson*, 403, cites an address Ann wrote to women in America that offers a glimpse of what women in India had to endure:

"Females in India receive no instruction; consequently they are wholly uninformed of an eternal state. No wonder mothers consider female existence a curse; hence their desire to destroy their female offspring, and to burn themselves with the bodies of their deceased husbands. This last circumstance might imply some attachment, were it not a well-known fact, that the *disgrace* of a woman who refuses to burn with the corpse of her husband is such, that her nearest relations would refuse her a morsel of rice to prevent her starvation."

because that meant accompanying him overseas, which, for a woman was "altogether inconsistent with prudence and delicacy."[15] The journey alone was fraught with danger, and once they arrived, the risk of death was high.

She eventually told Judson that he had to receive consent from her parents, and he wrote to her father:

> I have now to ask whether you can consent to part with your daughter early next spring, to see her no more in this world! Whether you can consent to her departure to a heathen land, and the hardships and sufferings of a missionary life! Whether you can consent to her exposure to the dangers of the ocean; to the fatal influence of the southern climate of India; to every kind of want and distress; to degradation, insult, persecution, and perhaps a violent death! Can you consent to all this for the sake of Him who left His heavenly home and died for her and for you; for the sake of perishing and immortal souls; for the sake of Zion and the glory of God! Can you consent to all this in the hope of soon meeting your daughter in the world of glory, with a crown of righteousness brightened by the acclamations of praise which shall redound to her Saviour from heathen saved, through her means, from eternal woe and despair?[16]

One can imagine the shock of receiving such a letter. However, Adoniram received her parents' consent, and Ann accepted his proposal, convinced this was God's plan for her life. In a revealing letter to her close friend Lydia Kimball, dated September 8, 1810, Ann explained her decision:

> I have ever made you a confidant. I will still confide in you, and beg for your prayers, that I may be directed in regard to this subject I shall communicate.
>
> I feel willing and expect, if nothing in providence prevents, to spend my days in this world in heathen lands. Yes, Lydia, I have about come to the determination to give up all my comforts and enjoyments here, sacrifice my affection to relatives and friends, and go where God, in his providence, shall see fit to place me. My determinations are not hasty, or formed without viewing the dangers, trials, and hardships attendant on a missionary life. Nor were my determinations formed in consequence of an attachment to an earthly object; but with a sense

---

[15] Knowles, *The Memoir of Mrs. Ann H. Judson*, 42–43.
[16] Courtney Anderson, *To the Golden Shore: The Life of Adoniram Judson* (Grand Rapids: Zondervan, 1956), 83.

of my obligation to God, and a full conviction of its being a call in providence, and consequently my duty. My feelings have been exquisite in regard to the subject. Now my mind is settled and composed, and is willing to leave the event with God—none can support one under trials and afflictions but Him. In Him alone I feel a disposition to confide.

How short is time, how boundless is eternity! If we may be considered worthy to suffer for Jesus here, will it not enhance our happiness hereafter? O pray for me. Spend whole evenings in prayer for those who go to carry the gospel to the poor heathen.[17]

In her journal a couple days later on September 10, 1810, she wrote, "O Jesus, direct me, and I am safe; use me in thy service, and I ask no more. I would not choose my position of work, or place of labor; only let me know Thy will, and I will readily comply."[18]

On February 5, 1812, Adoniram and Ann were married, and the next day Adoniram was ordained in Salem. Just a few days later on February 19, they set sail for India on the ship *Caravan*. This young, newlywed couple had no idea of the hardships they would face, but in the midst of each trial, they allowed God to be glorified. James Knowles wrote of Ann's contribution as the first woman missionary from America:

It is well for the cause of Missions that God assigned to Miss Hasseltine the honorable yet difficult office of leading the way in this great enterprise. Her adventurous spirit and her decision of character eminently fitted her to resolve, where others would hesitate, and to advance, where others might retreat. She did decide to go, and her determination, without doubt, has had some effect on the minds of other females, who have since followed her example.[19]

Journey Begins: Surprise on the Sea and a New Assignment

The journey took more than four months before the Judsons landed at Calcutta on June 18, 1812. During the trip, they read several books on baptism, and both Adoniram and Ann became convinced that true baptism was immersion of believers. In a letter to her parents, Ann said,

---

[17] Ibid., 84. This letter was prophetic. During her darkest hours in Burma, surrounding the loss of her children and the imprisonment of her husband, it was to her Savior that she turned for strength and comfort.
[18] Knowles, *The Memoir of Mrs. Ann H. Judson*, 45.
[19] Ibid., 43.

I confined my attention almost entirely to the Scriptures, compared the Old with the New Testament, and tried to find something to favor infant baptism, but was convinced it had no foundation there. I examined the covenant of circumcision, and could see no reason for concluding that baptism was to be administered to children, because circumcision was. Thus, my dear parents and sisters, we are both confirmed Baptists, not because we wished to be, but because truth compelled us to be.[20]

This was a problem since they were sent to India on behalf of pedobaptists. So they resigned their missionary appointments and were left without financial support. On September 6, 1812, both Judsons were baptized by William Ward in Calcutta. When news of this reached America, it sparked interest among Baptists to form what came to be known as the American Baptist Missionary Union.

In addition to a change in denominations, the Judsons faced many challenges during their first year overseas because the East India Company ordered them out of the country, fearing that missionary work would interfere with trading. The Judsons travelled to the Isle of France for a time and then returned to India, landing at Madras this time instead of Calcutta. However, they were ordered out again almost immediately by the East India Company. An avenue opened for them in Burma, and they moved to

---

[20] Ibid., 75. Dana Robert argues that Ann had no choice but to change her views regarding baptism saying, "In hindsight it is clear that given the expectations of lifelong marriage and her isolation from everyone except her husband, Ann Judson had no choice but to go along with her husband in his change of views. Baptist lore indicates that the Judsons reached their change of views on baptism independently, but the evidence from the Knowles biography suggests otherwise." Dana Robert, "Evangelist or Homemaker? Mission Strategies of Early Nineteenth-Century Missionary Wives in Burma and Hawaii," in *North American Foreign Missions, 1810–1914: Theology, Theory, and Policy*, ed. Wilbert R. Shenk (Grand Rapids: Eerdmans, 2004), 118 n4. Robert has an identical footnote in her work, *American Women in Mission: A Social History of Their Thought and Practice* (Macon, GA: Mercer University Press, 1997), 43 n7.

The problem with Robert's conclusion is that she assigns motives and a weakness of conviction to Ann without ample evidence. Robert cites p. 73 in the Knowles memoir as evidence for her conclusion, but a careful reading of pp. 73–75 reveals that while Ann was initially opposed to changing her views on baptism, when she studied the Scriptures herself, she became convinced of the truth. She was not afraid to disagree with her husband; Ann admitted that initially she argued for infant baptism: "I always took the Pedobaptists' side in reasoning with him, although I was as doubtful of the truth of their system as he," 75. In addition, Ann's letter to her parents cited in the body of this chapter makes clear that she studied Scripture for herself and became convinced of the truth of baptism by immersion. For Robert to argue that Ann had "no choice" but to change her views is inconsistent with Ann's testimony. Nowhere does she say she felt pressure to change her views in order to mirror her husband's convictions. To accept Robert's assertion is to disbelieve Ann's own testimony regarding her change of convictions.

Rangoon, Burma, between China and India. In her journal two days before they departed for Burma, Ann wrote,

> But I most sincerely hope that we shall be able to remain at Rangoon, among the Burmans, a people who have never heard the sound of the gospel, or read, in their own language, of the love of Christ. Though our trials may be great, and our privations many and severe, yet the presence of Jesus can make us happy, and the consciousness that we have sacrificed all for his dear cause, and are endeavoring to labor for the salvation of immortal souls, will enable us to bear our privations and trials, with some degree of satisfaction and delight.[21]

They departed Madras on June 22, and Ann, who was pregnant with her first child, became very ill on the journey in a rickety old boat known as the *Georgianna*.[22] On this voyage they faced a monsoon in the Bay of Bengal, and Ann gave birth to their first baby, attended only by her husband. The woman they brought to assist her in childbirth had died during the early days of the journey. The baby died and was buried at sea.[23]

They landed in Burma on July 13, 1813, not knowing what lay ahead of them. Brutal murders and robberies were common occurrences, and the mission house was close to the spot where public executions took place. It was a spiritually dark land in desperate need of the gospel.

---

[21] Knowles, *The Memoir of Mrs. Ann H. Judson*, 103.

[22] Edward Judson, *The Life*, 48.

[23] Some confusion exists in the secondary literature on the Judsons' life regarding whether Ann had three children or two. For instance, in Edith Deen's work, *Great Women of the Christian Faith* (New York: Harper and Row, 1959), 173, she remarks that Roger Williams was Ann's first child. However, in the book *Notable American Women: A Biographical Dictionary*, ed. Edward T. James and Janet Wilson James (Cambridge, MA: Radcliffe College, 1971), 296, the editors note that Roger Williams was the Judsons' second child. Courtney Anderson in *To the Golden Shore*, 167, states that Ann went into labor on the trip to Rangoon with only Mr. Judson as an attendant. Anderson quotes from a letter Ann wrote to her parents about the voyage stating that she had "no physician, no attendant but Mr. Judson." This letter that Anderson quotes is found in Edward Judson's *The Life*, 49. Ann's letter and Adoniram's account regarding the same voyage are not clear as to whether Ann was just sick or sick and pregnant, and this may be why the secondary literature is not clear on this matter. In fact, neither of the Judsons' letters regarding this voyage mention a baby or Ann's pregnancy. However, later in Edward Judson's book, he refers to Roger as his father's second child and the first child as sleeping "beneath the waters of the Bay of Bengal" (267).

Missionary Endeavors: Times of Great Faith and Perseverance

When the Judsons began their work, Burma was the equivalent of a modern-day closed country. All previous missionaries had either died in service or abandoned the area.[24] During the first few years in Burma, Ann devoted herself to learning the Burmese language, and she proved to be a gifted linguist, learning Siamese as well. She assisted her husband in his translation work and produced a catechism that she used in the school they opened for Burmese girls. She decided to adopt the colorful dress of the Burmese women and to learn their customs in order to reach them with the gospel. She formed a society of native women that met together on Sunday to pray and read Scripture, and she conducted classes for women. Seeing the mistreatment of Burmese women increased her burden for them.

Ann's writing proved to be one of her greatest contributions on the mission field. Through her pen the world learned of her husband's imprisonment for almost two years, the child marriages popular in Burma and India, female infanticide, and other difficulties faced by Burmese women. She also wrote to women in America, enlisting them to help her in the missionary endeavor through prayer, giving, or, in some cases, coming to the field.

On September 5, 1815, the Judsons learned of their official appointment as missionaries by the American Baptist Board of Foreign Missions. Six days later, Ann gave birth to their second child, Roger Williams Judson, named for the great American Baptist. Unfortunately, Roger caught jungle fever, died several months later on May 4, 1816, and was buried under a mango tree. Ann wrote upon his death:

> Our little Roger was the only legitimate child of foreign parents in the place; consequently he was quite a curiosity to the Burmans. But what shall I say about the improvement we are to make of this heavy affliction? We do not feel a disposition to murmur, or to inquire of our Sovereign why he has done this. We wish rather, to sit down submissively under the rod and bear the smart, till the end for which the affliction was sent, shall be accomplished.[25]

In the midst of such great tragedy, Ann demonstrated her reliance upon the Savior and her trust in His unseen, sovereign hand.

---

[24] Anderson, *To the Golden Shore*, 134–35.
[25] Knowles, *The Memoir of Mrs. Ann H. Judson*, 152.

In December 1817, Adoniram embarked for Chittagong to visit an abandoned mission and to look for a native helper. From December 25 until the next July, Ann did not receive any word from her husband though she had only expected him to be gone three months. One challenge after another met her during those months. Disease swept through the city, the government harassed the missionaries, rumors circulated that all foreigners would be banished, and a war loomed on the horizon. One by one English ships left the area; and when only one remained, fellow workers with the Judsons prepared to leave on it and urged Ann to accompany them. She went initially; but after reaching the ship, she did not have a peace about leaving so she returned to the mission house alone. If Adoniram was still alive, she wanted him to find her carrying on their mission. She said upon returning to the mission house, "I know I am surrounded by dangers on every hand, and expect to see much anxiety and distress; but at present I am tranquil, and intend to make an effort to pursue my studies as formerly, and leave the event with God."[26] A few days later, her husband returned unharmed to find his wife busy about the Lord's work.

On the 27th of June 1819, more than seven years after leaving America, and almost six after arriving in Rangoon, Adoniram baptized his first Burmese believer, Moung Nau. Ann wrote, "This event, this single trophy of victorious grace, has filled our hearts with sensations hardly to be conceived by Christians in Christian countries."[27] Adoniram jotted in his journal: "Oh, may it prove to be the beginning of a series of baptisms in the Burman empire which shall continue in uninterrupted success to the end of the age."[28] Converts were added slowly, and both Adoniram and his wife labored faithfully among the Burmese people, though lesser men and women most assuredly would have become discouraged that it took so long to bear fruit.

Ann had to leave Burma in 1821 because of illness. Although she was gone two years before her health was restored, her husband resolved to remain at his post. Her visit to America aroused much interest in missionary endeavors. Francis Wayland, who became acquainted with her during this visit said, "I do not remember ever to have met a more remarkable woman."[29] While home, she wrote a 326-page history of the Burmese work entitled *An Account of the American Baptist Mission to the Burman Empire*, which was published in 1823 and educated believers in America about the work she and her husband and others were doing.

---

[26] Ibid., 174.
[27] Edward Judson, *The Life*, 133.
[28] Ibid., 132.
[29] Ibid., 197.

Ann came back from America in December 1823 with additional missionary helpers; and soon after her return to Rangoon, she and her husband sailed up the Irrawady for a new assignment in the city of Ava. They landed on January 23, 1824, and the natives, who had never seen a white woman before, flocked to see Ann. Shortly, the Judsons were established in the home assigned them by the king, and this new chapter of their ministry in Ava proved to be one of the most perilous.

Imprisonment: Strength under Fire

In 1824, as war broke out between Burma and the English Government of India, the few Englishmen in Ava were immediately imprisoned. Americans were not always distinguished from Englishmen, and on June 8, 1824, orders were issued for the arrest of the foreign teachers. Judson was taken at his home in front of Ann by an armed band headed by an executioner whom Ann called the "spotted man."[30] She did all she could to secure her husband's well-being and that of many other prisoners, and her memoir recounts her persistent entreaties for her husband's release.[31] Judson was imprisoned for 17 months in the jails of Ava and Oung-pen-la, being bound during nine months of this period. His memoir includes the following description of the prison in Ava:

> The *Let-ma-yoon* was a building about forty feet long and thirty feet wide. It was five or six feet high along the sides, but as the roof sloped, the centre of it was perhaps double that height. There was no ventilation except through the chinks between the boards and through the door, which was generally closed. On the thin roof poured down the burning rays of a tropical sun. In this room were confined nearly one hundred prisoners of both sexes and all nationalities.[32]

Henry Gougher, one of Judson's fellow captives, described the sights as he first entered the prison:

---

[30] Knowles, *The Memoir of Mrs. Ann H. Judson*, 286.

[31] Henry Gouger, a trader who was imprisoned at the same time as Adoniram, called Ann a "guardian angel" because of her ministries to the prisoners at Ava. Henry Gouger, *Personal Narrative of Two Years' Imprisonment in Burmah, 1824–1826* (London: John Murray, 1860), 196. In addition, another author states, "It was due to the indefatigable exertions of Mrs. Judson that the horrors of the imprisonment in Let-ma-yoon were somewhat mitigated after a time." Norman Macleod, "Eastern Prisons: Prisoners in Burmah," in *Good Words for 1861* (London: Groombridge and Sons, 1861), 177.

[32] Edward Judson, *The Life*, 219.

Before me, stretched on the floor, lay forty or fifty hapless wretches, whose crimes or misfortunes had brought them into this place of torment. They were all nearly naked, and the half-famished features and skeleton frames of many of them too plainly told the story of their protracted sufferings. Very few were without chains, and some had one or both feet in the stocks besides. A sight of such squalid wretchedness can hardly be imagined. Silence seemed to be the order of the day; perhaps the poor creatures were so engrossed with their own misery that they hardly cared to make any remarks on the intrusion of so unusual an inmate as myself.

If the *ensemble* be difficult to portray, the stench was absolutely indescribable, for it was not like anything which exists elsewhere in creation. I will therefore give the facts, and leave the reader's nose to understand them by a synthetic course of reasoning—if it can.

The prison had never been washed, nor even swept, since it was built. So I was told, and have no doubt it was true; for, besides the ocular proof from its present condition, it is certain no attempt was made to cleanse it during my subsequent tenancy of eleven months.[33]

As often as possible Ann bribed the jailer so she could whisper words of hope and consolation to her husband and bring food, for the prisoners were not supplied with food by the jailers. She also smuggled his "work in progress," the Burmese translation of Scripture, into the prison in a pillow. Almost eight months into his imprisonment, her daily visits stopped because she went into labor, and she did not appear for three weeks. On January 26, 1825, she gave birth to her third child, Maria, and when she returned to the prison, she bore the baby her arms.

Soon Adoniram was secretly moved to another death prison. To reach the new prison, Ann, along with Maria, travelled by boat and cart. An epidemic of smallpox raged through Oung-pen-la, and little Maria caught the dreaded disease. Due to the double strain of concern for her husband, who had a serious fever at the time, and the suffering baby, Ann found herself unable to nurse Maria and begged local women to help nurse her. One jailer consented to give her a room, half full of grain, close to the prison, and she lived there for six months.[34] Recalling this time, Ann said, "The annoyance,

---

[33] Gouger, *Personal Narrative of Two Years' Imprisonment in Burmah*, 148.
[34] Knowles, *The Memoir of Mrs. Ann H. Judson*, 305–6.

the exhortations, and the oppressions, to which we were subject, during our six months' residence at Oung-pen-la, are beyond enumeration and description."[35]

One incident illustrates Ann's incredible courage on behalf of her husband. There was a lioness' cage close to the prison, and the animal made horrible noise day and night. The prisoners feared it was being starved before being turned loose upon them. However, the animal died, and Ann received permission for her husband to be moved to its cage. She cleaned it out, and it proved much nicer than the prison cell. At the time, Adoniram suffered terribly with a fever and could have died had Ann not secured the cage for him.[36] Finally, through the influence of Sir Archibald Campbell, Adoniram was released at the end of almost two years.[37]

End of the Journey: Gone but Never Forgotten

The war made a change of location necessary, and the Judsons chose Amherst, a city under British protection. But before they were settled, Adoniram, in hope of securing religious freedom, went with the English commissioner to obtain a treaty with the king at Ava. Ann was favorable to his going, and he departed with good courage. When he returned home though, he found his wife deathly ill. She recovered, and they moved on to a new station where she started a girls' school. However, while Judson was in Ava on business, Ann was stricken again with a fever and died at age 37 on October 24, 1826. She was buried under a hopia (hope) tree in Amherst. One biographer aptly applied a poem to her situation:

> By foreign hands thy dying hands were clos'd
> By foreign hands thy weary limbs compos'd
> By foreign hands thy humble grave adorn'd
> By stangers honor'd and by strangers mourn'd.[38]

---

[35] Ibid., 312.

[36] Edward Judson, *The Life*, 225.

[37] Both *Let-ma-yoon* and *Oung-pen-la* prisons have been destroyed. However, in 1915 a small white stone marker was put over the site of the *Let-ma-yoon* prison that described how Judson "in this prison of horror which stood here sustained in his faith in the Lord Jesus Christ, and by the devotion of his heroic wife, endured unrecorded sufferings from June 1824 to May 1825." Colin Metcalfe Enriquez, *A Burmese Enchantment* (Calcutta: Thacker, Spink and Co, 1916), 240–41.

[38] G. W. Hervey, *The Story of Baptist Missions in Foreign Lands* (St. Louis, MO: Chancy R. Barns, 1886), 278.

Ann's daughter Maria lasted only six months more before she too died, and Adoniram buried her beside her mother on April 24, 1827. Despite losing his wife and all three children during his first 14 years overseas, he decided not to go home on furlough, though he had earned one. Instead, as he would later encourage prospective missionaries to do, he stayed on the mission field.[39]

Interestingly, God used the lives and deaths of Ann and Maria to play instrumental roles in the spiritual journeys of both Sarah Hall Boardman and Emily Chubbuck, Adoniram's second and third wives. When Sarah Boardman learned of Maria's death, she wrote a poem in tribute. Within the poem is a stanza on Ann:

Thy mother's tale, replete with varied scenes,
Exceeds my powers to tell; but other harps,
And other voices, sweeter far than mine,
Shall sing her matchless worth, her deeds of love,
Her zeal, her toils, her sufferings, and her death.[40]

SARAH HALL BOARDMAN JUDSON (1803–45)

I have been pained by thinking of those who have never heard the sound of the Gospel. When will the time come that the poor heathen, now bowing to idols, shall own the living and true God?[41]

Road to Burma: Determined for Christ

Born November 4, 1803, in Alstead, New Hampshire, Sarah was the oldest of 13 children of Ralph and Abiah Hall. Her family was poor, and Sarah spent most of her youth as a second mother to her brothers and sisters. Consequently, she went to school irregularly but devoted many evenings to study and the writing of poetry. Her family moved a few times during her childhood—first to Danvers, Massachusetts, and later to Salem, Massachusetts. At age 17, she became a Christian and joined the First Baptist Church

---

[39] See "Advice to Missionary Candidates" letter referenced earlier in Edward Judson, *The Life*, 577.
[40] Sarah H. Boardman, "To the Dying Little Maria," *The Judson Offering*, ed. John Dowling (New York: Lewis Colby, 1848), 144–46. This collection was assembled in honor of Adoniram Judson's one furlough to America in 1845.
[41] Sarah wrote these words in her journal shortly after her baptism, recorded in Emily Chubbuck Judson's *Memoir of Sarah B. Judson: The American Mission to Burmah* (New York: L. Colby and Company, 1848), 21.

of Salem, Massachusetts. She was active in ministry there, becoming a Sunday school teacher and tract distributor. Soon after her conversion, though, her heart turned toward the mission field. In contemplating the life of missionary Samuel J. Mills, she wrote, "I have almost caught his spirit and been ready to exclaim: Oh that I, too, could suffer privations, hardships and discouragements, and even find a watery grave for the sake of bearing the news of salvation to the heathen."[42]

Edward Judson wrote of his mother:

> Those who knew her speak of "faultless features, molded on the Grecian model, beautiful transparent skin, warm, meek blue eyes, and soft hair, brown in the shadow and gold in the sun." She was pronounced by her English friends in Calcutta to be "the most finished and faultless specimen of an American woman that they had ever known." From her earliest years she had possessed an enthusiasm for missions. When ten years old, she wrote a poem upon the death at Rangoon of Mrs. Judson's infant, Roger. Little did the child dream that many years after she was to take the place of the ideal heroine of her childhood, who, worn out with the prolonged horrors of Ava and Oung-pen-la, lay down to rest beneath the hopia-tree at Amherst.[43]

Indeed, it was an interesting path that Sarah took from Salem to the mission field in Burma. As a child, she had no idea that the missionary whom she so admired would become her second husband. A childhood friend of Sarah's wrote these words as a tribute to her devotion to follow God's call to serve Him overseas:

> I see thee now by memory's light as then, —
> So calm in dignity, so strong in faith,
> Thy soft blue eye half-veiled; —thy angel face
> Half-bowed, —the mirror of thy modest mind;
> Placid and gentle, as thou always wast . . .
>
> How beautifully in thee were blended
> Meekness with majesty, by blessed hands,

---

[42] Ibid., 21–22.
[43] Edward Judson, *The Life*, 285.

As leaning on Omnipotence, on God,
Weak in thyself, but all-possess'd in Him,

Thou mad'st thy purpose known to go far hence,
And bear to heathen lands the wealth of Christ;
Yet if His presence went not with thee, there—
Thou would'st not go—thy strength was in the Lord.[44]

Sarah met George Dana Boardman, of Livermore, Maine, through unusual circumstances, and they found in each other a like-mindedness to serve as missionaries on the foreign field. When a young missionary named Colman died only two years after arriving in Chittagong, Sarah penned an elegy in his honor. George Dana Boardman, upon learning of Colman's death, felt the call to serve as his replacement. He read the elegy and desired to meet the authoress, since her sentiments were so similar to his own. Only 12 days after George and Sarah were married on July 4, 1825, they left for Burma as missionaries.

On account of the Burmese war, the Boardmans had to remain in Calcutta nearly 18 months. They finally arrived in Burma in 1827 a few months after Ann Judson's death and a week before Maria Judson passed away. They worked in Amherst, then Moulmein, and then Tavoy. About a month after her settlement at Moulmein, Sarah wrote to a friend: "We are in excellent health, and as happy as it is possible for human beings to be upon earth. It is our earnest desire to live, and labor, and die, among this people."[45] In 1829 Adoniram joined the Boardmans briefly in Moulmein, which became the chief seat of Baptist mission work in Burma. There schools and a house of worship were built (the missionaries were aided by Sir Archibald Campbell), and a number of converts were added to the church.

During her early years on the field, Sarah had three children, but only her second child, George Dana, survived past infancy.[46] The death of her first child (named Sarah as well) in 1829 served as a catalyst to rejuvenate her faith in God.[47] Emily Judson later wrote of this in her memoir of Sarah:

---

[44] Stephen Hill, "A Reminiscence of Mrs. S. B. Judson," in Dowling, *The Judson Offering*, 233–34.
[45] Emily Chubbuck Judson, *Memoir of Sarah B. Judson*, 66.
[46] George was sent back to America as a young child to pursue his education. He graduated from Brown University in 1853 and then studied theology and became a pastor and an author, see Hervey, *The Story of Baptist Missions in Foreign Lands*, 301.
[47] Ibid., 295.

She hesitated not to acknowledge, that it was a strange, an almost incredible forgetfulness, and that her bereavement, bitter as it was, was a reminder from Heaven, sent, not only in justice, but in mercy; and in tearful, repentant, sorrowing humility, she bowed beneath her Father's rod, grateful for the love which directed the blow, though it descended crushingly upon her spirit. She knew that this affliction was sent to call back her wandering heart to its place, the foot of the Cross; and with the confiding submission of a little child, she obeyed the summons.[48]

As God used this death to renew her passion for Him, it also prepared her for the many other losses she would face. Mr. Boardman succumbed to illness and died on February 11, 1831, just a few years after he had arrived with Sarah in Burma.[49] She found herself a widow with a young son in a foreign land with an important decision to make. Mrs Boardman wrote,

---

[48] Emily Chubbuck Judson, *Memoir of Sarah B. Judson*, 92–93.

[49] On March 4, 1831, while in Rangoon, Adoniram wrote a beautiful letter to Sarah upon learning of her husband's death, see Edward Judson, *The Life*, 374–75:

"My Dear Sister: You are now drinking the bitter cup whose dregs I am somewhat acquainted with. And though, for some time, you have been aware of its approach, I venture to say that it is far bitterer than you expected. It is common for persons in your situation to refuse all consolation, to cling to the dead, and to fear that they shall too soon forget the dear object of their affections. But don't be concerned. I can assure you that months and months of heartrending anguish are before you, whether you will or not. I can only advise you to take the cup with both hands, and sit down quietly to the bitter repast which God has appointed for your sanctification. As to your beloved, you *know* that all his tears are wiped away, and that the diadem which encircles his brow outshines the sun. Little Sarah and the other have again found their father, not the frail, sinful mortal that they left on earth, but an immortal saint, a magnificent, majestic king. What more can you desire for them? While, therefore, your tears flow, let a due proportion be tears of joy. Yet take the bitter cup with both hands, and sit down to your repast. You will soon learn a secret, that there is sweetness at the bottom. You will find it the sweetest cup that you ever tasted in all your life. You will find heaven coming near to you, and familiarity with your husband's voice will be a connecting link, drawing you almost within the sphere of celestial music.

"I think, from what I know of your mind, that you will not desert the post, but remain to carry on the work which he gloriously began. The Karens of Tavoy regard you as their spin Uial mother; and the dying prayers of your beloved are waiting to be answered in blessings on your instructions. As to little Georgie, who has now no earthly father to care for him, you can not, of course, part with him at present. But if you should wish to send him home, I pledge myself to use what little influence I have in procuring for him all those advantages of education which your fondest wishes can desire. Or if you should be prematurely taken away, and should condescend, on your dying bed, to commit him to me, by the briefest line or verbal message, I hereby pledge my fidelity to receive and treat him as my own son, to send him home in the best time and way, to provide for his education, and to watch over him as long as I live. More than this I can not do, and less would be unworthy of the merits of his parents."

> When I first stood by the grave of my husband, I thought I must go home with George. But these poor, inquiring and Christian Karens, and the school boys, and the Burmese Christians, would then be left without any one to instruct them; and the poor, stupid Tavoyans would go on in the road to death, with no one to warn them of their danger. How then, oh, how can I go? We shall not be separated long. A few more years, and we shall all meet in yonder blissful world, whither those we love have gone before us.[50]

So, instead of returning home, she continued the missionary work at Tavoy among the Karens. She founded a school for girls and made several treacherous journeys through jungles and adverse weather conditions with George strapped to her back in order to continue the work.[51]

Marriage to Judson: Mission and Ministry Joined

On April 10, 1834, Adoniram and Sarah married, an event noted only with a brief, matter-of-fact entry in Adoniram's journal.[52] Sarah could speak and write fluently in Burmese. After eight years of loneliness, Adoniram found her companionship to be sweet; and she was a great asset to him, conducting Bible studies and prayer meetings for the women. During the 11 years of their married life, eight children were born to them, three of whom died at an early age.

Sarah's ministry to and with Adoniram was fruitful over the ensuing years. She translated part of *Pilgrim's Progress*, several hymns, and other materials into the Burmese language. She wrote four volumes of a Scripture catechism, and she learned the language of the Peguan tribe to help translate the New Testament and tracts. Unfortunately, like Ann before her, Sarah's health declined even while her passion for ministry burned brightly.

In 1844, Sarah's health began to fail, so Adoniram and Sarah travelled to the Isle of France. She began to feel so much better that they decided to return home. However, in 1845, it seemed best that she return to the United States as her health continued to deteriorate. Leaving the youngest three children behind with missionaries and taking

---

[50] Emily Chubbuck Judson, *Memoir of Sarah B. Judson*, 149; Edward Judson, *The Life*, 400; see also Henry Burrage, *Baptist Hymn Writers and Their Hymns* (Portland, ME: Brown Thurston & Company, 1888), 303.
[51] Emily Chubbuck Judson, *Memoir of Sarah B. Judson*, 166–67.
[52] Edward Judson, *The Life*, 399.

the eldest three with them (two children had already died by this time), they started the journey back to America.

On September 1, 1845, while their boat was off St. Helena, Sarah died. Judson remembered her final moments:

> I sat alone by the side of her bed during the hours of the night, endeavoring to administer relief to the distressed body and consolation to the departing soul. At two o'clock in the morning, wishing to obtain one more token of recognition, I roused her attention and said, "Do you still love the Savior?" "Oh yes," she replied, "I ever love the Lord Jesus Christ." I said again, "Do you still love me?" She replied in the affirmative, by a peculiar expression of her own. "Then give me one more kiss;" and we exchanged that token of love for the last time. Another hour passed—life continued to recede—and she ceased to breathe. For a moment I traced her upward flight, and thought of the wonders which were opening to her view.[53]

Judson prepared the body for burial. That afternoon it was carried ashore and buried in the public burial ground, a small stone marking the grave. Sarah's grave was beside that of an English Baptist missionary to Ceylon who had died in similar circumstances on her passage home. That evening Adoniram and three of his children continued the journey to America. He had the following inscription etched on her gravestone:

> Sacred to the memory of Sarah B. Judson, member of the American Baptist Mission to Burmah, formerly wife of the Rev. George D. Boardman, of Tavoy, and lately wife of the Rev. Adoniram Judson, of Moulmein, who died in this port, September 1, 1845, on her passage to the United States, in the forty-second year of her age, and the twenty-first of her missionary life.[54]

Sarah had written a poem called "The Parting," which she meant to give Adoniram when her death was near. It began and ended with the following sentiments:

We part on this green islet, love,—
    Thou for the eastern main,—

---

[53] Emily Chubbuck Judson, *Memoir of Sarah B. Judson*, 245–46.
[54] Ibid., 248.

I for the setting sun, love;
  Oh! when to meet again! . . .

Then gird thine armor on, love,
  Nor faint thou by the way—
Till Boodh shall fall, and Burmah's sons
  Shall own Messiah's sway.[55]

Judson found the lines after she had died, and when he copied them, he wrote after the last verse: "Gird thine armour on—And so, God willing, I will yet endeavor to do; and while her prostrate form finds repose on the rock of the ocean, and her sanctified spirit enjoys sweeter repose on the bosom of Jesus, let me continue to toil on all my appointed time, until my change, too, shall come."[56] Sarah was, as he testified, "in every point of natural and moral excellence, the worthy successor of Ann H. Judson."[57]

EMILY CHUBBUCK JUDSON, "FANNY FORESTER" (1817–54)

> I have felt ever since I read the memoir of Mrs. Ann H. Judson when I was a child, that I must become a missionary.[58]

Early Notoriety: "Fanny Forester"

Born in Eaton, New York, on August 22, 1817, Emily Chubbuck came from very humble beginnings. At a young age she had to work in a factory for 12 hours a day in order to help support her family. After the death of her sister, Emily's health began to fail and her family moved to a farm outside of town. During these years she studied on her own and demonstrated a keen mind. She later taught school in Utica and was one of the earliest advocates in America for the higher education of women. However, God planted within young Emily an interest in the missionary life:

---

[55] Mrs. Sarah B. Judson, "The Parting," in Dowling, *The Judson Offering*, 213–14.
[56] Wayland, *Memoir*, 2:212.
[57] Ibid., 2:207.
[58] Taken from a letter Emily wrote to a friend, recorded in Edward Judson's *The Life*, 483.

At the age of twelve Emily had her dreams about mission life. She had already read, and her sister had told her some things about missionaries. One day, in reading the *Baptist Register*, her eyes fell on the words, 'Little Maria lies by the side of her fond mother.' She knew at once that the letter was from Mr. Judson, and that this little daughter was dead. She dreamt that her missionary life was to be one of suffering and toil and pain, and though these ended in death, the death always came as death does in our dreams, pleasantly. After reading (two or three years later perhaps) the memoir of Mrs. Ann H. Judson, she felt that she must become a missionary.[59]

Emily struggled with her sense of calling to serve as a missionary and her sense of duty to help her parents and her younger siblings. During her time teaching in Utica, she was able to earn money writing books and articles and sent a portion of that money to her parents. The burden she felt for her parents weighed heavily upon her, driving her to pursue her writing as she saw fruits from the endeavor.[60] "Fanny Forester" was the nom de plume she took when she submitted her works, and though she gained notoriety from works like *Trippings in Author-land* and *Alderbrook*, very few people at the time knew much about the real woman behind the pseudonym "Fanny Forester."

Encounter with Rev. Judson: The Challenge

When Judson returned to America after Sarah's death, it was the first and only time during 30 years of mission service that he set foot back on American soil. He used this time to raise awareness of his work and was somewhat shocked by his celebrity status among the churches. During a trip from Boston to Philadelphia, a friend procured a book by Fanny Forester for him to read. He quickly saw the capabilities of the writer and said, "The lady who writes so well ought to write better. It's a pity that such fine talents should be employed on such subjects."[61] The friend replied that she was a guest at his home, and Judson asked if he could meet her. When Judson arrived, Emily was in the middle of getting a vaccination. After the procedure was complete, he guided her to a couch and encouraged her to use her skills as a writer for nobler subjects than fiction. He asked her to consider writing the life story of his second wife, Sarah. She accepted the challenge, and this encounter led to courtship and marriage.

---

[59] Hervey, *The Story of Baptist Missions in Foreign Lands*, 307.
[60] A. C. Kendrick, *The Life and Letters of Mrs. Emily C. Judson* (New York: Sheldon & Co., 1860), 41.
[61] Edward Judson, *The Life*, 484.

Emily was a vivacious and talented woman, and many wondered when they heard that she was to become Judson's wife—she was 29 and he was 57 after all. Some feared this marriage would spoil her literary career and his missionary service.[62] However, she made a noble partner for the missionary and a loving mother for his children.

Off to Foreign Lands: Ministry with a Purpose

Addressing a note to her home church, Emily wrote:

> Dear friends of Jesus at Morrisville, ye whose prayers first drew me to the protection of your church; whose prayers sustained me through the many years that I remained with you; whose prayers, I trust have followed me during the little time that we have been separated, will you pray for me still? When dangers and difficulties are about me, will you plead earnestly, "God help her!" Will you pray for me, now that we are to see each other's faces no more in this world? Ah, I know you will; so let me ask the same for those among whom I go to labor; those who know not Christ and his salvation, and yet "are without excuse." Pray for them, and for me, that I may do them good.[63]

On July 11, 1846, Judson, with his wife, left his children in America to be educated and sailed for Burma with some new missionaries. During the 18 months of Adoniram's absence, one of his three children in Burma had died and only two greeted him. Adoniram, Emily, and his two youngest children lived in Rangoon in a house Emily named the "Bat Castle."[64] A new king was on the throne—the "most bloodthirsty monster" Adoniram had ever known.[65] Only fear of the British kept his soldiers from persecuting the missionaries, though much of their work had to be kept secret from the king. Adoniram continued work on his English-Burmese dictionary, and Emily began the memoir of Sarah while also learning the Burmese language. On their first anniversary, she wrote, "It has been far the happiest year of my life; and, what is in my eyes still more important, my husband says it has been among the happiest of his."[66] Emily finished the memoir of Sarah Judson in 1847 just a few months before she gave birth to her first

---

[62] Ibid., 485.
[63] Letter from Emily Judson dated 6 July 1846, in Dowling, *The Judson Offering*, 271.
[64] Kendrick, *Life and Letters*, 270.
[65] Edward Judson, *The Life*, 504.
[66] Anderson, *To the Golden Shore*, 391.

child, Emily Frances. Adoniram completed his work on the dictionary in January 1849, but his health began to decline. In April 1850 as Emily was expecting her second child, they decided to return to America to try to regain Adoniram's health.

However, he died during the journey on April 12, 1850, three days out from Burma. That evening his body was lowered into the Indian Ocean. "He could not," wrote Emily, "have a more fitting monument than the blue waves which visit every coast; for his warm sympathies went forth to the ends of the earth, and included the whole family of man."[67] Emily gave birth 10 days later, but her son Charles died the same day he was born. She returned to America to help her ailing parents and care for her children. She died in Hampton, New York, in 1854, of tuberculosis.

A. C. Kendrick, a professor who compiled Emily's biography, noted that she proved to be a wonderful companion to Adoniram in his last years:

> Ann Hasseltine more than met all the demands of Judson's earlier years of youthful and heroic action; Sarah Boardman shed the light of one of the most exquisite of womanly natures over the calmer scenes of his manhood; Emily, with heroism not less devoted, with a womanliness not less pure and gentle, met his ripe culture, his keen intellectuality, his imaginative and poetic temperament, with gifts and acquirements which belonged to neither of those admirably endowed women.[68]

THE LEGACY OF THE JUDSON WIVES

Trusting the Lord through the loss of a child, courage in the midst of persecution, love for those who do not know Christ, deep convictions based upon the Word of God, a sense of urgency to accomplish God's mission, complete surrender and obedience to the Heavenly Father's call—these are just some of the traits exhibited by Ann, Sarah, and Emily. Adoniram Judson's son Edward once wrote in his memoir of his father:

> O that some young man might rise from the reading of these memoirs and lay down his life in all its freshness and strength upon the altar of God, so that he

---

[67] Edward Judson, *The Life*, 542.
[68] Kendrick, *Life and Letters*, 190.

might become, like Paul of old, a chosen vessel of Christ, to bear His name before the gentiles and kings and the children of Israel![69]

May the story of Judson's wives who faithfully served alongside him have a similar effect. May their testimonies inspire other women—young and old—to follow in their footsteps by being obedient to God's plan. The legacy of each of these women is not just the thousands of female believers in Burma, but also the inspiration they gave and continue to give Christians around the world to be faithful to God in each step of their journey.

---

[69] Edward Judson, *The Life*, 559.

Missiological and Theological Evaluation

Chapter 6

The Enduring Legacy of Adoniram Judson's Missiological Precepts and Practices

Keith E. Eitel

In a few lives the temporal kisses the eternal. They embrace the truths and calling of heaven, pouring themselves out for others. They are viewed as odd by some because they do not regard this world as their home. To others, they seem heroic. Yet, in a New Testament sense, they simply live out the normal cost of discipleship—denying self and clinging to the cross. Such was the life of Adoniram Judson. A glimpse of this can be gleaned from a poem he made his children memorize:

> 'Tis religion that can give sweetest pleasure while we live.
> 'Tis religion will supply solid comfort when we die.
> Be the living God my friend, then my joys shall never end.[1]

This was the Judsons' family motto. The lines were likely in Adoniram's mind during his trials as a missionary.

Historically, Judson stands out from other missionaries because of his many and varied achievements. Two centuries later, his dedication, techniques, and core principles continue to instruct missionaries. Indeed, he changed the world. Certainly there are embellishments to his life story. Clarifying and defining his influences, achievements, and particularly his missiological methods are the subjects of this chapter.

---

[1] Adoniram B. Judson, *How Judson Became a Baptist Missionary* (Philadelphia: The Griffith & Rowland Press, 1913), 3. Though no date is indicated, the face page of the copy held by Yale Divinity School is stamped "New York, 1913." Additionally on page 10 there is a reference to the events of the 1812 ordination service and "last February" is mentioned in reference to the centennial service held to commemorate his father's ordination. Additionally, note that use of the term *religion* in the early nineteenth century (when the verses would have been used by Judson himself) did not intend to portray an organizational structure per se; in his context it meant a personalized, dedicated, and purposeful relationship with Christ. The pamphlet makes this clear.

Historical Groundwork

Delving into the history of larger-than-life figures usually means encountering exaggerations. One example is the minor, but also significant, detail regarding when the Judsons decided to change their commitments from the Congregationalists, who practiced of infant baptism, to the Baptists, who baptized only believers. It is commonly believed that "en route, the Judsons converted to Baptistic principles and sought the support of the Baptist community in the United States."[2] But many have misinterpreted the sequence of events.[3] Their change of mind happened over a longer period and with investigation and argumentation on land and sea. Judson indicated in a letter "to the Third church of Plymouth, Mass," that it was "on board the vessel, in prospect of my future life among the heathen, that I was led to *investigate* this important subject."[4] In a letter to her parents dated February 14, 1813, while in exile from India on the Isle of France, Ann Judson described the process they went through to embrace Baptist beliefs, noting that Judson studied the subject in route: "Knowing he should meet the Baptists at Serampore, he felt it important to attend to it more closely, to be able to defend his sentiments."[5] Ann goes on to say that after they arrived in India, they commenced with resettlement issues.

---

[2] William H. Brackney, "The Legacy of Adoniram Judson," *International Bulletin of Missionary Research* 22, no. 3 (1998): 123.

[3] See for example Robert G. Torbet, *A History of the Baptists*, 3rd ed. (Valley Forge, PA: Judson Press, 1982), 249, and Kenneth Scott Latourette, *A History of the Expansion of Christianity*, 7 vols., Contemporary Evangelical Perspectives (Grand Rapids: Zondervan, 1970), 6:228.

[4] Adoniram Judson Jr., *A Letter to the Rev. Adoniram Judson, Sen., Relative to the "Formal and Solemn Reprimand." To Which Is Added, a Letter to the Third Church in Plymouth, Mass., on the Subject of Baptism* (Boston, MA: Lincoln & Edmands, 1820), 15. Emphasis added.

[5] Francis Wayland, *A Memoir of the Life and Labors of the Rev. Adoniram Judson, D.D.* (Boston, MA: Phillips, Sampson, and Company, 1853), 1:107. For the same letter see also Edward Judson, *The Life of Adoniram Judson* (New York: Ansom D. F. Randolph, 1883), 40–41. Wayland notes that the originals of many of Judson's correspondences and diaries were lost to historians by various means. Fires, shipwrecks, and the like were some of the hazards of life in the settings where Judson lived and worked. Also, Wayland indicates that Ann Judson destroyed some documents at the time of his imprisonment for security reasons. Yet, Judson also wanted to limit his legacy out of humility. He had "peculiar views of duty . . . and caused to be destroyed all his early letters written to his family together with all his papers of a personal character," 3. During the Judson centennial celebrations by Baptists, many notable missions writers addressed Judson's significance. One common observation was that he wished to put to death the self-centered ambition that haunted him in earlier years. W. O. Carver concluded that "he sought to destroy all the correspondences and records that could be used to lionize him." W. O. Carver, "The Significance of Adoniram Judson," in *The Review and Expositor* 10, no. 4 (October 1913): 476. Nevertheless Wayland and Edward Judson were able to compile replacements of many sources through family members, associates, and missionary newspapers where letters were privately held, published, or circulated.

While waiting for another ship from America that had fellow missionaries onboard, they studied baptism more extensively: "I now commenced reading on the subject, with all my prejudices on the Pedobaptist side. . . . But after closely examining the subject for several weeks, we were constrained to acknowledge that the truth appeared to lie on the Baptists' side." Judson petitioned William Carey, Joshua Marshman, and William Ward for believers' baptism on August 27, 1812. It was a four-month process, beginning on board ship but ending only "after much laborious research and painful trial."[6]

This may seem an unnecessary detail, but it demonstrates Judson's serious and thoughtful decision-making process. Given what he eventually faced in Burma, especially his imprisonment, knowing this trait helps explain his reactions to mental challenges, physical trials, and intense adversity.[7]

Lore has also entered the accounts of the Judsons' move to Rangoon. Contrary to legend, when authorities forced the original set of missionaries out of Calcutta with threat of arrest, they sailed together to the Isle of France. Some of the band departed from there to return to New England, but Judson and Ann, after some time there, attempted to re-enter India through the port of Madras. Within three weeks the threat of arrest resurfaced; the fact that Britain and the United States had been at war for nearly a year likely provided the rationale for issuing a warrant for their arrest.[8] Rogue Americans, especially missionaries, were not welcome in British territories at that time. Judson's diary said an arrest order was forthcoming and noted, "Our only safety appeared to consist in escaping from Madras before such order should arrive."[9] Judson found "in the roads of Madras" while escaping that there was only one vessel departing and it was "bound to Rangoon." The Judsons lamented having to flee for their lives, but resigning themselves to the providence of God they experienced "something of that peace which our Saviour bequeathed to his followers."[10] This circumstance shows that Judson both held a high view of God's sovereignty and felt compelled to share the gospel with others. Such views reflected new theological trends that shaped Judson's missionary service.

---

[6] Wayland, *Memoir*, 1:109.

[7] Adoniram B. Judson, *How Judson*, 9.

[8] Robert Thomas Middleditch, *Burmah's Great Missionary: Records of the Life, Character, and Achievements of Adoniram Judson* (New York: E. H. Fletcher, 1854), 380. Middleditch indicated this as the reason why the Judsons were "driven into Burma" and the hostility was from "war between this country [the United States] and Great Britain."

[9] Wayland, *Memoir*, 1:119.

[10] Ibid., 1:120–21. Possibly a reference to Jesus' remarks in John 14:27; 16:33; or 20:21.

INFLUENTIAL BACKGROUND DEVELOPMENTS

Evangelism in New England

A century earlier Jonathan Edwards sparked a brand of Calvinism, different than that of the Puritans, that took root in New England and beyond. Certain forms of Puritanism collided with a "New Light" or "New Divinity," which provided a "handbook for revivalistic Calvinism during the Great Awakening."[11]

Leonard Woods's 1812 ordination sermon for Judson and four other missionaries illustrated well the theology of the New Divinity. Woods affirmed that faith is the mark of born-again believers and results in obedience to the Great Commission. Life should be spent publishing the Good News to all who have not believed, or even heard it. The tone of the sermon was anything but dry. It brimmed with passion. It is hard to imagine that anyone would be unmoved to pray, give, or go by the end of the message. Woods listed six motivations for going and sending missionaries. First, they should go because of the worth of souls. Woods challenged the audience, "In the name of him who died on Calvary, I call upon you O Christians, to labor for the salvation of beings that will never die." The second motive was Christ's provision for the salvation of the nations. The third motivation was that the Great Commission was "binding upon Christians 'always even to the end of the world.'" Fourth, the original recipients of the Great Commission went themselves. Woods saw apostolic precedents as motivating examples for believers in his day. Fifth, God valued the souls of every race of people. Finally, Woods said biblical prophecy told of increasing obedience of the Great Commission leading up to Christ's return.[12]

David W. Kling, in agreement with British historian David Bebbington, cites four characteristics of British and American evangelicals at the turn of the nineteenth century: "conversionism," "activism," "biblicism," and "crucicentrism."[13] These four characteristics were central to "New Divinity" thought. Indeed, New Light Calvinism believed

---

[11] Charles L. Chaney, *The Birth of Missions in America* (South Pasadena, CA: William Carey Library, 1976), 60. See further in Robert Caldwell's chapter in this book.

[12] Woods, *A Sermon Delivered at the Tabernacle in Salem, Feb. 6, 1812* (Boston, MA: Samuel T. Armstrong, 1812), 11, 13, 15, 17, 18, and 19.

[13] David W. Kling, "The New Divinity and the Origins of the American Board of Commissioners for Foreign Missions," *Church History* 72, no. 4 (2003), 798. Kling echoes Bebbington's formulation from *Evangelicalism in Modern Britain: A History from the 1730s to the 1980s* (1989; repr., Grand Rapids: Baker Books, 1992), 2–17. For specific understanding of how these influences affected Baptists, see also Mark A. Noll, *A History of Christianity in the United States and Canada* (Grand Rapids: Eerdmans, 1992), 100.

that "Christ's death was sufficient to save each and every sinner, salvation was freely offered to all."[14] This conviction propelled Judson.

Judson's Baptist Journey

Becoming Baptist was no simple path for the Judsons. As noted, it was an arduous decision because they knew full well the economic, social, and religious consequences it would bring on them. Yet it was also a decision longer in the making than is commonly believed. Judson's mother's maiden name was Abigail Brown, and there is far too little written about her influence on him. A cursory trace of her family tree indicates the possibility that she was distantly related to John, Nicholas, and Moses Brown, signatories of the original charter for the College of Rhode Island (later Brown University), and Nicholas Brown Jr., who later donated significantly enough to have the college renamed in honor of his father.[15] Judson's son, Adoniram B. Judson, was unsure why his father went to Brown, but he surmised that financial necessity and the close proximity of Providence to their home played into the decision.[16] Possibly the family selected Brown because of his father's reaction against prevailing influences at both Harvard and Yale in that day. Brackney concurs with this assumption: "The school, under denominational patronage of Baptists, was the preferred choice of his father, since Harvard was theologically unacceptable and Yale was suspected of infidelism by many contemporary evangelicals."[17]

The possibility of a familial connection, his father's theological preferences, and the cost effectiveness of staying close to home each could have played roles in selecting Brown over Harvard or Yale. Denominational identification of the university was probably not the reason he attended Brown, as Brackney concluded, because the university prided itself, from its early days, on not having a distinctly Baptist atmosphere. George Edwin Horr's celebrative address at the 150th anniversary of the university entitled, "The University and Christian Missions," states the nonsectarian philosophy of the university. It was amazing to Horr that it could be both nonsectarian, even having a multidenominational governing board, and yet make a distinctly Baptist mark on missions through

---

[14] Kling, "The New Divinity," 804.
[15] Abigail Brown was born at Tiverton, Rhode Island, December 15, 1759, and Adoniram Brown Judson, Judson's son, was born April 7, 1837, in Burma. Edward Judson, *The Life*, 1 and 420 respectively. The name "Brown" seems prominent in the family's tradition. Also, there is evidence of this connection found in existing family trees found December 10, 2010, on www.Ancestry.com.
[16] Adoniram B. Judson, *How Judson*, 4.
[17] Brackney, "The Legacy," 122.

Judson.[18] Adoniram B. Judson thought it was at Brown where his father "incidentally became acquainted with Baptist principles," particularly the Baptist view of religious freedom that set it apart from Harvard, Princeton, or Yale. At Brown, Judson learned "to walk with the Bible as his sole guide, striving to follow the example of Jesus."[19]

Later in life, in July 1826, Judson's sentiments regarding religious freedom manifested themselves when he was asked to translate for settlement negotiations between the Burmese government and the English government. Initially he refused to entangle himself with government affairs, only recently having been released from his dismal imprisonment. An English representative coaxed him to assist in the translation by telling Judson that "every effort would be made to secure the insertion of a clause in the treaty granting religious liberty to the Burmans, so the whole country would be thrown open to the gospel." In recounting his father's life, Edward Judson argued that Baptists "ought to be willing to stand for what they really are—the only true representatives of religious freedom in the world."[20] It is possible that religious freedom, the primary principle that set Brown apart from the prevailing attitudes of the New Divinity thinkers in New England, played a role in Judson's choice of a college. To the New Light thinkers he owed the theological framework for his foreign missions impetus; from Brown he gained a desire to plant Baptist churches and to preach the gospel freely without fear of social retribution for new believers. Religious freedom is evident in his missiological practices.

Andover Associations

Adoniram B. Judson described his father's halting turn from deistic thought and stated that Adoniram Judson Sr., "arranged for his admission as an experiment to a new theological school in 1807 at Andover, Mass."[21] There he altered his life focus to turn from self-centered ambitions and "to please God [which was now] more delightful than all the

---

[18] William V. Kellen, ed., *The Sesquicentennial of Brown University, 1764–1914* (Providence, RI: The University, 1915), 61–64.

[19] Adoniram B. Judson, *How Judson*, 4.

[20] Edward Judson, *The Life*, 288 and 409. The latter citation is quoted from a letter Judson's third wife, Emily, wrote within three years of his death. Reuben Aldridge Guild, *Life, Times, and Correspondence of James Manning, and the Early History of Brown University* (Boston: Gould and Lincoln, 1864), 3, records the atmosphere at Brown University that surely helped form Judson's thoughts. "They advocated liberty of conscience, the entire separation of church and state, believer's baptism by immersion, and a converted church membership;—principles for which they have earnestly contended from the beginning."

[21] Adoniram B. Judson, *How Judson*, 5.

other forms of ambition which had beset him."[22] A generation earlier, the New Divinity thinkers, especially Samuel Hopkins, spoke of "disinterested benevolence."[23] This concept was popular at Andover and was prevalent during Judson's time there. Essentially the term described unconditional surrender to the lordship of Christ. This conviction, popularized by Hopkins, Chaney concludes, "was so significant that it became one of the slogans for the great missionary advance of the Nineteenth Century."[24]

Andover's spiritually charged atmosphere so changed Judson's convictions that "he gave his heart to the Saviour . . . and was ready to give up worldly preferment."[25] There he encountered men with whom he was later ordained and commissioned to form the first set of overseas missionaries sent from the American Board of Commissioners of Foreign Missions in 1812. Samuel J. Mills Jr., James Richards, Luther Rice, and Gordon Hall, while they attended Williams College, had formed something akin to a spiritual secret society. They committed to spend their lives for the spread of the gospel among those of distant lands, especially those who had not heard of Christ's provisions. Judson's own journey intersected theirs at Andover, and the circle broadened to include Samuel Nott, Jr. and Samuel Newell.[26] Together their zeal solidified. It is best described by Adoniram B. Judson a century later:

> In the ecstasy of prayer and consecration they saw with the eye of faith the bright vision of a world converted. . . . These young theologians desired to reach the field and begin their chosen work, but men of age and experience controlled the ways and means and counseled delay.[27]

The young Judson turned to fields unknown. The puzzle was nearly complete. The missing piece was finding his bride. January 1, 1811, Judson wrote to his fiancée, Ann Hasseltine, as follows: "May this be the year in which you will change your name, in which you will take final leave of your relatives and native land, in which you will cross the wide ocean, and dwell on the other side of the world, among a heathen people."[28]

---

[22] Ibid.
[23] Chaney, *The Birth*, 75.
[24] Ibid. See also Robert Caldwell's chapter in this book.
[25] Adoniram B. Judson, *How Judson*, 5.
[26] Wayland, *Memoir*, 1:36–42. As to the secrecy of the society see, Adoniram B. Judson, *How Judson*, 6. Note that James Richards did not become an ABCFM missionary with the others.
[27] Adoniram B. Judson, *How Judson*, 6. Since organized missions had not been attempted by New England's churches before, the older leaders saw that logistical planning was needed.
[28] Ibid., 5.

Later Ann reminisced, "I feel that there is not a better man on the globe than my husband."[29]

A fact-finding journey to England to gather information on ways and means of facilitating foreign missions resulted in less than anticipated. Eventually, formation of the ABCFM launched the set of five off to regions beyond. The newlywed Judsons and the Newells set sail for India from Salem on February 19, 1812. The Notts, Hall, and Rice sailed from Philadelphia on the eighteenth of the same month.[30]

MISSIOLOGICAL CONVICTIONS AND PRACTICES

Defining the missionary process is of utmost importance. Do historical precedents, contemporary best practices, or random ideas provide the basis for a missionary's task? At various times, all of these have guided the missionary task. At the beginning of the American missions experience, however, Judson laid a firmer foundation. His source was the unchanging Word of God. After more than 30 years on the mission field, he attended the ninth annual meeting of the American and Foreign Bible Society, held May 15, 1846.[31] Judson's voice was frail, and the society's president delivered his address on his behalf. In it Judson explained his missiological principles. Speaking to the debate over oral versus written communication of the gospel, he stated his convictions, especially regarding the nature of God's Word, and the basis for missiological practice:

> Protestant missions have patronized the translation and distribution of the Scriptures; *but of late years there has appeared, in one or two instances, a tendency to promote the oral communication of the Gospel, not, indeed, to an undue pre-eminence, but in such a manner as to throw a shade over the written communication by means of tracts and Scriptures* . . . all missionary operations, to be permanently successful, must be based on the written Word. Where that Word is most regarded and honored, there will be the most pure and permanent success. . . . The Bible, in the original tongues, comprises all the revelation now extant which God has given to the world. It is, in all its contents, and parts, and appendages, just the book, the one book, which Infinite Wisdom saw best

---

[29] Wayland, *Memoir*, 1:31.
[30] See the preface to Woods, *A Sermon*, 8, for these dates, ports of departure, and the name of the ships, *Caravan* and *Harmony* respectively.
[31] Middleditch, *Burmah's Great*, 388.

adapted to answer the end of a written revelation. . . . [The Bible is] like all the works of God, perfect and unique.³²

The word *inerrancy* was not in vogue then, but Judson embraced the concept. Consequently, his convictions about baptism, the nature of the New Testament church, and evangelism and church planting, along with his own sense of purpose in life, stemmed from the Bible.

Baptism and the New Testament Church

On September 27, 1812, Judson preached in Calcutta and explained his change to a Baptist view of baptism. Luther Rice recounted that sermon, which was designed to define "what is baptism; & [sic?] to whom it is to be administered."³³ Judson's sermon was later published and widely distributed.

In this sermon, Judson illustrated his hermeneutical assumptions, drawn from the text itself. He affirmed that the normal sense of language is the basis for interpretation of the Bible and that it should not, "require us to depart from the etymological and established interpretation of the word. We must believe that the writers of the New Testament used words according to their usual acceptation, in the Greek language, unless the connexion [context and syntax] requires some other interpretation." He said to do otherwise distorts the logic and that the writers, "knew that their readers would naturally and necessarily interpret every word in the usual way."³⁴

Judson recognized consistent New Testament teachings for personal faith and baptism, then linked them with the corollary ordinance of communion. If it is logical to affirm infant baptism, then why do its advocates not likewise implement "infant communion"? Judson asserted that infants "are incapable of remembering Christ, of examining themselves, and discerning the Lord's body. . . . They are equally incapable

---

[32] Ibid., 388–89. Emphasis is Judson's.
[33] Rice recorded his piqued interest in affirming Baptist principles from that date on through to November 1, 1812 when he, "Was baptized into the name of the Holy Trinity." William H. Brackney, ed. *Dispensations of Providence: The Journal and Selected Letters of Luther Rice: With an Introduction and Appendices*, commemorative ed. (Rochester, NY: American Baptist Historical Society, 1984), 71–73. Carver viewed this sermon as the main influence on Rice as well. He stated that it "led him two months after Judson to accept baptism." Carver, "The Significance," 479.
[34] Adoniram Judson, *Christian Baptism: A Sermon on Christian Baptism, with Many Quotations from Pedobaptist Authors, to Which Are Added a Letter to the Church in Plymouth, Mass., and an Address on the Mode of Baptizing*, 5th American ed. (Boston, MA: Gould, Kendall & Lincoln, 1846), 12.

of repenting and believing, which are required of those who receive baptism."[35] Included in the 1846 edition of that sermon, there is an appendix with a reprint of the letter Judson wrote to the Third Church in Plymouth on August 20, 1817. To that church he argued that the New Testament church and its ordinances are designed for regenerate members only. To baptize the unregenerate would violate the New Testament and initiate "unqualified persons . . . into the church."[36]

These principles relate to Judson's missiological convictions and practices. Robert G. Torbet notes that one's concept of the missionary's work is intertwined with each element above. He concluded that

> the evangelizing zeal of Baptists, arising out of their emphasis upon regeneration through Christ and the need of a conversion experience as a requisite to church membership, has been a leading factor in the development of Protestant foreign missions.[37]

Evangelism and Contextualization

On February 10, 1817, Judson wrote a letter to Thomas Baldwin in Boston, pleading for reinforcements in Burma. Knowing funds were necessary for both distribution of materials and personnel, Judson said, "O that all the members of the Baptist Convention could live in Rangoon one month! Will the Christian world awake? O Lord send help! Our waiting eyes are unto Thee!"[38] Eventually help arrived.

Since the Judsons had hitherto been a lone unit of missionaries, there was little need to draft a memorandum of agreement as to what their objective was and to define the means to accomplish it with a team dynamic. When George H. Hough and family arrived October 15, 1816, they developed such a working agreement. Judson and Hough drafted a letter stating their mission principles and sent it to the corresponding secretary of the Baptist society in America. It listed eight missiological concepts that guided their work. Item 3 is pertinent to the whole work and may rightly be termed their ultimate aim.

---

[35] Ibid., 91.
[36] Ibid., 101. See also Adoniram Judson, *A Letter to the Rev. Adoniram Judson, Sen.*, 18.
[37] Torbet, *A History*, 522.
[38] Edward Judson, *The Life*, 84, and Wayland, *Memoir*, 1:186–87.

3. We agree in the opinion that our sole object on earth is to introduce the Religion of Jesus Christ into the empire of Burmah; and that the means by which we hope to effect this are translating, printing, and distributing the Holy Scriptures, preaching the Gospel, circulating religious tracts, and promoting the instruction of native children.[39]

A clear objective gave them direction in their day-to-day tasks. All would, of course, hinge on acquisition of Burmese which in turn would open doors to the culture and maximize the effect of Scripture translation, evangelization, and church planting. Cross-cultural communication of the gospel was the Judsons' heartbeat.

Judson understood that translation work could commence more quickly in Burma than in some settings because, as Wayland surmised from Judson's letters, "The Burmans are a reading people. They have their religious books, and possess the teachings of Gaudama in their own language."[40] However, Judson prioritized proclamation, "The press can never supplant the pulpit."[41]

Language acquisition came gradually with parallel cultural knowledge, giving them the ability to interpret nuanced Burmese meanings, and worldview complexes of belief and practice. One of Judson's first forays in adapting his technique to the culture was to build a *zayat*, a speaking point at the edge of his house where passersby would stop to inquire about this foreigner and his teaching. Eventually it became a place to hold public worship.[42] Even though he borrowed the *zayat* idea from Buddhist priests, he clearly distinguished his *zayat* from theirs. His diary described the design and function of the building and recorded that it "is whitewashed, to distinguish it from the other *zayats* around us."[43]

Emily Chubbuck Judson, his third wife, was a creative writer and described the *zayat* in "Wayside Preaching." She described how they arranged it to be intriguing to those passing by; even at day's end, "the mats were still spread invitingly upon the floor."[44] Working daily on translation, he prioritized people whenever they stopped.

---

[39] Edward Judson, *The Life*, 108.
[40] Wayland, *Memoir*, 1:157. See also Edward Judson's similar conclusion when he stated in *The Life*, 83, "There were only two channels through which the truths of the Gospel could be conveyed to the conscience of the Burman—the eyes and the ears. The natives were emphatically a reading people."
[41] Edward Judson, *The Life*, 85.
[42] Ibid.
[43] Ibid., 122.
[44] Ibid., 589.

If several gathered, Judson began reading aloud from a translated tract conveying the essence of the Christian gospel. Some scoffed, others were interested, and some stopped to ask questions. Once a man and his young son stopped to see the curious foreigners. The boy referred to Judson as "Jesus Christ's man."[45] The boy's father said that religion was not too important to him and joked with Judson that neither of them believed the "fables" of their respective religions. Judson probed and told the fellow perhaps the little boy might hear and believe Judson's truths and asked if the father was worried. The father was not, but Judson made clear his intent:

> What if I should tell you I do believe everything I preach, as firmly as I believe you sit on the mat before me; and that it is the one desire of my life to make everybody else believe it—you and your child among the rest?[46]

Because of the conviction behind Judson's statement, the father took a tract to investigate further. This episode illustrates his daily engagements with the Burmese. On June 27, 1819, Judson baptized Moung Nau, his first Burman convert, nearly six years after he first arrived in Rangoon.[47] Persistent proclamation is vital to all well-established mission work. Short-term work has its place but cannot replace effective and continuous influence.

Language and Culture

When the Judsons arrived, they "knew not a word of the language." They were reduced to childlike attempts to understand the people, places, and things around them. The few traces of work by others was of little assistance to them. By persistent cultural immersion they acquired the language and began to understand the people.[48]

Immersion means living embedded in the culture in order to learn the ways of the people. Abandoning an earlier mission station, they adopted typical Burmese lifestyle. In 1830, an English traveler passed through and described Judson's dwelling. To enter his house she had "to ascend by a ladder . . . after the fashion of Burman houses."[49]

---

[45] Ibid., 590.
[46] Ibid., 597.
[47] Ibid., 564.
[48] Wayland, *Memoir*, 1:156–63.
[49] Edward Judson, *The Life*, 363–64.

To some degree the Judsons adopted Burmese clothing as well. When attending to her husband's needs while he was incarcerated, Ann entered the prison dressed like the Burmans. Edward Judson explained that "Mrs. Judson had long previous to this adopted the Burmese style of dress."[50] Judson, himself, engaged the culture and wanted the Burmese to perceive him as a religious teacher. One historian notes that

> Adoniram only tried dressing differently to see if it would help him be more clearly identified as a public teacher of religion. . . . [A]nd he once dressed in a robe of the same color as a Buddhist priest and later dressed in the same color as a Catholic priest. . . . When he found no advantage in dressing like other religious figures the Burmese would recognize he stopped trying to imitate them.[51]

Attempts to be both Burmese-like and still distinctly live for Christ piqued Burmese interest in their message.

Linguistic and cultural immersion led to the most significant contributions the Judsons made over the years, their literary work. Both Judsons were translators. Dana L. Robert explains the literary contributions Ann made. In 1817 she took interest in the Thai people living in Rangoon and learned enough of their language to translate the Gospel of Matthew. Robert notes, "Her translation of the Gospel of Matthew in 1819 was the first translation of the Scriptures into Siamese."[52]

Judson translated Matthew into Burmese first. In a list of important dates he noted the project's completion on May 20, 1817. Nearly a year earlier, on July 20, 1816, he wrote a tract that he described as "a view of the Christian Religion, in three parts, Historical, Didactic, Perceptive."[53]

This tract proved essential to creating interest in the gospel among the Burmese. Though brief, the document evidences serious study of Burmese Buddhist beliefs in his day. It presents a keen critique of Buddhism without being rude to the legacy of Gautama Buddha or to Buddhists. He contrasts Buddhism's life assumptions with the Bible. For example, the first sentence reads, "There is one Being who exists eternally; who is

---

[50] Ibid., 268.

[51] Phyllis Rodgerson Pleasants, "Beyond Translation: The Work of the Judsons in Burma," in *Baptist History and Heritage* 42:2 (2007): 26.

[52] Dana L. Robert, "Evangelist or Homemaker? Mission Strategies of Early Nineteenth-Century Missionary Wives in Burma and Hawaii," in *North American Foreign Missions, 1810–1914: Theology, Theory, and Policy*, ed. Wilbert R. Shenk (Grand Rapids: Eerdmans, 2004), 119.

[53] Edward Judson, *The Life*, 563.

exempt from sickness, old age, and death; who was, and is, and will be without beginning and without end. Besides this, the true God, there is no other God."[54]

The concept of an eternal, personal deity, who is not captive to cycles of pain and suffering and who claims to be the one true God, contrasts with historic Theravada Buddhism.[55] Judson's tract shows unusual care in representing the Bible's truth with cultural sensitivity. His simple closing admonition was, "May the reader obtain light. Amen."[56] Buddha's enlightenment began his departure from Hinduism and is now the aim of every devout Buddhist. Here Judson wishes readers "light" and adds the Christian term "Amen," which means "so let it be." It was a cogent appeal to reason that addressed Burmese Buddhists and contrasted their views with the alternative of Christianity.

La Seng Dingrin, a Burmese theologian, takes issue with Judson's tracts. He contends that Judson utilized the Burmese language of his day hypocritically. In his opinion, Judson borrowed heavily from Buddhist categories of thought and vocabulary, from what Dingrin terms, "Burmanized Pali." He argues that Judson was indebted to the very religion he wished the gospel would supplant. Yet Dingrin admits that successive Burmese Kings, "Bodawpaya (reigned 1782–1819) and Bagyidaw (reigned 1819–37) . . . had been patronizing Buddhism, and encouraging Pali scholarship and translation of Pali texts into Burmese."[57] Pali was a linguistic import to Burman culture and needed to be "Burmanized."

It is delicate communicative surgery, so to speak, to take religiously packed words with specific meaning drawn from Buddhism and then repack them with distinctly Christian theology. It must be done without misrepresenting either religion but posing a different way of thinking about the same realities. What Dingrin criticizes is a common cross-cultural communication technique for proclamation of the gospel. Judson tried to position the gospel in such a way as to critique the culture and guard the gospel at the same time so the culture did not supersede it. Two hundred years after Judson, this process is termed contextualization. Had Judson tried to equate the gospel with Buddhist truth-claims or to minimize the differences between them with the intent to

---

[54] Ibid., 568.
[55] Klaus K. Klostermaier, *Buddhism: A Short Introduction* (Oxford: Oneworld, 1999). This is still the most prominent form of Buddhism in Burma and Thailand.
[56] Edward Judson, *The Life*, 571.
[57] La Seng Dingrin, "The Conflicting Legacy of Adoniram Judson: Appropriating and Polemicizing against Burmese Buddhism," in *Missiology* 37, no. 4 (2009): 492. See also La Seng Dingrin, "Is Buddhism Indispensable in the Cross-Cultural Appropriation of Christianity in Burma?" in *Buddhist-Christian Studies* 29, no. 1 (2009): 3–22.

reverse himself later, he would be guilty of Dingrin's charges. This was not the case. The first sentence of the tract, as cited above, demonstrates that he clearly asserted personal theism. It was a different point of departure for interpreting life. Paul used the Greek concept of an unknown god as an opening to present the God of the Bible, and he went on to critique Greek beliefs and practices. Judson followed suit. The God Paul spoke about did not live in temples made by humans (Acts 17:22–32). The God Judson spoke about was a personal Being that Buddhism did not know. Integrity of the speaker makes a difference in how the message is heard, and the Judsons had integrity. As Ann wrote in a letter, "We are endeavoring to convince the Burmans by our conduct, that our religion is different from theirs; and I believe we have succeeded in gaining the confidence and respect of those with whom we have any concern, so that they tell others who know us not, that they need not be afraid to trust us."[58]

Church Planting

The Judsons' translation work bore fruit. Moung Nau's profession of faith, according to Judson, showed that "from the darknesses, and uncleannesses, and the sins of his whole life, he has found no other Saviour but Jesus Christ; nowhere else can he look for salvation; and therefore he proposes to adhere to Christ and worship Him all his life long. It seems almost too much to believe that God has begun to manifest His grace to the Burmans."[59] Judson later recorded on June 27, 1819, and July 4, 1819, respectively that Moung Nau participated in public baptism and took the Lord's Supper.[60]

As others came to faith and joined the church, it was distinctly a Baptist gathering. As Edward Judson states, "He was a strong, thorough Baptist."[61] National workers emerged. Judson started with (and later changed) a subsidy-based system for their support. He referenced this fact in his visit to the United States in 1845–46 during a session held at the First Baptist Church in Providence, Rhode Island. He thanked that church "for their contributions to the support of the pastor of the native church in Rangoon."[62] This practice of subsidizing leaders changed as the work developed. Especially the Karen work, in a different area of Burma, demonstrated greater strength in self-support, and it vested confidence in the new believers from the beginning so that a sense of

---

[58] As cited by Pleasants, "Beyond Translation," 26.
[59] Edward Judson, *The Life*, 127.
[60] Ibid., 132.
[61] Ibid., 409.
[62] Ibid., 464.

personal responsibility before God resulted. C. H. Carpenter, one of Judson's colleagues who worked in the Karen zones noted concern over external dependency and that *"in permanently successful missions, they have never subsidized their converts."*[63]

As the gospel spread into adjacent areas, including Siam (Thailand), there were 112 churches and 540 baptized believers documented in 1852–53 by the American Baptist Missionary Union.[64] Self-support principles stimulated church growth so much that today there are significant concentrations of Christians in these same areas, and among these particular people groups, in Burma and Northern Thailand.[65] One historian attributes the growth to self-support:

> This policy of deliberate self-reliance in Bassein caused a good deal of misunderstanding and irritation among the missionaries on the field and at the home office in Boston. The Bassein Sgaw Karen churches . . . took full responsibility of their own work. They even took care of the expenses of the American missionaries in the region. . . . [P]astors and evangelists from the Bassein Karen churches took an active part in the establishing of the first Christian community among the Karen in the *muang nua*.
>
> —Karen pastors and evangelists, rather than missionaries, led the evangelistic outreach of the Christian community;
>
> —there was a marked movement towards self-reliance and individual districts and churches were prepared to support their own work as well as evangelistic outreach to hitherto unreached areas; and
>
> —the production of literature in the Sgaw and Pwo Karen—promoting and/or presupposing the spread of literacy—was a most important factor in the spread of Christianity among the Karen.[66]

---

[63] Chapin Howard Carpenter, *Self-Support, Illustrated in the History of the Bassein Karen Mission from 1840 to 1880* (Boston, MA: Rand, Avery, 1883), 134–35. Emphasis his. Additionally noted is the practice of decentralization of the missionaries in a letter from Judson to a friend dated October 21, 1847, regarding the tendency for missionaries to be too concentrated in the city of Maulmain and "infected with the *Maulmania*."
[64] Wayland, *Memoir*, 2:522.
[65] Todd M. Johnson and Kenneth R. Ross, *Atlas of Global Christianity 1910–2010* (Edinburgh: Edinburgh University Press, 2009), 147. From 1910 to 2010 Myanmar's Christian population increased from 259,000 to 4,002,000 and Thailand's increased from 44,500 to 849,000.
[66] Anders P. Hovemyr, "In Search of the Karen King: A Study in Karen Identity with Special Reference to 19th Century Karen Evangelism in Northern Thailand" (D.Th. Thesis, University of Uppsala, 1989), 99–100.

By 1850, when Judson died, varieties of Burmese work were well rooted and have since made lasting contributions to the Christian world.

Advice to Missionary Recruits Revisited

Part of Judson's enduring legacy is the manifold ways his life inspired others to invest themselves in missionary work and influenced their practices. By June 25, 1832, Judson's investments in the spiritual well-being of Burma through his sacrificial life were renowned, especially in America. Missionaries in training wanted his advice, especially after his then nearly 20 years on the field.

On that date, he wrote to advise the missionary candidates at the Foreign Missionary Association of the Hamilton Literary and Theological Institute in New York. The 10 principles given have proved to be timeless and insightful. Though the concepts now have familiar sounding labels, essentially these ideas still apply. Selected examples are here elaborated.

> *First*, then, let it be a missionary *life*; that is, come out for life, and not a limited term. Do not fancy that you have a true missionary spirit, while you are intending all along to leave the heathen soon after acquiring their language. Leave them! For what? To spend the rest of your days in enjoying the ease and plenty of your native land?[67]

The future ease of international travel, of course, Judson had no way of anticipating. Short-term missions have proven helpful in casting vision and mobilizing churches. Indeed, Judson commented that if all the Baptists in America could just spend a limited time in Burma, they would invest their lives in activities aimed at taking the gospel there.[68] However, discontinuity still plagues missions. So Judson warned about halfhearted motives. He cautioned those wanting to go to the new field to stay there until and unless God Himself moved them. Leaving to build self-centered legacies in one's homeland is a disservice to the people one goes to serve. If someone goes, he should devote his whole heart to serving the host people. Knowledge of a foreign language makes veteran missionaries very valuable to the sustenance of the work. That tongue will

---

[67] Edward Judson, *The Life*, 577–78.

[68] Writing to Baldwin in Boston from Rangoon February 10, 1817, Judson pleads for others to come. While the modern idea of short-term, month-long missions was not practical in that time, he imagined the effect of such journeys on the sending churches. See Wayland, *Memoir*, 1:186–87.

hardly be utilized except in some esoteric linguistic academic setting in the missionary's home country.

> *Fifthly.* Beware of the reaction which will take place soon after reaching your field of labor. . . . You will see men and women whom you have been accustomed to view through a telescope some thousands of miles long. Such an instrument is apt to magnify. Beware [not to] take up a prejudice against some persons and places which will embitter all your future lives.[69]

Judson here is describing the phenomenon of culture shock, or the mental and emotional adjustments needed when one arrives on the mission field, if not before. The people are different than imagined before living among them. Two centuries later, with broadband information transfer, this is no less valid and may actually be more important. There is a tendency to study a people as objects under a microscope and forget that they are people, broken and in need of redemption and right standing before God. Judson refers to lingering bitterness that can set in if what is happening is not noticed early and dealt with quickly. If bitterness takes root, it is very difficult to overcome and will undermine the very thing the missionary is there to accomplish. Burnout not only impacts a missionary and his family but can ruin the witness of other missionaries. Judson says to be prepared, recognize this, and deal with it early.

> *Seventhly.* Beware of pride; not the pride of proud men, but the pride of humble men—that secret pride which is apt to grow out of the consciousness that we are esteemed by the great and good. . . . In order to check its operations, it may be well to remember how we appear in the sight of God, and how we should appear in the sight of our fellow-men, if all were known. Endeavor to let all be known.[70]

If Satan cannot stop a missionary from going to the field, his next best tactic is to steal vision and motivation for the work by disrupting relationships, both with the nationals and other missionaries. Judson's assessment is that this is a complicated web of pride that works its way into hearts. While perhaps not always visible, it manifests as habits in a person's life. Judson's antidote is transparency, being open with others,

---

[69] Edward Judson, *The Life*, 578.
[70] Ibid., 579.

not hiding self-serving agendas. Deception can take many forms and missionaries are not exempt from practicing it. In fact, pride is even more complicated cross-culturally. This is just another reason to acquire the language, because along with it comes the understanding of cultural signals and nuances that assist in relationship building.

> *Tenthly.* Beware of genteel living. Maintain as little intercourse as possible with fashionable European society. The mode of living adopted by many missionaries in the East is quite inconsistent with that familiar intercourse with the natives which is essential to a missionary.[71]

Judson's caution here is ongoing. Missionaries need to relate well to their adopted people. Living in vastly different ways from them alienates the indigenous people and inhibits the work. Missionaries should venture out of the "little Americana" they may have established for themselves, as Judson termed it, living in a "genteel" manner. Failure to do so may erect barriers. In the words of his day, Judson described materialistic shock. It relationally separates missionaries from people, as half a world's distance lies between them. Electronic technologies, as prolific as they are in many mission settings today, can become relational barriers. Judicial use of technology and careful observation of one's lifestyle enhances relationships with nationals.

Judson ends with a prayer for would be missionaries. He specifically asks that they be "guided in all [their] deliberations, and that I may have the pleasure of welcoming some of [them] to these heathen shores."[72]

Conclusion

Judson research is by no means exhausted. The richness of so many diary entries, letters, and records left by his spouses show the means that God used to woo Judson to faith and missionary life. Analysis of how God called him and his spouses into missionary work,

---

[71] Ibid.

[72] Ibid. For Judson's admonitions regarding discipleship and obedience to Christ, see his final public address during his American visit entitled *Obedience to Christ's Last Command a Test of Piety*. He delivered it July 5, 1846. His voice was still ailing so the manuscript was read aloud. The event was a concert of prayer by the network of Baptist churches in Boston. The essence of his appeal was to cherish what Christ most cherishes and work to redeem those for whom He died. Whether senders or goers, all must pass this test of piety. Wayland, *Memoir*, 2:519–21.

and to change part of the world through the investment of their lives, is still not fully mined. More can and should be done regarding his mother's influence on his life and his eventual affirmation of Baptist doctrines. His understanding of religious freedom, and how that impacted the missiological methods he employed, is hardly addressed and herein only raised. Scholarship has focused largely on his unselfish sacrifices to broadcast the gospel to the Burmese and his meticulous translation work, and rightly so. Yet, these other themes are ripe for exploration. His insights into what moderns would term contextualization, evangelization, discipleship, and church planting should be investigated more extensively.

Judson's lifestyle was exemplary. If someone holds an idealistic or faulty understanding of missions, that quickly fades when reading these historical records. Missionaries are real people with real problems and victories. Over the years, the Christian world tended to prize Judson, his spouses, and their legacies far beyond what Judson himself would ever have wanted. He fought cycles of pride before he was a Christian. When spiritually arrested by Christ, he ordered his life to do God's bidding and tried to avoid the personal fame that came with his work.

Behind his work stands a man who desired full consecration to Christ, and he was diligent at his post until death. Emotional crises, struggles, loneliness, and ill health all took tolls. Yet, in spite of it all, he likely maintained emotional equilibrium by the jingle of verse he taught his children to recite in their earliest years: "Be the living God my friend, then my joys shall never end."[73] This coupled with another often-repeated retort surely provided anchorage and endurance: Once an inquirer asked whether "he thought the prospects bright for the speedy conversion of the heathen." Judson replied, "As bright as the promises of God."[74] So it is, still two centuries later. This is Judson's enduring legacy.

---

[73] Adoniram B. Judson, *How Judson*, 3.
[74] Edward Judson, *The Life*, 92.

Chapter 7

From Congregationalist to Baptist
Judson and Baptism

Gregory A. Wills

On September 6, 1812, Adoniram and Ann Judson submitted to baptism at the Lal Bazar Baptist Chapel at Calcutta, India.[1] It was a fateful step with consequences that they deeply dreaded. It meant severing their relationship with the churches of their parents, their friends, and their dear missionary colleagues. It severed also their relationship with the mission board that Judson had helped create and upon which their entire support depended. They felt themselves thoroughly alone, cast upon a threatening sea with no visible harbor.

It was a dramatic reversal of their prospects. Just seven months earlier, on February 6, 1812, an august gathering of Congregationalist pastors and laypersons celebrated the ordination of Judson, together with four of his fellow students at Andover Theological Seminary, to the ministry of the gospel as missionaries to India. They had been meeting and praying secretly to devise some means of going to preach the gospel in Asia. In 1810 they revealed their aspirations to their professors and to leading Congregationalist ministers in Massachusetts, who embraced the cause and formed the American Board of Commissioners for Foreign Missions. Judson had assumed a leading role among the students, and with strong support and leadership from the Andover professors and influential pastors, he and his companions had realized their long cherished ambition

---

[1] In 1903, a memorial tablet was unveiled in the chapel that reads: "Dr. Judson was born in Malden Massachusetts, 9th August 1788, was educated in Brown University and Andover Seminary, and sailed for India under the auspices of the American Board of Commissioners for Foreign Missions. ON the voyage he and his wife, ANN HASSELTINE, embraced Baptist views and were baptized in this Church, 6th September 1812, by the REV. WILLIAM WARD, Serampore. This incident called into existence, in 1814, the American Baptist Missionary Union with Dr. Judson as its first Missionary. In the providence of God he was then led to Burmah, which country was blessed with thirty-eight years of heroic endeavour in the cause of CHRIST. He died at sea 12th April 1850. This tablet erected by one of his countrymen who revered his memory, was unveiled by the Counsul-General for the United States of America, 24th Februrary 1903." A photograph of the tablet appears in *The Baptist Missionary Magazine* 83, no. 8 (August 1903): 633.

to go abroad to preach the gospel where it was not known. Becoming a Baptist now jeopardized the objects for which he had longed and labored.

Judson saw it as an unfortunate consequence of following God's revealed will regarding baptism. Baptists viewed his sacrifices and trials as evidence of his sincerity. Many Congregationalists viewed the matter in a different light. They viewed it as a self-serving act. Judson's defection was a scripturally unjustified betrayal of those who had nurtured and supported him. But it was also a tragic blow to the prospects for a new evangelical unity driven by the missionary cause and its spirit of public benevolence. It seemed a step backward toward the divisive denominationalism of the past. In fact, it was a reminder that ecclesiology imposed some practical limits on evangelical unity.

JUDSON AND THE MISSIONARY CAUSE

Judson's defection to the Baptists caused such offense in part because he was the best known of the five missionaries, since he had taken the leading role on behalf of the students. The five were members of a small cadre of Andover Theological Seminary students who had committed themselves to missionary service. The group originated in 1806 when several Williams College students, seeking refuge in a rainstorm, prayed that God would use them to undertake a mission to the unevangelized peoples of Asia. Samuel Mills was the student who challenged them to commit themselves to do it at a time when no organization existed in the United States to send missionaries abroad. Two years later Mills and other students formed a Society of the Brethren, whose members pledged themselves to missions. They kept the organization and its meetings secret, since many Christians would consider a scheme to establish missions in Asia impractical—or rather, impossible. Mills and several of the other brethren enrolled at Andover and kept up the secret meetings there. They recruited a few like-minded students, including Adoniram Judson.[2]

Although Judson was a newcomer to the group, he quickly assumed a leading role. He had only recently come to personal faith in Jesus Christ, in December 1808, during his first term at seminary. In February 1810 he committed his life to missionary service.[3] His heart had been kindled with a strong desire to preach the gospel in Asia, but he could

---

[2] See Margaret L. Bendroth, *A School of the Church: Andover Newton Across Two Centuries* (Grand Rapids: Eerdmans, 2008), 50–52; Thomas C. Richards, *The Haystack Prayer Meeting: An Account of Its Origin and Spirit* (New York: De Vinne Press, 1906).

[3] Francis Wayland, *A Memoir of the Life and Labors of the Rev. Adoniram Judson, D.D.* (Boston, MA: Phillips, Sampson, and Company, 1853), 1:27–39.

see no possible means to accomplish it, not least because no organization existed in the United States at that time for sending and supporting missionaries. But as he prayed and reflected alone one day, "the command of Christ, 'Go into all the world, and preach the gospel to every creature,' was presented to my mind with such clearness and power that I came to a full decision, and though great difficulties appeared in my way, resolved to obey the command at all events."[4]

He did not know of any other students who shared his ambition. But the Society of Brethren members heard him declaiming passionately in favor of missionary service, and they invited him to join them. His ardent nature, his daring impetuousness, his intelligent grasp, and his focused ambition to accomplish their missionary hopes won their affection and trust. And Judson immediately began to draw in others. They were all men of independent mind, with strength of conviction, courage, and ambition. And they recognized in Judson a spokesman who could represent their cause well.

Samuel Spring, pastor of the Second Church in Newburyport, and Samuel Worcester, pastor of the Tabernacle Church in Salem, suggested to Judson that he write a petition on behalf of the student group and present it at the upcoming meeting of the Massachusetts General Association. Spring and Worcester played the leading role among the clergy in establishing the new mission board. Judson agreed to compose the petition, and read it before the association on behalf of the four men who signed it: Judson, Samuel Mills, Samuel Nott, and Samuel Newell. The petition related that the four had long been impressed with their personal duty to attempt a mission to the heathen and that they had solemnly devoted themselves for life to this work. They then asked the association to advise them regarding the feasibility of their object and the practical measures necessary to attain it. After Judson read the petition, the delegates questioned each of the four young men and dismissed them. On the following day the association established the American Board of Commissioners for Foreign Missions, the first society in the United States whose purpose was to send and support missionaries across the globe.[5]

The Board of Commissioners selected Judson to petition the London Missionary Society for help. The board needed information about the unevangelized parts of the

---

[4] Adoniram Judson to Stephen Chapin, 18 December 1837, quoted in Wayland, *Memoir*, 1:51–52.

[5] Minutes of the First Annual Meeting of the American Board of Commissioners for Foreign Missions, in American Board of Commissioners for Foreign Missions, *First Ten Annual Reports of the American Board of Commissioners for Foreign Missions* (Boston, MA: Crocker and Brewster, 1834), 9–10; Adoniram Judson to Mr. and Mrs. Judson, 29 June 1810, in Wayland, *Memoir*, 1:55–56; Courtney Anderson, *To the Golden Shore: The Life of Adoniram Judson* (New York: Little, Brown and Company, 1956), 64–71, 81.

world, that it might judge best where to send them and how to arrange their mission. It also needed money. The new board had no funds. The best way to secure the necessary information and funds would be to establish a cooperative venture with the London Missionary Society, which had large revenues and considerable experience in managing a missionary enterprise. The London Society had been established in 1795 by evangelical Anglicans and dissenters, especially Congregationalists. The board therefore appointed Judson to invite the London Society to provide funds for the support of the American missionaries with the condition that the American board would govern the American missionaries jointly with the London Society. The London Society expressed a willingness to send and support the Americans but only if they alone governed their mission. They officially offered appointment to the Americans, but they would not cede partial control of their mission to the American board.[6]

When the American board met in September 1811, they agreed that it would be unwise to surrender the missionaries to the London Society. They asked the young men not to accept their appointment with the London Missionary Society. They officially appointed them as "missionaries to labor under the direction of this board in Asia" and agreed to send them abroad as soon as they had sufficient funds. Some members of the board urged strongly that they should delay sending the missionaries. Raising sufficient funds for such an expensive undertaking would be difficult, as business conditions were poor due to the long war between England and France. Judson, supported by Nott, opposed a policy of caution and delay. He judged that war would soon erupt between the United States and England, in which case it might be years before the missionaries could be sent. Time was short. It was now or never.

Judson's passionate interchange offended some members of the board. He deepened the offense when he told them that if the board did not take action to send them right away, they would find some other way. They would go as missionaries of the London Missionary Society.

This was too much for many members. They were prepared to dismiss him. He seemed to feel little loyalty or obligation to the board that had been organized for the purpose of supporting him and his companions. He had placed himself under the patronage of the board in 1810. They had expended considerable effort and were raising the necessary funds. Judson, however, was prepared to abandon the board and spurn its patronage. Indeed, his actions in London had already given considerable offense, for he

---

[6] For a full account of the early years of the American Board of Commissioners, see Joseph Tracy, *History of the American Board of Commissioners for Foreign Missions*, 2nd ed. (New York: M. W. Dodd, 1842).

had practically pledged the American missionaries to the London Missionary Society and induced the London society to accept them "as missionaries, to be employed by this society in India."[7] Now he expressed willingness once again to abandon the men who had adopted the missionaries and their cause. Only the wise and strong leadership of Samuel Spring prevented catastrophe. Spring convinced the board to make arrangements to send the available students as missionaries at once. Spring however also delivered a public rebuke to Judson for his independent policy both in London and in the board's meeting.[8]

In January the board learned that two ships planned to sail for India the following month. They had insufficient funds and preparations would have to be made in great haste, but they decided to send five young men as missionaries on the two ships. Judson married Ann Hasseltine on February 5. He was ordained on February 6 along with Samuel Newell, Samuel Nott, Gordon Hall, and Luther Rice. The Judsons, along with Newell and his new wife, departed Salem harbor in their native Massachusetts on February 19, 1812, aboard the brig *Caravan*. Nott, Hall, and Rice sailed the following day from Philadelphia aboard the *Harmony*.

BAPTISM AND IMMERSION

About midway in the four-month voyage Judson began to examine the Bible's teachings on baptism. He had no thought of becoming a Baptist. Although he had not seriously examined Baptists' arguments for their views, he had "strong prejudices" against them as a "sect that is everywhere spoken against."[9]

Three considerations spurred his examination. First, he had begun translating the New Testament from the Greek, which raised new questions in his mind concerning the proper meaning of the Greek words for baptism and baptize. Second, since they would be consulting with William Carey and the other Baptist missionaries in India, he wanted to be fully prepared to answer any arguments they might raise against infant baptism. Third, in anticipation of receiving the first converts in a pagan land and gathering them

---

[7] Minutes of the Board of Directors, London Missionary Society, 27 May 1811, quoted in Wayland, *Memoir*, 1:77.

[8] See Anderson, *To the Golden Shore*, 93–95, 98–102; and Wayland, *Memoir*, 1:81–92.

[9] Adoniram Judson to the Third Congregational Church, Plymouth, Mass., 20 August 1817, in Adoniram Judson, *A Sermon on Christian Baptism*, rev. ed. (Boston, MA: Gould, Kendall and Lincoln, 1846), 96.

into a church, he reflected upon his duty to baptize not only converts but their entire households with them.[10]

Ann Judson summarized these developments to a friend:

> As Mr. Judson was continuing a translation of the New Testament which he had begun in America, he had many doubts respecting the meaning of the word *baptize*. This, with the idea of meeting the Baptists at Serampore, when he would wish to defend his own sentiments, induced a more thorough examination of the foundation of the pedobaptist system. The more he examined, the more his doubts increased. And, unwilling as he was to admit it, he was afraid the Baptists were right and he was wrong.[11]

Doubt concerning the proper mode of baptism seems to have arisen first. As Judson translated the New Testament, he reflected on the fact that the Greek nouns and verbs translated as baptism and baptize referred straightforwardly to immersion or dipping. This meant that the English Bible did not in fact translate the Greek words but rather borrowed them from Greek and Anglicized them. The Greek noun *baptismos*, which meant immersion or dipping, was transliterated to become "baptism," and the verb *baptizein*, which meant to immerse or dip, was transliterated as "baptize."[12] Greek linguists agreed that "immersion is the native and proper signification of the word." Judson quoted an array of pedobaptist authors, including Luther and Beza, to demonstrate that "immersion is the exclusive signification of the word."[13] He cited Calvin also asserting that when the Scriptures show John "plunging the whole body under water," we must recognize "how baptism was administered among the ancients, for they immersed the whole body in water."[14]

The circumstances of the Bible's baptisms strongly suggested immersion. John and the apostles resorted to rivers and went into the water, the Bible records. Pouring or sprinkling could be administered with much less trouble than this, since they do not require going into the water. And the metaphorical uses of the words for baptism also strongly implied immersion. Paul's comparison of baptism to burial in Romans 6, for example, works well if baptism means immersion but poorly if it means sprinkling. If

---

[10] Adoniram Judson, *A Sermon on Christian Baptism*, 96.
[11] Ann Judson to a friend, 7 September 1812, quoted in Wayland, *Memoir*, 1:105.
[12] See Judson, *Sermon on Baptism*, 5–7.
[13] Ibid., 9–10.
[14] Ibid., 24.

baptism meant sprinkling, the Christians were "buried with him by sprinkling" and "they were all sprinkled unto Moses." Immersion always suited the metaphorical uses, but sprinkling rarely did.[15] He noted also that the Greek-speaking churches had always understood baptism to mean immersion, from the period of the apostles to the present.[16]

The more he studied the Greek texts, the more convinced he was that immersion was the act commanded. To speak of a "mode of baptism" was therefore to confuse the matter, since the command itself included the mode. The thing commanded was an immersion. It was a relatively uncomplicated lexical matter. "The terms *baptism* and *immersion* are equivalent and interchangeable," and therefore "when Christ commanded his disciples to be baptized, he commanded them to be immersed."[17] Baptism was, by definition, an immersion.

WHO SHOULD BE BAPTIZED?

The question of the proper subjects of baptism was more complicated. When Judson began the voyage to India, he was certain enough that baptizing the dependents of converts was the biblical pattern. The apostle Paul had done this when persons converted in response to his missionary preaching. He baptized Lydia's household after she converted and the Philippian jailer's household when he converted. The requirement was taught in the Old Testament as well, since God commanded the circumcision of the males of Abraham's household and of his descendants, a command reiterated in the covenant at Sinai. The obligation in the new covenant church was unchanged from that of the old covenant church. The sign had changed from circumcision to baptism, but the obligation to apply it to all within the household had not. All persons in a believer's household should therefore receive baptism.

Judson thus recognized that he had a duty to baptize the entire household when a father converted. The mission board expected him to do this. Their instructions directed the missionaries to baptize only "credible believers and their households."[18] Samuel Spring, who delivered the charge at the ordination of Judson and his fellows, reminded

---

[15] Ibid., 20–21.
[16] Ibid., 21–31.
[17] Ibid., 32.
[18] "Instructions Given by the Prudential Committee of the American Board of Commissioners for Foreign Missions to the Missionaries, February 7, 1812," *First Ten Annual Reports of the American Board of Commissioners for Foreign Missions,* 41.

them of their solemn duty to "apply the seal of the covenant to the children and domestics of believers, agreeably to the practice of Abraham, the father of the faithful."[19] But as he reviewed the arguments and the scriptural passages that supported them, he began to doubt his position.

It struck him forcefully that the baptism of believers was the unvarying expectation of the New Testament. Jesus commanded that believers should be baptized. In His commission to the apostles, Jesus commanded them to "Go therefore make disciples of all nations, baptizing them in the name of the Father and of the Son and of the Holy Spirit" (Matt 28:19 ESV). They should baptize those who first became disciples. Every baptism recorded in the Bible was the baptism of a professing believer. And the apostles spoke of baptism as an act undertaken by those who had believed. "As many of you as have been baptized into Christ," Judson quoted Paul (Gal 3:27), "have put on Christ." The Galatians who had been baptized had all been united to Christ by faith.[20]

But in pedobaptist churches, the pattern was quite different. The baptism of believers was quite rare, since almost all persons in the church were baptized as infants. And a large proportion of those baptized had never put on Christ by exercising faith in Him. The incongruity between the baptisms of the apostolic churches and those of the pedobaptist churches of New England deepened his doubt concerning the propriety of baptizing infants.[21]

He discovered no command in the Bible to baptize infants and no examples of baptized infants. In the instances where households received baptism, the context suggests that those who were baptized had believed.[22] But pedobaptists held that the command to baptize infants derived from the covenant of circumcision, which was still in force; therefore no explicit command in the New Testament was necessary. Upon reflection Judson concluded that pedobaptist churches were inconsistent in their observance of the covenant of circumcision. Circumcision was commanded on the eighth day after birth, was commanded to be applied to males only, and was imposed for servants as well as sons. There was no intimation in the New Testament that God had remanded or relaxed any of these requirements. Permission is nowhere given to baptize other than on the

---

[19] Samuel Spring, "The Charge," in Leonard Woods, *A Sermon Delivered at the Tabernacle in Salem, Feb. 6, 1812, on the Occasion of the Ordination of the Rev. Messrs. Samuel Newell, Adoniram Judson, Samuel Nott, Gordon Hall, and Luther Rice Missionaries to the Heathen in Asia* (Boston, MA: Samuel T. Armstrong, 1812), 35.

[20] Judson, *Sermon on Baptism*, 32.

[21] Ibid., 33.

[22] Ibid., 34–36.

eighth day, to apply it to females in the household, or to withhold it from the male servants in the household. Yet pedobaptists neglected to obey these parts of the covenant.[23]

If baptism has been substituted for circumcision in the new covenant, Judson thought, it is strange that the New Testament failed to mention this fact in its discussions of circumcision. The New Testament stated explicitly that circumcision has been abolished. There were many in the early church, however, who found this difficult to accept. The church at Galatia thought that circumcision was binding upon Christians. If Christ had substituted baptism for circumcision, then the apostles surely would have mentioned this when they explained why circumcision was no longer obligatory. It would have constituted a powerful answer to the Judaizers who insisted on circumcision.[24]

Judson concluded that the covenant of circumcision was not the same as the covenant of grace; the church under the old covenant was not the same as the church under the new covenant. The covenants had different obligations, different promises, and different conditions for admission. Most important in this regard, Israelites were admitted to the church based on natural descent, whereas Christians were admitted to the church based on faith.[25]

Judson's investigations aboard the *Caravan* had only deepened his doubts concerning the validity of infant baptism. Ann feared that he was about to become a Baptist. She argued at length with him, pressing upon him the arguments in favor of infant baptism. She sought to dissuade him also by pointing out the "unhappy consequences" of such a change. She told him repeatedly that if he became a Baptist, "I would not."[26]

Although Judson was growing in his conviction that the Baptists were correct, he patiently kept up the investigation. He had to be thorough, for the consequences were severe. Some time after their arrival in India, Adoniram and Ann had to spend two weeks in Calcutta with little to occupy their attention. They were pleasantly surprised to find in their temporary lodgings an extensive collection of books on baptism. They studied carefully the books on both sides of the matter of infant baptism. After comparing all the authors with the Scriptures, they "examined and reexamined the sentiments of Baptists and pedobaptists, and were finally compelled, from a conviction of truth," to

---

[23] Ibid., 36–39.

[24] Ibid., 59–60.

[25] For a fine summary of Judson's evaluation of the covenant of circumcision and the covenant of grace, see Adoniram Judson to the Third Congregational Church, Plymouth, Mass., August 20, 1817, in Judson, *A Sermon on Christian Baptism*, 100–110.

[26] Ann Judson to Her Parents, 14 February 1813, in Wayland, *Memoir*, 1:107; Ann Judson to a friend, 7 September 1812, in ibid., 106.

embrace Baptist views. They were now convinced that the Bible taught that "the immersion of a professing believer is the only Christian baptism."[27]

What Did Christ Require?

The practical implication of this conviction came upon Judson with force. If the immersion of a professing believer was the only baptism, then he was not baptized, since he had been sprinkled as an infant, before he was even capable of repentance and faith. He was mortified at the prospect of seeking baptism and becoming a Baptist. Ann had pressed upon him the painful and humiliating consequences of such a change, and now he had to confront them.

> Must I, then, forsake my parents, the church with which I stand connected, the society under whose patronage I have come out, the companions of my missionary undertaking? Must I forfeit the good opinion of all my friends in my native land, occasioning grief to some, and provoking others to anger, and be regarded henceforth, by all my former dear acquaintance, as a weak despicable Baptist, who has not sense enough to comprehend the connection between the Abrahamic and the Christian systems?[28]

He entertained the thought of continuing on as he was, unbaptized, rather than overturning his ambitions and hopes for his life and ministry. What need was there to put him and Ann through so much humiliation, difficulty, and inconvenience? But even if he could quiet his conscience regarding his own baptism, he could not escape the question of whether he could with integrity administer baptism to the children and servants of the converts who responded in faith to his missionary preaching. He knew that he could no longer agree to baptize them and treat them as members of the church. He now knew that it was contrary to the command of Christ. He resolved finally that he must seek the praise of Christ rather than the praise of men. He must become a Baptist.[29]

---

[27] Ann Judson to a friend, 7 September 1812, in Wayland, *Memoir*, 1:106; Ann Judson to her parents, 14 February 1813, in ibid., 1:107; Adoniram Judson to William Carey, Joshua Marshman, and William Ward, 27 August 1812, in ibid., 109.

[28] Adoniram Judson to the Third Congregational Church, Plymouth, Mass., 20 August 1817, in Judson, *A Sermon on Christian Baptism*, rev. ed., 104.

[29] Ibid., 104–5.

Judson wrote a letter to the English Baptist missionaries explaining that he and Ann had come to Baptist convictions and requesting baptism in their church. To this point, the two had not discussed the matter with any of the Baptist missionaries. William Ward, one of the Baptist missionaries, immersed them upon their profession of faith in Christ. They had obeyed Christ. They were now baptized. And they had never felt so alone.

TRUTH, OBEDIENCE, AND EVANGELICAL UNITY

Early missions leaders invested high hopes in the burgeoning missionary movement. They did not view it as a denominational enterprise. It was a social cause of general benevolence, and it represented the advance of Christian civilization. New England Congregationalists did not intend the American Board of Commissioners for Foreign Mission to be a Congregationalist entity. They wanted an evangelical entity. All evangelical denominations could unite in it, since it involved essentially the proclamation of the basic gospel message of the forgiveness of sins through repentance and faith in Christ Jesus, on the foundation of the orthodox convictions shared by all evangelical denominations. The Presbyterians, in fact, united with the Congregationalists in operating the American Board of Commissioners. The two already cooperated closely in calling ministers, establishing new congregations, and in missionary efforts in North America, having adopted in 1801 a formal "Plan of Union" that established rules for such cooperation.

Congregationalist leaders expected that missions would serve to unite the evangelical denominations generally. The constitution of the American Board of Commissioners described their effort in general Christian terms only, avoiding any suggestion that it was denominational in any sense. In the February 6 ordination sermon, Leonard Woods expressed the ecumenical hopes of the missionary enterprise. "Episcopalians, Presbyterians, Congregationalists, Baptists, Moravians, new divinity men, and old divinity men," Woods observed, were relinquishing their former "party spirit" and "narrow prejudices." Denominational partisanship was being displaced by an evangelical religion of "greater love and harmony." The grand cause of missions—the "spread of the gospel and the conversion of the world"—was purifying and unifying Christians into one great family and might soon induce them to forget their party names.[30]

---

[30] Woods, *A Sermon Delivered at the Tabernacle in Salem*, 23–24.

Baptist views proved a greater obstacle to this evangelical harmony than Woods imagined. Congregationalists could find no means for including Baptists in their missionary efforts. Perhaps they could unite well enough on a mission board, raising money and sending missionaries. But they could hardly unite in the establishing of new churches, since Baptist missionaries could not in good conscience support baptizing infants, and pedobaptist missionaries could not in good conscience refuse to uphold infant baptism.

For Adoniram and Ann Judson, the heartaches were both more personal and more practical. "A renunciation of our former sentiments has caused us more pain than anything which ever happened to us through our lives," Ann confided to her parents.[31] Many of their Massachusetts friends and colleagues did not understand. For most of them it seemed, as Enoch Pond described it, as "one of the most mysterious and unaccountable events which has ever occurred in the Christian world."[32] Pond thought it inconceivable that Judson could became a Baptist based on the biblical evidence and the theological arguments. When Judson published a sermon delineating his arguments, his Congregationalist friends in Massachusetts judged his arguments too weak to persuade a sound mind. They could not see "how they could have induced his present belief."[33] They therefore sought another explanation. They ascribed the change to personal pique, suggesting that his change "had been induced by resentment" toward the board of commissioners.[34]

The board had found fault with some of his actions when they deputized him to go to England to arrange some plan of cooperation with the London Missionary Society. They concluded that in some respects he had not acted prudently in the best interests of the American Board, and they admonished him. Pond and other Congregationalists concluded that Judson resented the board's action when they rebuked him for his independent policy in London and in the board's 1811 meeting. They imagined that he was nursing his wounded pride all the way to India and that he leaped at a chance to take revenge on them by becoming a Baptist. The deep mental distress of personal humiliation before his Massachusetts brethren, not scriptural arguments, had induced him to take such an irrational and injurious step. The board had "cramped" his ambition and "mortified"

---

[31] Ann Judson to her parents, 7 September 1812, quoted in Wayland, *Memoir*, 1:108.
[32] Enoch Pond, *A Treatise on the Mode and Subjects of Christian Baptism, in Two Parts, Designed as a Reply to the Statements and Reasonings of Rev. Adoniram Judson* (Worcester, MA: William Manning, 1818), 5.
[33] Ibid., 6.
[34] Ibid., 8.

his pride. He embraced Baptist views in order to get his revenge. Pond included a summary of the opinion of Judson's pedobaptist friends in New England: "Shortly before he sailed, he received a reprimand from the Board, which so offended him, that he resolved to have nothing more to do with them, and in no way could he escape so honorably as by becoming a Baptist."[35]

For their part, Adoniram and Ann Judson saw little enough honor in becoming Baptists. They felt deep pain as they reflected that becoming Baptist would cost them dearly. They tried to count the cost, Ann told a friend the day after their baptism, and expected "severe trials" as a result.

> We anticipate the loss of reputation, and of the affection and esteem of many of our American friends. But the most trying circumstance attending this change, and that which has caused the most pain, is the separation which must take place between us and our dear missionary associates. Although we are attached to each other, and should doubtless live very happily together, yet the brethren do not think it best we should unite in one mission."[36]

They wept and poured out their hearts before God concerning all these trials. And they committed themselves to their Savior. "We feel that we are alone in the world, with no real friend but each other, no one on whom we can depend but God."[37]

Ann explained the matter similarly to her parents a few months later:

> We knew it would wound and grieve our dear Christian friends in America—that we should lose their approbation and esteem. We thought it probable that the commissioners would refuse to support us. And, what was more distressing than anything, we knew we must be separated from our missionary associates, and go alone to some heathen land. These things were very trying to us and caused our hearts to bleed with anguish. We felt we had no home in this world and no friend but each other.[38]

---

[35] Ibid., 9, 11.
[36] Ann Judson to a friend, 7 September 1812, quoted in Wayland, *Memoir*, 1:106.
[37] Ibid.
[38] Ann Judson to her parents, 14 February 1813, quoted in Wayland, *Memoir*, 1:107.

A few days before their baptism, Adoniram wrote Samuel Worcester, the corresponding secretary of the American Board of Commissioners, resigning his appointment. He could no longer pledge in good conscience to carry out the board's instructions to baptize "credible believers with their households." His new views were incompatible with continuing as a missionary of the board and with his serving in the same mission as his fellow missionaries. Their only prospect was going alone "to some distant island" without any financial support and without another missionary associated with them. "The dissolution of my connection with the Board of Commissioners, and a separation from my dear missionary brethren, I consider most distressing consequences of my late change of sentiments, and indeed, the most distressing events which have ever befallen me."[39]

Adoniram Judson did not become a Baptist from personal alienation and desire for revenge. Nor out of a calculating opportunism. Nor instability. He acted because he was sincerely convinced that the Baptists had interpreted the Bible correctly. When Christ commanded baptism, He commanded the immersion of a professing believer and nothing else. Judson obeyed "from a single regard for truth and duty."[40] His obedience damaged the movement toward unity and harmony among evangelicals. It injured his reputation, jeopardized his hopes of serving as a missionary, and alienated him and his wife from their entire circle of friends and colleagues. Conscience compelled them to take the fateful step, nevertheless. Once they became fully convinced of Baptist views, their only course was submission. "We are confirmed Baptists," Ann told a friend, "not because we wished to be, but because truth compelled us to be."[41]

Does that truth still compel?

> Come, Holy Spirit, Dove divine!
> On these baptismal waters shine,
> And teach our hearts, in highest strain,
> To praise the Lamb for sinners slain.
>
> We love thy name, we love thy laws,
> And joyfully embrace thy cause;

---

[39] Adoniram Judson to Samuel Worcester, 1 September 1812, quoted in Wayland, *Memoir*, 1:110. One of their colleagues afterward joined them. Luther Rice, who had argued forcefully in August 1812 against Judson's emerging Baptist convictions, became a Baptist two months after the Judsons were baptized.

[40] Adoniram Judson to the Third Congregational Church, in Judson, *A Sermon on Christian Baptism*, 111.

[41] Ann Judson to a friend, 7 September 1812, quoted in Wayland, *Memoir*, 1:106.

We love thy cross, the shame, the pain;
O Lamb of God! for sinners slain!

We plunge beneath thy mystic flood,
O plunge us in thy cleansing blood;
We die to sin, and seek a grave
With thee, beneath the yielding wave.

And as we rise with thee to live,
O let the Holy Spirit give
The sealing unction from above,
The breath of life, the fire of love![42]

---

[42] "Come Holy Spirit, Dove Divine," words by Adoniram Judson, c. 1829, published as Hymn 511 in James M. Winchell, "A Supplement of More Than Three Hundred Hymns" in *An Arrangement of the Psalms, Hymns, and Spiritual Songs of the Rev. Isaac Watts, D.D.* (Boston, MA: James Loring, 1832).

Homiletical Interpretation

Chapter 8

Marked for Death, Messengers of Life
Adoniram and Ann Judson[1]

Daniel L. Akin[2]

ROMANS 8:28–39

And we know that for those who love God all things work together for good, for those who are called according to his purpose. For those whom he foreknew he also predestined to be conformed to the image of his Son, in order that he might be the firstborn among many brothers. And those whom he predestined he also called, and those whom he called he also justified, and those whom he justified he also glorified. What then shall we say to these things? If God is for us, who can be against us? He who did not spare his own Son but gave him up for us all, how will he not also with him graciously give us all things? (Rom 8:28–32 ESV)

Adoniram Judson is the father of the American Baptist missionary movement. Eugene Harrison calls him "the apostle of the love of Christ in Burma."[3] He left American soil as a Congregationalist. Arriving in India, having carefully studied the New Testament, he became a Baptist. He was baptized by an associate of William Carey. He would eventually go to Burma where he labored for nearly 40 years. He would translate the whole Bible into Burmese, spend 21 months in a brutal prison, and bury two wives and more than five children. Divine providence indeed marked him for death, while also making him a messenger of life.

---

[1] Significant biographical information for this sermon came from Courtney Anderson, *To the Golden Shore: The Life of Adoniram Judson* (New York: Little, Brown and Company, 1956).

[2] This sermon has been previously published in Daniel L. Akin, *Five Who Changed the World* (Wake Forest, NC: Southeastern Baptist Theological Seminary, 2008), 19–34. Republished here with permission.

[3] Eugene Myers Harrison, *Giants of the Missionary Trail: The Life Stories of Eight Men Who Defied Death and Demons* (Chicago, IL: Scripture Press, 1954), available online at http://www.wholesomewords.org/missions/giants/biojudson2.html.

Born in 1788 in Massachusetts, he died in 1850 and was buried at sea. No earthly grave marks his departure from this world into the world of his King Jesus. Fred Barlow said it well when he wrote, "By whatever measurement you measure the man Judson—the measurement always is the same—he was a mighty man!"[4]

Romans 8:28–39 is written "all over the life" of this wonderful Baptist missionary. Indeed, had he not been confident of the truths contained in these verses, he would have never "finished the race" and "kept the faith" (2 Tim 4:7). Many of us will likewise be sustained only by the same.

Four lessons leap from this text for our blessing and benefit. Each was marvelously lived out by Adoniram and Ann Judson. Each comes in the form of a divine promise.

WE HAVE HIS PROVIDENCE, ROMANS 8:28–32

Paul affirms that there are no accidents in the life of the child of God, only providence. In 8:28 we are given: a certain promise (we know), a comprehensive promise (all things), a comforting promise (work together for good), a chosen promise (those who love God), and a clear promise (called according to His purpose). Paul also affirms the signed, sealed, and settled nature of our salvation through what has been called the "golden chain of redemption."

The chain has five links, located in vv. 29–30. First, God foreknew. Second, He predestined. Third, He called. Fourth, He justified. Fifth, He glorified. These are certain realities in the plan and purpose of God. Such a glorious and certain salvation has very definite and wonderful consequences: God is for us (v. 31), and He will give us everything we need for His glory and our good (v. 32).

How did this divine providence work itself out in Judson's life? Let me note three ways.

First, his family and education. Mentally, he was a giant. He began reading at the age of 3, took navigation lessons at 10, studied theology as a child, and entered Providence College (now Brown University) at 17. Despite the fact that his father was a Congregational preacher, and in spite of his mother's "tears and pleadings," Judson was not saved until he was 20 years of age. In college he became a confirmed deist—due largely to the influence of a brilliant unbelieving student at Brown who set out to win

---

[4] Fred Barlow, *Profiles in Evangelism: Biographical Sketches of World-Renowned Soul Winners* (Murfreesboro, TN: Sword of the Lord, 1976), 103.

Judson to his deistic faith. That man was Jacob Eames of Belfast, Maine. Keep that name in mind.

Second, his conversion. No conversion, save the apostle Paul's, is any more providential in its character than that of Adoniram. After graduation he left home to become a wanderlust (a traveler in search of excitement), confirmed and growing in his deistic convictions. One night, while traveling, he stopped to stay in a country inn. His room was adjacent to the room of a dying man. The moaning and groaning of that man through the long night permitted Judson no sleep. His thoughts troubled him. All night questions assailed his soul: "Was the dying man prepared to die? Where would he spend eternity? Was he a Christian, calm and strong in the hope of life in Heaven? Or, was he a sinner shuddering in the dark brink of the lower region?" Judson chided himself for even entertaining such thoughts contrary to his philosophy of life beyond the grave and thought how his brilliant college friend would rebuke him if he learned of these childish worries.

But the next morning, when Judson was leaving, he was informed that the man had died. He inquired of the proprietor as to the identity of the dead man. He was shocked by the reply: he was a brilliant young person from Providence College. Eames was his name.[5]

Jacob Eames was the unbeliever who had destroyed Judson's faith. "Now he was dead—and was lost! Was lost! Was lost! Lost! Lost!" Those words raced through his brain, rang in his ears, roared in his soul—"Was lost! Lost! Lost!" There and then Judson realized he was lost, too. He immediately ended his traveling, returned home, and entered Andover Theological Seminary. Soon he "sought God for the saving of his soul." Shortly thereafter he was saved, and he dedicated his life to the Master's service.

Joining a group at Andover called "the Brethren," an outgrowth of the famous "Haystack Revival," he would answer God's call to be a missionary. This would lead him to turn down golden opportunities both at Brown and at an influential church in Plymouth. The latter broke the heart of his mother who on hearing of the offer rejoiced and said, "And you will be so near home."

Judson, however, replied, "I shall never live in Boston. I have further than that to go." Neither the tears of his mother and sister nor the hopes and dreams of his father could deter him from his call to go to the nations for Jesus' sake.

Third, his wife. God led Judson both to the right woman and, I should add, the right father-in-law. Ann (Nancy) Hasseltine would become the first woman missionary from America to go overseas. She would die at the young age of 37. The two children she bore

---

[5] Anderson, *To the Golden Shore*, 44.

(she also miscarried at least once) would die in infancy, Roger Williams at 8 months and Maria at 27 months.

Ann was saved at 16 and married Adoniram when she was 23. Brilliant in her own right, she learned Burmese and Siamese, did translation work, and cared for her husband tirelessly during his imprisonment. There is little doubt this dedication cost Ann her life.

Having been smitten by Ann, Adoniram wrote a letter to her father asking for her hand in marriage, and also one to Ann where he laid bare his heart for her and the mission with which God had burdened his soul. Both letters are legendary among missionaries.

The letter to Mr. Hasseltine:

> I have now to ask whether you can consent to part with your daughter early next spring, to see her no more in this world? Whether you can consent to her departure to a heathen land, and her subjection to the hardships and sufferings of a missionary life? Whether you can consent to her exposure to the dangers of the ocean; to the fatal influence of the southern climate of India; to every kind of want and distress; to degradation, insult, persecution, and perhaps a violent death? Can you consent to all this, for the sake of Him who left His heavenly home and died for her and for you; for the sake of perishing, immortal souls; for the sake of Zion and the glory of God? Can you consent to all this, in hope of soon meeting your daughter in the world of glory, with a crown of righteousness brightened by the acclamations of praise which shall redound to her Savior from heathens saved, through her means, from eternal woe and despair?[6]

The letter to Ann (January 1, 1811):

> It is with the utmost sincerity, and with my whole heart, that I wish you, my love, a happy new year. May it be a year in which your walk will be close with God; your frame calm and serene; and the road that leads you to the Lamb marked with purer light. May it be a year in which you will have more largely the spirit of Christ, be raised above sublunary things, and be willing to be disposed of in this world just as God shall please. As every moment of the year will bring you nearer the end of your pilgrimage, may it bring you nearer to

---

[6] Edward Judson, *The Life of Adoniram Judson* (New York: Ansom D. F. Randolph, 1883), 20.

God, and find you more prepared to hail the messenger of death as a deliverer and a friend. And now, since I have begun to wish, I will go on. May this be the year in which you will change your name; in which you will take a final leave of your relatives and native land; in which you will cross the wide ocean, and dwell on the other side of the world, among a heathen people. What a great change will this year probably effect in our lives! How very different will be our situation and employment! If our lives are preserved and our attempt prospered, we shall next new year's day be in India, and perhaps wish each other a happy new year in the uncouth dialect of Hindostan or Burmah. We shall no more see our kind friends around us, or enjoy the conveniences of civilized life, or go to the house of God with those that keep holy day; but swarthy countenances will everywhere meet our eye, the jargon of an unknown tongue will assail our ears, and we shall witness the assembling of the heathen to celebrate the worship of idol gods. We shall be weary of the world, and wish for wings like a dove, that we may fly away and be at rest. We shall probably experience seasons when we shall be "exceeding sorrowful, even unto death." We shall see many dreary, disconsolate hours, and feel a sinking of spirits, anguish of mind, of which now we can form little conception. O, we shall wish to lie down and die. And that time may soon come. One of us may be unable to sustain the heat of the climate and the change of habits; and the other may say, with literal truth, over the grave—

"By foreign hands thy dying eyes were closed;
By foreign hands thy decent limbs composed;
By foreign hands thy humble grave adorned."

but whether we shall be honored and mourned by strangers, God only knows. At least, either of us will be certain of *one* mourner. In view of such scenes shall we not pray with earnestness "O for an overcoming faith," etc.?[7]

Thirteen months later they would marry. A few days after that they sailed for Calcutta on their way, by unseen providence, to Rangoon, Burma. Yes, the child of God has the Lord's providence.

---

[7] Ibid., 20–21.

WE HAVE HIS PRAYERS, ROMANS 8:33–34

The child of God has a double divine blessing in the department of prayer. In vv. 26–27 we learn that the Spirit of God prays in us. In vv. 33–34 we learn that in heaven the Son of God prays for us. In heart and in heaven deity intercedes for the child of God.

In v. 33 the theme of our justification is brought forward once again (see v. 30). Using a courtroom analogy, Paul points out that no one can successfully bring a charge or accusation that will stick against a believer because God has declared us just from His bar as judge.

Verse 34 builds on v. 33 and settles the issue decisively. Who can charge or condemn us at the judgment with the hope that we will be found guilty? Again the answer is no one! Why? Four reasons are given. First, Christ died for us. Second, He is raised for us. Third, He is exalted at God's right hand for us. Fourth, He continually makes intercession for us (see Heb 7:25).

Hallelujah! What a Savior!

Knowing of the intercession of Jesus was crucial to Judson. Sometimes it was all he had to lean on in the midst of sorrow and suffering. How so?

Arriving in India, the East India Company forced the Judsons to leave as they tried to settle at different places. They lived four months on the Isle of France, where they learned of the death of Mrs. Harriett Newell, Ann's best friend, a 19-year-old who had sailed with them from America to serve as a fellow missionary. Harriett died while giving birth to her baby girl on the cabin floor of a ship with only her husband at her side. The baby also died, and so would her husband soon thereafter. The Judsons finally found a resting place on July 13, 1812, at Rangoon, Burma. Here, by their sweat, labor, and blood the gospel would be planted among the hostile Burmese peoples.

In Rangoon the first 10 years of missionary labors were given mainly to mastering the Burmese language. They had no grammar, dictionary, or English-speaking teacher. Three years after their arrival, Adoniram completed a grammar for the Burmese language. On May 20, 1817, he finished the translation of Matthew; he also wrote tracts—concise, clear statements of Bible truth—and gave them out discriminately and prayerfully.

After almost seven years in Burma, on April 4, 1819, Adoniram ventured to preach his first public sermon. Sitting in a traditional Burmese *zayat* by the roadside he would call out, "Ho! Everyone that thirsteth for knowledge!"[8] On June 27 he baptized Moung

---

[8] Anderson, *To the Golden Shore*, 221.

Hau, his first Burmese convert. Soon others who had also been taught would follow. By 1822 there were 18 converts he could count after 10 years of laboring.

In 1824 war broke out between Burma and the English government of India, and the Judsons were looked upon as English spies. On June 8, 1824, Judson was arrested and put first in what many called "the Death Prison," the horrible prison of Oung-pen-la. The dimensions of "the Death Prison" were 40 by 30 feet, 5 feet high, with no ventilation other than the cracks between the boards.

> In this room were confined one hundred persons of both sexes and all nationalities, nearly all naked, and half famished. The prison was never washed or even swept. Putrid remains of animal and vegetable matter, together with nameless abominations, strewed the floor. In this place of torment Mr. Judson lay with five pairs of fetters on his legs and ankles, weighing about fourteen pounds, the marks of which he carried to his dying day. At nightfall, lest the prisoners should escape, a bamboo pole was placed between the legs and then drawn up by means of pulleys to a height which allowed only their shoulders to rest on the ground while their feet depended from the iron rings of the fetters.[9]

Mosquitoes would often land and eat away the broken flesh of their feet, nearly driving them mad. Adoniram endured 21 months of prison life, nearly dying on several occasions. Of the British Prisoners of War, all but one would die.

Judson was not the only sufferer. His wife Ann was without support or protection. Yet she brought food to the prison day after day and with bribes passed the officials and gave relief to her husband and some of the other suffering prisoners. She gave birth to a child, and after 21 days carried the little girl in her arms to show to her father in prison. The child contracted smallpox; then the mother was inflicted with the same disease, followed closely by spotted fever, which brought her close to death. After many petitions, she secured permission for her husband to come out of prison, and he, with fetters on and a guard following, carried their crying baby about the streets, begging Burman mothers to nurse the child. Ann could not nurse her own little girl, she was so emaciated and weak.

During this time Adoniram and Ann tried to remain strong, despite the fact that their health deteriorated and death nearly claimed each of them on numerous occasions.

---

[9] Cited in Galen B. Royer, *Christian Heroism in Heathen Lands* (Elgin, IL: General Mission Board of Churches of the Brethren, 1917), 63.

Judson once remarked, "It is possible my life will be spared; if so, with what [zeal] shall I pursue my work! If not—His will be done. The door will be open for others who will do the work better."[10]

Later, toward the end of his imprisonment, his faith would be severely tested. Courtney Anderson summarizes the situation: "His daughter was starving before his eyes; [Ann] was nearly dead, his translation was lost; he himself was marked for death."[11]

I am convinced it was the prayers of the Savior that sustained him during those days.

WE HAVE HIS POWER, ROMANS 8:35–37

Life, by its very nature, is filled with sorrow and suffering, hardships and disappointments. Yet, nothing in this life can conquer the child of God. Why? We have His prayers (v. 34) and His love (vv. 37, 39) which gives us the victory.

In v. 35 Paul notes the realities that will come against but cannot conquer the child of God. In v. 36 he passionately notes the precious lives given for the sake of King Jesus. This destiny was foretold in Ps 44:22.

Yet in all of this and more, we are "more than conquerors," *hupernikomen*, "super conquerors" through Him who loves us. Do you see it? His great power is wedded to and made active by His great love, a power that can keep us going "against all odds."

Adoniram Judson desperately needed to know this. Eventually he was released from prison. He quickly made his way to Ann and little Maria. Read what he met in the words of Eugene Harrison:

> One of the most pathetic pages in the history of Christian missions is that which describes the scene when Judson was finally released and returned to the mission house seeking Ann, who again had failed to visit him for some weeks. As he ambled down the street as fast as his maimed ankles would permit, the tormenting question kept repeating itself, "Is Ann still alive?" Upon reaching the house, the first object to attract his attention was a fat, half-naked Burman woman squatting in the ashes beside a pan of coals and holding on her knees an emaciated baby, so begrimed with dirt that it did not occur to him that it could be his own. Across the foot of the bed, as though she had fallen there,

---

[10] Anderson, *To the Golden Shore*, 334.
[11] Ibid., 349.

lay a human object that, at the first glance, was no more recognizable than his child. The face was of a ghastly paleness and the body shrunken to the last degree of emaciation. The glossy black curls had all been shorn from the finely-shaped head. There lay the faithful and devoted wife who had followed him so unwearily from prison to prison, ever alleviating his distresses and consoling him in his trials. Presently Ann felt warm tears falling upon her face and, rousing from her daze, saw Adoniram at her side.[12]

She suffered from spotted fever and cerebral meningitis. Amazingly she survived, but only briefly. In less than a year, while away out of necessity, he received what is known as "the blacked sealed letter." He opened it to read: "My Dear Sir: To one who has suffered so much and with such exemplary fortitude, there needs but little preface to tell a tale of distress. It was cruel indeed to torture you with doubt and suspense. To sum up the unhappy tidings in a few words—Mrs. Judson is no more."[13]

Ann had died a month earlier while he was away. His beautiful and faithful helper had gone to be with her King. Six months later, on April 24, 1827, little Maria slipped into eternity and into the arms of Jesus, united so quickly to her mother.

Death seemed to be all about Adoniram. For a period of months he was plunged into despair and depression. He would flee to the jungle and live the life of a hermit, for some time questioning himself, his calling, even his faith. He demanded all his letters to America be destroyed.[14] He renounced the D.D. degree bestowed upon him by Brown. He gave all his private wealth, a sizable sum, to the Baptist Mission Board. He requested a cut in salary. Then Judson dug a grave near his hermitage and for days sat beside it staring into it.

On October 24, 1829, the third anniversary of Ann's death, he wrote, "God is to me the Great Unknown. I believe in Him, but I find Him not."[15] However, God's power and love did not fail him. He would emerge from the valley of the shadow of death in the strength of his Good Shepherd. He would say of these days, "There is a love that never fails. If I had not felt certain that every additional trial was ordered by infinite love and mercy, I could not have survived my accumulated sufferings."[16]

---

[12] Harrison, *Giants of the Missionary Trail*.
[13] Anderson, *To the Golden Shore*, 370.
[14] Ibid., 390.
[15] Ibid., 391.
[16] Harrison, *Giants of the Missionary Trail*.

Adoniram Judson would marry twice more. In 1834 he married Sarah Boardman, a precious and wonderful lady who had lost her missionary husband in death. They were married for 11 years, and she would bear him eight children, five of whom would survive into adulthood. In 1846 he married Emily Chabbuck. They would spend not quite four years together before Adoniram died on April 12, 1850. Emily died four years later in New York of tuberculosis, another slaughtered sheep for her Savior.

WE HAVE HIS PROMISE, ROMANS 8:38–39

These final verses of Romans 8 constitute what some call "the grand persuasion." Added to the seven items of v. 35 are nine additional realities that have no hope, no chance, of separating the child of God from the love of God found in Christ Jesus our Lord.

This promise accompanied Adoniram, who would finish his Burmese translation of the Bible on January 31, 1834. He did a complete revision that was finished in 1840.

Adoniram would live to see about 7,000 people baptized in Burma by the time of his death, and 63 congregations were established under 163 missionaries, native pastors, and assistants. Today the Myanmar Baptist Convention has more than 600,000 members in 3,513 churches. All of this goes back to the work of God accomplished through the Judsons.

Then there is the matter of the Karen people and the movement of God among them. This in and of itself is a remarkable evidence of the providence of God preparing a particular people for the gospel. Here is the historical record of what occurred.

> In the year 1828 an event of vast significance took place. Having come in contact with the Karens, a race of wild people living in remote and almost inaccessible jungles, Judson longed for the opportunity of winning a Karen for Christ and thus reaching his race. This opportunity came to him through Ko Tha Byu, a Karen slave who was sold one day in the bazaar in Moulmein and bought by a native Christian, who forthwith brought him to Judson to be taught and, if possible, evangelized. Ko Tha Byu was a desperate robber bandit. He had taken part in approximately thirty murders and was a hardened criminal with a vicious nature and an ungovernable temper. Patiently, prayerfully, and lovingly, Judson instructed the wretched, depraved creature, who eventually not only yielded to the transforming power of Christ but went through the jungles as a flaming evangelist among his people. The hearts of the Karens had been remarkably and

providentially prepared for the reception of the gospel message by a tradition prevalent among them to this effect:

> Long, long ago the Karen elder brother and his young white brother lived close together. God gave each of them a Book of Gold containing all they needed for their salvation, success and happiness. The Karen brother neglected and lost his Book of Gold and so he fell into a wretched type of existence, ignorant and cruelly oppressed by the Burmese. The white brother, however, prized his Golden Book, or Book of God, and so, when he sailed away across the oceans, God greatly blessed him. Some day the white brother will return, bringing with him God's Book, which, if the Karen people will receive and obey, will bring to them salvation and untold blessings.
>
> Accordingly, as Ko Tha Byu went on his unwearying preaching tours through the jungles, declaring that the long-looked-for white brother had returned with God's Book, hundreds received the message with gladness.[17]

When a depraved slave, a bandit and murderer, was brought to Judson in 1828, who would have imagined that, a century later, the Christian Karens would have many splendid high schools, hundreds of village schools, some 800 self-supporting churches, and a Christian constituency of more than 150,000?

Conclusion

On March 4, 1831, Adoniram Judson wrote a letter to his fellow missionary Cephas Bennett, who was a printer, requesting 15,000 to 20,000 tracks. Attending the great annual Buddhist festival at the Shwe Dagon in Rangoon, they experienced a mighty movement of God's Spirit and an increased interest in the gospel. May his words burn deep into our hearts, never to depart:

> [We have distributed] nearly ten thousand tracts, giving to none but those who ask. I presume there have been six thousand applications at the house. Some come two or three months' journey, from the borders of Siam and China—"Sir, we hear that there is an eternal hell. We are afraid of it. Do give us a writing that will tell us how to escape it." Others come from the frontiers of Kathay, a

---

[17] Ibid.

hundred miles north of Ava—"Sir, we have seen a writing that tells about an eternal God. Are you the man that gives away such writings? If so, pray give us one, for we want to know the truth before we die." Others come from the interior of the country, where the name of Jesus Christ is a little known—"Are you Jesus Christ's man? Give us a writing that tells about Jesus Christ."[18]

---

[18] Anderson, *To the Golden Shore*, 399.

Conclusion
Please Come and Dig

Jason G. Duesing

The rocks signified a specific event in Israel's history. The crossing of the Jordan into the Promised Land—a supernatural event—revealed God acting on behalf of His people to keep His promise, show His faithfulness, and display His might. While the generation who migrated across the divided river would never forget walking through that divinely-made aisle, human nature and subsequent circumstances likely would have prevented those distinct memories from remaining with the next generation. So, the Lord God instructed Joshua to create the small tower—not a man-made object of worship or a magical location for accessing divine favor but rather a catalyst of remembrance, a memorial (Josh 4:19–24). Prone to wander, the Israelites needed a physical object to remind them of the great work of God so that they might remain both grateful for and faithful to Him. However, the establishment of the memorial also conveyed a message to the watching world. Only a God of great might could act to deliver His own people in this manner. The memorial stones were meant to witness to the world that the God of Israel was faithful and true.

Not long after the international celebration of the Judson Centennial in 1913, Baptists in Burma erected a sizable memorial stone on the site of the Let-Ma-Yoon prison to commemorate Judson's missionary legacy and sacrifice for the Burmese. Pictures of the stone are difficult to find today, but an inscription on one side tells how Judson, "in this prison of horror which stood here sustained in his faith in the Lord Jesus Christ, and by the devotion of his heroic wife, endured unrecorded sufferings from June 1824 to May 1825."[1] After the political winds changed in Burma and it became Myanmar, the government sought to eradicate all references to Judson throughout the country. In 1988, the bicentennial year of Judson's birth, Myanmar authorities tried to bulldoze the stone and throw it in the river. Due to its immense size, all attempts failed and the authorities determined their only option was to bury it. For the last 24 years, the monument designed to introduce Judson and Judson's God to future generations has been covered.[2]

---

[1] Colin Matcalfe Enriquez, *A Burmese Enchantment* (Calcutta: Thacker, Spink and Co, 1916), 240–41.
[2] Rosalie Hall Hunt, *Bless God and Take Courage* (Valley Forge, PA: Judson Press, 2005), 253.

As Paige Patterson tells the story in the beginning of this volume, I had heard for years of how my professor had, with the aid of friends, found his way to the Let-Ma-Yoon prison, describing both the enormous trees, leaning palace tower, and overgrown brush. During the summer of 2010, after teaching seminary students in a neighboring country, I set out to see if the prison or location of the memorial stone could still be found. However, it was not what I found, but what I heard, that made all the difference. After a day of dusty and cumbersome travel, I hoped that I would soon arrive at the Let-Ma-Yoon prison. But had my translator and I not sought the help of a local elderly man, we would not have found it. Remarkably, the local man not only knew where to take us but also knew the significance of what we sought. After surveying the scene, I walked out into a nearby field while my translator and the elderly man stayed and spoke in their native tongue under three large trees. Standing in the field, weeds taller than my shoulders grew wildly all around for several acres. As I took video footage and a few photographs on a very windy day, it took me a moment to realize that the elderly man and my translator's conversation had grown in volume and intensity. The old man kept pointing to the ground under the trees and repeated the same phrase again and again. My translator had tears in his eyes when he turned to me to explain.

"This man knows about the memorial stone that is buried here. He says he has lived in this area his entire life and remembers the time when the stone was visible for all to see. Now that it is buried, he knows there is a generation who knows nothing of Judson and what Judson did for Burma.

"He told me that he knows he is old and will soon die. He said to me that since I am young he would like me to make him a promise. He said that should the political situation ever change in this country, he wants me to promise him that I will come and dig up the stone and restore it so people will once again know of Judson.

"And then he started pleading and saying, 'Please come and dig. Please come and dig. Please come and dig.'"

As I write this, the cry of an elderly Burmese man to please come and dig still rings in my ears. For just as Paul heard the Macedonian call in Acts 16 to go and preach the gospel, such is the real substance of this elderly man's call to dig, whether or not he knows it.

Memorial stones and missionary legacies are important, but one day they, too, will permanently fade. The call to please come and dig is the call Adoniram Judson first answered when he left America for Burma 200 years ago. It is the call he continued to follow when he returned to Burma after his only return home in 1846. In his parting address, he said,

Let us not, then, regret the loss of those who have gone before us, and are waiting to welcome us home, nor shrink from the summons that must call us thither. Let us only resolve to follow them who through faith and patience inherit the promises. Let us so employ the remnant of life, and so pass away, as that our successors will say of us, as we of our predecessors, "Blessed are the dead that die in the Lord. They rest from their labors, and their works do follow them."[3]

It is the call Judson followed until the day he died when he heard the call to come home—the final call to which he said he would go "with the gladness of a boy bounding away from his school."[4]

It is the call that still goes out for many no longer to build upon others' foundations (Rom 15:20) but instead to go to the places where the name of Christ is suppressed, buried, or not known. There are peoples from every tribe, tongue, and nation ready to hear of the Lord Jesus that Judson proclaimed, but how will they hear unless a new generation of Judsons is sent (Rom 10:15)?

Regardless of the state of a buried rock under three trees in Myanmar, the life and mission of Adoniram Judson itself is truly a memorial stone that points to the mercies of God in Christ. Just as Josh 4:24 explains that Joshua's memorial stone existed "so that all the peoples of the earth may know that the hand of the LORD is mighty," so does Judson's life and mission. The purpose of this volume has been to unearth this metaphorical stone and present a call to imitate Adoniram Judson in taking the gospel to the ends of the earth. An old man in Myanmar holds out hope that someday someone will unearth the large granite stone and tell a new generation of Burmese about Adoniram Judson. However, what the people of Myanmar need more is a new generation of Judsons coming to tell them about Jesus.

Please go and dig.

---

[3] Adoniram Judson, "Parting Address of Mr. Judson," in *Southern Baptist Missionary Journal* (July 1846): 31–33.

[4] Statement made to his wife, Emily. Recorded in Arabella M. Wilson, *The Lives of the Three Mrs. Judsons* (Boston: Lee and Shepard, 1855), 353.

Name Index

Ahlstrom, Sydney 32, 34
Anderson, Christopher 16
Anderson, Courtney 2, 36, 39–40, 50–51, 68–69, 79, 81–83, 90–94, 96, 99, 106, 109–10, 123, 151, 153, 167, 169, 172, 174–75, 178
Anderson, Gerald H. 24, 87
Angus, Joseph 67

Balasundaran 24
Beck, James 23
Bellamy, Joseph 36, 38–39, 48
Boreham, F. W. xxiii, 65
Boston, Thomas 62
Brackney, William H. i, 80, 130, 137
Brainerd, David 18, 49–50, 65–66
Breitenbach, William 34, 38, 43, 46
Brumberg, Joan Jacobs xxi, xxii, 57–58, 60, 62–63, 65–67, 71, 74
Buchanan, Claudius 66–67
Budge, Thomas J. 30

Carey, Eustace 11–15, 28–29
Carey, S. Pearce 10
Carey, William xv, xvii, xxiii, 9–15, 17–24, 28–29, 66–67, 78–81, 84, 86, 131–32, 153, 158, 167
Carter, Terry G. 24
Carver, W. O. xxii, 130
Chauncy, Charles 34
Chesterman, A. de M. 18
Claghorn, George S. 48
Conant, H. C. 56, 67, 103
Conforti, Joseph A. 31, 35, 37, 39, 48–49

Dana, James 35
Dowling, John 4, 115, 117, 121, 123
Drewery, Mary 11, 14
Dwight, Timothy 38, 40, 58

Edwards, Jonathan xvii–xviii, xxiii, 18, 31–35, 37–38, 43–45, 47–51, 65–66, 132
Edwards, Jonathan, Jr. 43
Emmons, Nathanael 38, 40, 45–46, 49, 51
Enriquez, Colin Matcalfe 1, 114, 179

Farrer, Keith 12
Fletcher, Edward H. 58, 131

George, Timothy iii, x, 10, 17
Goen, C. C. 35
Gougher, Henry 60, 76, 112
Griffin, Edward Dorr 38–40, 44
Grose, Howard B. xxi
Guelzo, Allen C. 32

Haggard, Fred P. xxi
Hall, Gordon 42, 49, 70, 73, 77, 135, 153, 156
Hart, William 35
Haykin, Michael A. G. x, xv, xviii, xxiii–xxiv, 9, 16–17, 30
Hewitt, John H. 71
Hiney, Tom 10
Holifield, E. Brooks 34, 44, 46
Holmes, Edward A. 77
Hopkins, Samuel 35–39, 44, 48–49, 135
Hunt, Rosalie Hall 1, 85, 179
Hurd, D. Hamilton 39

James, John Angell 10
Judson, Adoniram B. 65, 129, 131, 133–35, 148
Judson, Ann iii, vii, xvi, xxi, 30, 61, 68–69, 72, 76–8, 82, 88–89, 96–97, 99–100, 103, 108, 117, 130, 149, 154, 157–58, 160–62, 167–68
Judson, Edward 1, 36, 50, 56, 59–60, 64, 71–72, 84–85, 89, 97, 99–101, 105,

109, 111–12, 114–16, 118–19,
121–25, 130, 133–34, 138–43,
145–46, 148, 170

Kidd, Thomas S. 33
Kiker, Thomas H. 55, 69–70
Kingdon, David 18, 29
Klauber, Martin I. 76
Kling, David W. 31, 38–39, 41–42, 46, 75, 132–33
Knowles, James D. 36
Kuklick, Bruce 35

Leile, George xxi, 77

Macleod, A. Donald xxii
Manetsch, Scott M. 76
Marsden, George 32
Maxcy, Jonathan 32
Mayhew, Jonathan 34
Messer, Asa 59
Middlebrook, J. B. 19
Murray, Iain H. 15, 17, 66
Music, David W. 27

Neill, Stephen 25
Nettles, Thomas J. 76
Noll, Mark 34

Owen, John 19

Park, Edwards Amasa 32, 49
Parsons, Levi 50–51
Payne, Ernest A. 20, 29
Pearce, Samuel 23, 30
Pease, Paul 23
Perkins, Frank H. 55
Pettit, Norman 49
Phillips, Clifton Jackson 41
Pierard, Richard V. 80
Piper, John xxiii, 87, 88, 90, 92–94, 96, 99
Potts, E. Daniel 24

Ramsey, Paul 43, 47
Raymond, David B. 74, 78
Redford, George 10
Rogers, William 30
Rowe, Henry K. 62

Smith, A. Christopher 11, 24
Smith, John E. 47
Spring, Gardiner 42, 50
Stanley, Brian 16
Stein, Stephen J. 32
Stiles, Ezra 34, 39
Stowe, Harriet Beecher 36–37
Sweeney, Douglas A. viii, 32
Symes, Michael 68

Taylor, John 76
Thompson, Evelyn Wingo 79
Tooze, George H. 69
Torbet, Robert G. 79, 130, 138
Trueman, Carl xxii

Valeri, Mark 36

Walker, F. Deaville 17
Walls, Andrew F. 21–22
Warburton, Stacy R. 57, 63, 75
Ward, William 16, 23–24, 26, 78, 84, 86, 108, 131, 158–59
Wayland, Francis 40–42, 59, 61–62, 64–65, 68–74, 77–80, 82–84, 86–87, 89–90, 96, 99, 105, 111, 121, 130–31, 135–36, 138–40, 144–45, 147, 150–51, 153–54, 157–58, 160–62
West, Stephen 37–38
Woods, Leonard 38, 40–42, 63–64, 66, 75, 132, 156, 159
Worcester, Samuel 72–74, 151, 162
Worcester, Samuel M. 74

Yarnell, Malcolm B., III x, 17